ARE YOU LANGUAGE POOR?

One of the greatest treasures in modern life is absolutely free. That treasure is the English language.

With total command of English, you can swiftly advance in business, score high in school, communicate better with people, and fully express your knowledge and talents.

Yet all too many of us benefit from just a tiny part of this vast potential. Our lives and careers are crippled by our limited understanding of how English works and should be used.

This book is uniquely designed to answer all questions about English; fill in all information gaps; and supply all of the vital tips for top-notch performance. It is more than just a reference book; it offers an enjoyable, step-by-step, complete course in self-improvement— one that you can benefit from without formal instruction or excess time spent. You easily can achieve results to make this the most valuable book that you have ever used.

HENRY THOMAS, who wrote BETTER ENGLISH MADE EASY, is the author of more than thirty books, among them THE STORY OF THE HUMAN RACE, THE COMPLETE BOOK OF ENGLISH, FIFTY GREAT AMERICANS and the LIVING BIOGRAPHY SERIES. His writing has been highly praised by such distinguished authors as Bernard Shaw, Sinclair Lewis and Theodore Dreiser.

Mr. Thomas studied at Harvard University, where he won his A.B., A.M., and Ph.D. degrees. As a professional writer and an educator (he has taught at Boston University and other well-known educational institutions) he has an excellent grasp of the problems we face in speaking and writing, and here he presents quick sure ways to solve them.

BETTER ENGLISH MADE EASY

by Henry Thomas, Ph.D.

WARNER BOOKS

A Warner Communications Company

CONTENTS

1

HOW TO GET THE MOST OUT
OF THIS BOOK

The purpose of this book is to show you how to improve
your English without the help of a teacher. You will be your
own instructor, and you will find the method easy, exciting,
and full of fun.

For the book is designed not as a task, but as a game.
Don't feel tense as you read these pages. Take it easy. Relax
as you learn.

But learn as you relax. Even the playing of a game requires
a certain amount of work. Read this book leisurely but carefully. Set aside, if possible, a definite period every day—two
hours, an hour, even half an hour if that is all you can spare.
But, once you have decided upon the schedule, stick to it.
Make your studying a daily habit.

Select, if you can, a quiet place for your study. But this is
not of the utmost importance. You can learn to concentrate
even in noisy surroundings. Newspaper editors and business
executives do some of their best thinking in the hubbub of
their daily work. And one of the highest grades in the history
of Harvard was made by a student who did his home lessons
amidst the clatter of a large family in the slums.

It is therefore not a question of *where* you study, but *how*
you study. Select your place, and then go ahead with your
schedule. Arrange this schedule to fit your time. And remember the old Roman adage: *Make haste slowly*. Don't try to
read too many pages at one sitting. Knowledge, like food,
must be chewed and swallowed a little at a time.

On the average, you should be able to do about sixteen
pages in two hours, eight pages in one hour, four pages in
half an hour. But don't let these figures misguide you. Do as
many or as few pages as your allotted time will allow you to
understand and digest. No matter what your speed, you will
be through with the book, and on the way to becoming a

9

master of Better English, in a few weeks or months at the most.

You will get the most out of this book if you approach it not as a casual reader but as an active thinker. Don't skip or skim. Don't merely dip into a subject. Plunge your whole mind into it. You will find it an invigorating experience in mental gymnastics to get your knowledge and pleasure at the same time.

Easy does it. Various tests have shown that the best way to learn a new subject is to stop after every two or three pages and to ask yourself how much of the material has become firmly fixed in your mind. That is how Benjamin Franklin acquired his fluent style—words that flow as easily as the waters of a rippling brook. He always tried to reconstruct, from memory, the best passages that he had come across in his daily reading.

This has been the experience of many other successful thinkers and writers and men of affairs. They have learned to read with their memory as well as with their eyes. As a guide to your memory, it is a good plan to begin each day's lesson with a review of the previous day's work. You will find your progress most satisfactory, as repeated experiments have shown, if you keep a pad and pencil always at hand, take notes as you go along, and review your notes as well as your text. The best way to make another person's ideas your own is to condense them in your own words.

As you learn each lesson and complete each word game, try your newly acquired knowledge on your friends. See if you can stump *them* with the quizzes that have stumped *you*. It's a great satisfaction to take a friend over a road that you have just discovered for yourself. Unlike your money, your knowledge increases as you share it.

But, most important of all, keep at this book steadily—as a game, let me repeat, and not as a chore. Don't fret if there are some sections that may require a little more concentration and a little slower progress. You will find these sections few and far between. On the whole, the book is designed to give you a minimum of trouble and a maximum of fun. And it is so paced that you can take it at your own best speed.

So go ahead, in a relaxed mood, and with the certain knowledge that an enthusiastic persistence will carry you successfully to the end.

Are you ready? Then turn to the next page and we'll begin.

2

HOW GOOD IS YOUR ENGLISH?

Have you ever taken stock of your mental equipment? You know your assets in dollars and cents. Do you know your assets in ideas and words? The English language has over 600,000 words. How many of them are yours? And how well can you combine them into sentences that will persuade other people and increase your own chances for success?

At school, the average child learns about 4,000 words a year. After leaving school, the average adult learns only about 40 words a year. This amazing fact has been demonstrated in a number of experiments conducted at various educational institutions.

A limited stock of words is one of the main reasons why so many people remain in the lower ranks. For words are the materials out of which we build our thoughts. The most successful people in the world are those who understand the cash value of their words. Their self-confidence increases with their superior power to express themselves. Winston Churchill, Lowell Thomas, Dale Carnegie, the statesman, the radio announcer, the writer, the business executive, the star salesman, the popular lecturer, the persuasive lawyer, the man who "talks himself" into a prize job—all those, in short, who have "arrived"—are members of that select circle, the magical weavers of words. Your best capital, in this competitive age of ours, is an adequate vocabulary and a knowledge of how to put it to work.

Yet the majority of Americans today are language-poor. They haven't enough words to define their wants, or ideas to attain them.

How about you? Are you rich, or poor, in the currency of your mother tongue? Suppose you find out for yourself. Here are several quizzes—in vocabulary, spelling, pronunciation, and grammar. These quizzes will test your ability to understand and to use better English. The questions—100 in all—

11

are neither too difficult nor too easy. Give yourself one credit for every correct answer. You will find the answers to all the 100 questions after the final quiz.

And, whatever your score, don't worry. It will be very much better at the end of this book than it is at the beginning. For this is precisely the purpose of the book—to show you how to correct your grammatical faults, to increase your vocabulary, to build up your self-confidence, and to guide you to greater power through the superior expression of your thoughts.

Here, then, are the questions for your entrance examination to the Academy of Better English:

I. Vocabulary

A

Check the correct word in each of the following pairs enclosed by parentheses:

1. He (effected, affected) his friends with his pathetic story.
2. The general predicted that war was (imminent, immanent).
3. Her insinuations (implied, inferred) that Mr. Smith was guilty.
4. Honest people are (ingenious, ingenuous).
5. Bachelors, as a rule, are (uninterested, disinterested) in marriage.
6. I shall (illiterate, obliterate) the scoundrel from my mind.
7. It was diagnosed as a (septic, skeptic) infection.
8. He amused them with a number of humorous (antidotes, anecdotes).
9. The little boy has a (veracious, voracious) appetite.
10. The man in the desert suffered from an optical (allusion, illusion).

B

Indicate whether the answer to each of the following questions is *yes* or *no*:

11. Is an *orthopedist* a specialist in children's diseases? Yes No
12. Is an *altruist* a man who speaks the truth? Yes No

13. Is an *optician* a grinder of lenses?   Yes   No
14. Is a *uxorious* person a person who loves luxury?   Yes   No
15. Is a *loquacious* woman very talkative?   Yes   No
16. Can a *censer* ban a book?   Yes   No
17. Do we *felicitate* a man on his good fortune?   Yes   No
18. Does a *council* plead cases in court?   Yes   No
19. Is Eisenhower a *progeny* of military genius?   Yes   No
20. Is a disease existing from birth *congenital*?   Yes   No

C

In this test, match the words of the first column with the definitions of the second column:

21. ascetic   a. appreciative of beauty
22. synthetic   b. replacing parts, in surgery
23. esthetic   c. severely abstinent
24. prosthetic   d. extremely enthusiastic
25. ecstatic   e. consisting of chemical substitutes

D

After each of the following five words, check the definition that fits it best:

26. entomology
    (a) the science of human races, (b) the study of words, (c) a branch of zoölogy dealing with insects, (d) a disease of the liver
27. fortuitous
    (a) strongly fortified, (b) courageous, (c) dangerous, (d) occuring by chance
28. cacophony
    (a) a disagreeable sound, (b) a fake, (c) slander, (d) praise
29. parsimonious
    (a) belonging to a parish, (b) stingy, (c) prejudiced, (d) inactive
30. prurient
    (a) economical, (b) discreet, (c) lustful, (d) excessively modest

13

II. Spelling

A

In each of the following groups, check the one word that is spelled *wrong:*

31. (a) accessible, (b) allege, (c) annoint, (d) admissible
32. (a) inoculate, (b) billious, (c) colossal, (d) license
33. (a) tyrannize, (b) embarrassment, (c) appraise, (d) wierd
34. (a) indispensible, (b) coalesce, (c) disappoint, (d) connoisseur
35. (a) giraffe, (b) persistant, (c) fuselage, (d) idiosyncrasy
36. (a) licorice, (b) mischievious, (c) omitted, (d) parochial
37. (a) naphtha, (b) parallel, (c) occurence, (d) perseverance
38. (a) acheive, (b) committee, (c) operetta, (d) plebeian
39. (a) removable, (b) sedentery, (c) scissors, (d) resuscitate
40. (a) roguishness, (b) sherriff, (c) separate, (d) toboggan

B

In each of the following groups, check the one word that is spelled *right:*

41. (a) exhilirate, (b) rebelious, (c) scythe, (d) releive
42. (a) perseverance, (b) rigamarole, (c) sacreligious, (d) geneology
43. (a) profficient, (b) pyjamas, (c) preceed, (d) acknowlege
44. (a) supprise, (b) avoirdupois, (c) incidently, (d) colusion
45. (a) bureaucracy, (b) calix, (c) aparrel, (d) callorie
46. (a) irrevelant, (b) coroborate, (c) dilemna, (d) newsstand
47. (a) dissapear, (b) sieze, (c) siege, (d) trapeeze
48. (a) truely, (b) tryst, (c) proffessor, (d) vaccilate
49. (a) usable, (b) tonnic, (c) sincopation, (d) sollicit
50. (a) stratagy, (b) battalion, (c) callendar, (d) batchelor

III. Pronunciation

Check the correct form or forms in each of the following pairs of pronunciations:

		(a)	(b)
51.	abdomen	(a) AB-doe-men	(b) ab-DOE-men
52.	accessory	(a) ak-SES-o-ree	(b) AK-ses-o-ree
53.	beatify	(a) BEE-ti-figh	(b) bee-AT-i-figh
54.	caricature	(a) KAR-i-ka-choor	(b) kar-IK-a-choor
55.	coupon	(a) KOO-pon	(b) KYOO-pon
56.	debris	(a) DEB-ris	(b) day-BREE
57.	decadent	(a) de-KAY-dent	(b) DEK-a-dent
58.	exigency	(a) EKS-i-gen-see	(b) ek-SIJ-en-see
59.	façade	(a) fah-SAYD	(b) fah-SAHD
60.	grimace	(a) gri-MAYSS	(b) GRIM-iss
61.	heinous	(a) HEE-nus	(b) HAYN-us
62.	inclement	(a) in-CLEM-ent	(b) IN-cle-ment
63.	itinerary	(a) eye-TIN-e-ree	(b) eye-TIN-er-a-ree
64.	lichen	(a) LAI-ken	(b) LITCH-en
65.	museum	(a) myoo-ZEE-um	(b) MYOO-zee-um
66.	nephew	(a) NEPH-yoo	(b) NEV-yoo
67.	pariah	(a) PAH-ree-a	(b) pa-RYE-a
68.	robust	(a) ro-BUST	(b) ROE-bust
69.	secretive	(a) SEE-kre-tiv	(b) se-KREE-tiv
70.	theater	(a) THEE-a-ter	(b) the-AY-ter

IV. Grammar

A

In each of the following sentences, check the correct word in parentheses:

71. I like the house, especially (it's, its) roof.
72. There is nobody here but (me, I).
73. I don't like (them, those) golf balls.
74. (Lie, lay) down, Fido!
75. He concurs (with, in) the decision of the other jurors.
76. Between you and (I, me), he is not altogether wrong.
77. Either the shoes or the hat (is, are) missing.
78. The murderer was (hung, hanged) by the neck.
79. He is much richer than (me, I).
80. He is one of those who (believe, believes) everything.
81. He shouldn't (have, of) done it.
82. The police commissioner tried to show that crime (didn't, doesn't) pay.

15

83. The scissors (is, are) on the table.
84. There is a good chance of (me, my) getting the job.
85. He loves her (regardless, irregardless) of her poverty.

B

Indicate whether the italicized word in each of the following sentences is right or wrong:

86. Neither of us *is* able to afford a yacht.	Right	Wrong
87. I don't like *these* kind of shoes.	Right	Wrong
88. *Leave* me tell you a funny story I've heard.	Right	Wrong
89. He goes very *slow*.	Right	Wrong
90. He *laid* down for a nap.	Right	Wrong
91. This lot of land, as well as the three adjoining lots, *belongs* to me.	Right	Wrong
92. He earns money *easier* than I do.	Right	Wrong
93. John can't walk any *further*.	Right	Wrong
94. He is angry *at* his friend's coldness toward him.	Right	Wrong
95. He has *laid* down to rest.	Right	Wrong
96. The flower *smells* pleasantly.	Right	Wrong
97. He acted *like* he meant it.	Right	Wrong
98. I know the man *who* I think will be elected.	Right	Wrong
99. When *it's* thirsty, the cat drinks its milk.	Right	Wrong
100. The man who fell down *raises* from the ground.	Right	Wrong

—*Answers*—

I A: 1-affected, 2-imminent, 3-implied, 4-ingenuous, 5-uninterested, 6-obliterate, 7-septic, 8-anecdotes, 9-voracious, 10-illusion

I B: 11-no, 12-no, 13-yes, 14-no, 15-yes, 16-no, 17-yes, 18-no, 19-no, 20-yes

I C: 21-c, 22-e, 23-a, 24-b, 25-d

I D: 26-c, 27-d, 28-a, 29-b, 30-c

II A: 31-c, 32-b, 33-d, 34-a, 35-b, 36-b, 37-c, 38-a, 39-b, 40-b

II B: 41-c, 42-a, 43-b, 44-b, 45-a, 46-d, 47-c, 48-b, 49-a, 50-b

III: 51-a and b, 52-a, 53-b, 54-a, 55-a and b, 56-b, 57-a and b, 58-a, 59-b, 60-a, 61-b, 62-a, 63-b, 64-a, 65-a,

66-a and b (the latter is British), 67-a and b, 68-a, 69-b, 70-a

IV A: 71-its, 72-me, 73-those, 74-lie, 75-in, 76-me, 77-is, 78-hanged, 79-I, 80-believe, 81-have, 82-doesn't, 83-are, 84-my, 85-regardless

IV B: 86-right, 87-wrong, 88-wrong, 89-right, 90-wrong, 91-right, 92-wrong, 93-right, 94-right, 95-wrong, 96-wrong, 97-wrong, 98-right, 99-right, 100-wrong

Your score, _____ out of 100.

Is your score low (50 or less), fair (50 to 70), creditable (70 to 85), or excellent (85 to 100)? In any case, you can use this book to your advantage. However bad your English, you *can* improve it; however good, you *should* improve it. Even the best of us make our verbal and grammatical mistakes. Nobody's English was ever perfect—not even Lincoln's, or Shakespeare's, or Bernard Shaw's.

As for the rest of us, we rarely succeed in making ourselves completely understood. We lack the precise word, the striking phrase, the proper expression at the proper time. We are like the famous screen actress who was invited to dine with a group of college professors. "I am honored," she said, "to be in the presence of so many extinguished gentlemen." And then she wondered why they greeted her speech with such an ominous silence.

If the world treats you with silence, or with an indifferent nod, one of the reasons may be your inability to express yourself. You say the wrong things, or say the right things in the wrong way. Bad English is like an unpressed suit or an untidy shirt. It betrays the carelessness of the person who uses it. Nobody will entrust an important job to a careless person.

This book, therefore, is designed to correct your mental appearance, to enrich your personailty, and to improve your position in life through a keener understanding of others and a clearer interpretation of yourself.

Through better English lies the way to success.

3

FIVE WAYS TO INCREASE YOUR VOCABULARY

A Greek philosopher once said that there is no royal road to learning. "The way of knowledge," he declared, "is difficult and steep." But today we know better. You can now have a royal time of adventure and fun as you learn. The process of education has been simplified and "streamlined" in accordance with the latest developments in practical psychology. The way to knowledge has become an interesting journey instead of an arduous climb.

Here are five pleasant ways that will lead you into the possession of a wider and richer vocabulary.

1. TALK TO ALL SORTS OF PEOPLE

While traveling on a train, I've often been drawn into conversation by strangers who sat next to me. And I have found that an exchange of ideas, even about the weather, may sometimes prove to be educational as well as stimulating. You may begin with a casual mention of today's sunshine or yesterday's thunderstorm, and end up with a discussion about geography, meteorology, floods, blizzards, avalanches, hurricanes, and the mysterious ways of God.

Several of my casual conversations with strangers have enriched my own mind with fresh knowledge and new words. One day a blind young man, who happened to be an ardent musician, was sitting beside me. He was traveling from Chicago, to study singing at the Juilliard School of Music, in New York. As a result of our conversation during that trip, I learned a number of facts—and words—about South American, African and Oriental music, as well as about the latest methods of education for the blind.

I have been able to use much of this information—together with the technical terms—in some of my articles and books.

18

Whatever your job, it's a good plan to trade ideas with people who have other jobs. You will all come out of the trade richer in good will and in good words.

2. READ THE BETTER MAGAZINES AND BOOKS

From your magazine reading you will get not only superior English, but important ideas about the current subjects of the greatest interest. And don't confine your magazine reading to the stories and the articles alone. You will find stimulating words and ideas even in some of the advertisements. The copy writers are chosen for their skill in putting their vocabulary to practical use. For magazine space is expensive, so that a good advertisement must pack a lot of meaning into a few expressive words. Try to learn some of these rich and meaningful words.

As for your book reading, try to keep it as varied as possible. History, biography, science, philosophy, psychology, religion, travel, current industry and interests and events— all these subjects will help to broaden your mind and to increase your chances for success. There are no tools so important for personal progress as a general understanding of the vocabulary in the diversified fields of human endeavor. Speak a man's language, and you win him over as a friend. And every occupation has its own peculiar language. You can master these languages through your reading. The wider your reading, the bigger your vocabulary, and the better your chances for successful contact with the world at many different angles.

3. USE THE DICTIONARY

It is said that Mark Twain, having heard a very fine sermon one day, spoke to the minister after the service. "Dr. Doane," he said, "I enjoyed your sermon this morning. In fact, it came to me like an old friend. For every word in it was copied out of a book I have at home."

The minister indignantly denied this, and challenged Mark Twain to prove his accusation.

"Very well," said the humorist, "I will let you see the book for yourself."

The next day, he sent Dr. Doane a copy of *Webster's Dictionary*.

The dictionary is, in a way, the most interesting book in the language. For it contains all the words of all the other books. And many a word, when you look up its derivation in one of the larger dictionaries, will paint a complete picture or tell a complete story.

Take, for example, such words as *gregarious, procrastinate,* and *carnival.*

Gregarious, as you will find in the dictionary, comes from the Latin word *grex,* which means a *flock.* Gregarious people are sociable; they like to *flock together* instead of living by themselves.

Procrastinate is related to the Latin word *cras,* which means *tomorrow.* To *procrastinate* is to *put off until tomorrow* the things that you ought to do today.

Carnival. This word is derived from the Latin phrase *carne vale, oh flesh, farewell!* Originally, a carnival was the last fling the merrymakers took before Lent. Nowadays it means any kind of exuberant festivity.

These are but a few hints of the many fascinating word-stories you can get out of the dictionary. You will also find, in the dictionary, the subtle distinctions between words whose meanings you may have confused in the past. Even the wife of Noah Webster, author of the famous dictionary, got her meanings mixed up at times. One day she found her husband kissing their maid. "Noah," she exclaimed, "I'm surprised!"

"Oh no, my dear," he replied. "*I* am surprised. *You* are astonished."

For the word *astonished* means *amazed,* while the word *surprised,* in one sense, means *caught in the act.*

The dictionary, you will find, is one of the best as well as one of the most fascinating sources for the development of your word power.

4. TRACK DOWN NEW WORDS

Another good way to develop your vocabulary is to *track down new words* and to look them up in the dictionary. Word-hunting can be turned into a very interesting sport. And it is much more civilized than bird-hunting. Make a game out of finding new words and their meanings. Write them down in a notebook. Ask yourself, every evening, how many words you have been able to bag today. And compare your daily achievement with that of your friends. For this sport you need no license, no skill in marksmanship, and no equipment other than a pair of open ears and eyes, and an eager mind.

As a help in keeping your mind alive to new words, this book will give you a number of word games—easy to grasp and interesting to play. These games, in turn, will give you ideas for other similar games that you can make up for yourself. You will thus get into the habit of building up your vocabulary stock in accordance with a well-laid and progressive plan.

5. HEAR GOOD SPEAKERS

The radio and the television set can bring some of the best spoken English into your home. And the subjects are so varied—from the Azores to the Zodiac and from statesmanship to sports—that everybody can find something to his taste almost every day.

In selecting your programs, it is a good idea to cultivate a taste for something beyond your immediate interests. In this way, you can widen your mental horizons and discover not only new words but new ideas.

As you listen to your radio, you will find it helpful to have your notebook at hand. You can then jot down the unfamiliar words and look them up at your leisure.

There is an interesting anecdote that shows the value of knowing your words. One day P. T. Barnum became exasperated because the visitors stayed too long at his museum. They kept drifting from room to room and preventing others from coming in. He therefore placed the following sign over one of the doors:

TO THE EGRESS

The patrons who read the sign, expecting to see a new and fascinating curiosity, went through the door in droves and found themselves out on the street.

It was only then that they learned the meaning of the strange word. *Egress* means *exit*.

Here, then, are the five royal roads to a better vocabulary: *Talk* to well-informed people. *Read* good books and magazines. *Use* the dictionary. *Track* down new words. *Hear* good speakers. Notice the initials of the five underlined words. They spell out the word T-R-U-T-H. Remember this key word; it will help you to fix the ideas of this chapter clearly in your mind.

We shall now take a brief intermission to play our first word game. You will find a number of these word games distributed, as breathing spells, throughout the book. They will provide you not only with plenty of fun, but with a bigger and more powerful vocabulary.

Time out for the First Word Game
SIMILAR AND OPPOSITE WORDS

Your words are a vital part of your personality. They represent a picture of your mind. The better the picture you reveal to the public, the more readily the public will respond to you.

The building of your vocabulary, therefore, is an important element in your study of better English. And you will find the process easy and full of fun. These word games will enable you to *learn as you play*.

Try this one for a start:

A

Words With Similar Meanings

Suppose you begin with your food. You've been invited to dinner at Mrs. Smith's, and you've been treated to filet mignon—tender, tasty, wholesome, spicy, and served with a lavish hand. You want to tell your hostess how much you've enjoyed the steak. But can you find the proper words, and a sufficient number of them, to express yourself in a manner worthy of the occasion?

Well, let's see. The meat has been *tender* to your bite, *tasty* to your palate, *wholesome* to your general health, *spicy* to your nostrils, and *lavish* in quantity as well as excellent in quality. Now take these five words and try to write, next to each one of them, four other words that have the same or similar meanings. As a help for a starter, I shall give you the first, the last, and some of the other letters of each required word, as well as dashes representing the number of letters in between.

Are you ready? Here they are:

tender   s_ft,   s_c__l_nt,   d_l_c__e,
           m_s___c_b_e

tasty	p_e_s__t, l_sc_o_s, s_v__y,
	a__e__z__g
wholesome	h__l__f_l, s__u_r_o_s, s_lt__y,
	b_n__i___l
spicy	a__m_t_c, p_q_a_t, f__g_a_t,
	p_n_e_t
lavish	g_n__o_s, u_s__nt_d, m_n__i_e_t,
	b__n__f_l

How many of the words have you been able to get? Very
few, perhaps. But you're going to get all of them right now,
and they will become a part of your permanent vocabulary.
As used in connection with food:

tender	is the same as *soft, succulent, delicate,*
	masticable
tasty	" " " " *pleasant, luscious, savory,*
	appetizing
wholesome	" " " " *healthful, salubrious, salutary,*
	beneficial
spicy	" " " " *aromatic, piquant, fragrant,*
	pungent
lavish	" " " " *generous, unstinted,*
	munificent, bountiful

You have just learned a number of *synonyms*—words that
mean the same thing, or nearly the same thing. Actually, no
two words are absolutely identical in their meaning, just as
no two faces are absolutely identical in their features. But,
for practical purposes, a good knowledge of synonyms will
add color to your vocabulary and increase your ability to
express yourself. The more ways you can present the same
idea, the better the chances that the idea will reach its mark
and produce results.

B

Words With Opposite Meanings

But this is only half of the game. The other half deals with
dissimilar instead of *similar* meanings. Many of the words you
come across in your daily use have not only *synonyms,* but
antonyms. An *antonym* is a word that means the direct opposite of another word.

Now see if you can write four antonyms after each of the
five key words in Section A. These antonyms need not neces-

sarily apply to food. But their meanings must be opposite to those of the key words.

As before, I shall give you the first, the last, and some of the other letters of each required word, together with the precise number of dashes for the remaining letters.

tender	t_u_h, c_l_o_s, i__l_x_b_e, t_n__i__s
tasty	u_s_v__y, i_s_p_d, v_p_d, fl_t
wholesome	u_s_n__a_y, n_x_o_s, h_r_f_l, __ju_i__s
spicy	d_ll, u_f__v___d, o_o_l__s, j_j_ne
lavish	c_o_e, s_in_y, m_s_r_y, n_g__r__y

Have you guessed most of the words? No? Well, here they are:

tender	is the opposite of			tough, callous, inflexible, tenacious
tasty	"	"	"	" unsavory, insipid, vapid, flat
wholesome	"	"	"	" unsanitary, noxious, harmful, injurious
spicy	"	"	"	" dull, unflavored, odorless, jejune
lavish	"	"	"	" close, stingy, miserly, niggardly

You have now looked at five basic words, together with twenty *synonyms* and twenty *antonyms*—forty-five words in all. Let's play around a little with these words, so that you may become more familiar with them.

C

In each of the following sentences, point out whether the *second italic* word is a synonym for the *first italic* word:

1. Hitler was *tenacious* in his opinions and *tough* in his actions   Yes   No
2. An *unsavory* reputation is *wholesome*.   Yes   No
3. A *noxious* attitude toward people is *pleasant*.   Yes   No
4. An *insipid* style in writing may be called *jejune*.   Yes   No
5. A *piquant* story is like a *spicy* dish.   Yes   No

24

6. Howard Jones is *niggardly* and *lavish* with his purse. Yes No
7. The food of the ancient gods was said to to be *ambrosial* and *aromatic*. Yes No
8. Carnegie's *munificent* gifts for education came out of a *bountiful* purse. Yes No
9. The squab at the banquet was *succulent* and *masticable*. Yes No
10. A thing *luscious* to the palate is generally regarded as *vapid*. Yes No

—Answers—

1-yes, 2-no, 3-no, 4-yes, 5-yes, 6-no, 7-yes, 8-yes, 9-yes, 10-no

D

And here are the words shuffled in a different way. Check, after the word in the *second* column, whether it is a *synonym* or an *antonym* of the word in the *first* column. S stands for synonym; A, for antonym:

1. invigorating	salubrious	S	A
2. piquant	jejune	S	A
3. delicate	callous	S	A
4. insipid	savory	S	A
5. noxious	injurious	S	A
6. wholesome	salubrious	S	A
7. fragrant	ambrosial	S	A
8. unstinted	niggardly	S	A
9. tough	succulent	S	A
10. lavish	munificent	S	A
11. callous	masticable	S	A
12. aromatic	odorless	S	A
13. inflexible	tender	S	A
14. healthful	nutritious	S	A
15. appetizing	unsavory	S	A
16. tasty	vapid	S	A
17. generous	bountiful	S	A
18. palatable	luscious	S	A
19. soft	tenacious	S	A
20. spicy	piquant	S	A

—Answers—

1-S, 2-A, 3-A, 4-A, 5-S, 6-S, 7-S, 8-A, 9-A, 10-S, 11-A, 12-A, 13-A, 14-S, 15-A, 16-A, 17-S, 18-S, 19-A, 20-S

Here is the proper pronunciation of the less familiar words that you have learned in this chapter:

ambrosial: am-BROE-zhul
aromatic: a-roe-MAT-ik
jejune: je-JOON
masticable: MAS-tik-abl
munificent: mew-NIF-iss-ent
piquant: PEE-kant
salubrious: sa-LEW-bree-us

You have added a number of words to your working vocabulary. The average adult, you will remember, learns only 40 new words a year. In these few pages you have played with 45 words—some of them familiar to you, but several of them most likely unfamiliar. From now on, they are part of your permanent stock.

It will be a good idea for you to go on with this sort of game. Try to get several synonyms and antonyms for the words you come across in your daily activities. And play this game with your friends. It's an easy and pleasant way to build your vocabulary. You will be amazed how rapidly your word-stock will pile up through this simple and practical plan.

4

HOW TO PUT YOUR IDEAS
INTO MOTION

THE KEY WORDS IN YOUR SENTENCES

In the following four sentences, do you see any difference in the use of the words *effect* and *censor?*

1. The doctor was able to *effect* a cure.
2. The *effect* of the cure was permanent.
3. He was appointed to *censor* the company mail.
4. He was made the *censor* of the company.

In the first sentence, *effect* is used as a *verb.*
In the second sentence, *effect* is used as a *noun.*
In the third sentence, *censor* is used as a *verb.*
In the fourth sentence, *censor* is used as a *noun.*
And thus, as you see, the same word can sometimes serve either as a *verb* or as a *noun.*
But what is the difference between a *verb* and a *noun?*

UNDERSTANDING THE VERB

A *verb,* derived from the Latin *verbum,* means a *word.* It is *the word* that gives life to a sentence. As you may recall from your school days, the textbook definition is somewhat as follows: A verb denotes an action, an occurrence, a fulfillment, or a state of existence. For example:

Action: The waves *lashed* against the ship.
Occurrence: The drowning *happened* by accident.
Fulfillment: At last he *succeeded* in his search for a true friend.
State of existence: Life *is* sweet.

And thus the verb is the word which helps to carry home the completed meaning of the sentence.

NOUNS ARE NAMES

A *noun* is quite a different sort of word. Derived from the Latin *nomen,* it means a *name.* It may name or denote a person, a place, a thing, an idea, a quality, or an emotion. Each of the following words in italics is a noun:

Person: *John Foster Dulles, statesman, student*
Place: *Central Park, bedroom, sky*
Thing: *pencil, shirt, table*
Idea: *democracy, militarism, art*
Quality: *goodness, charity, justice*
Emotion: *anger, pleasure, fear*

THE SECRET OF POWERFUL ENGLISH

We shall return to the *noun* in a later chapter. For the present, let us look a little more closely at the verb.

Turn back to the beginning of this chapter, and please notice the *action* of the word *effect* in the first sentence, and of the word *censor* in the third sentence. In each of these sentences, the verb is of the utmost importance. It is the verb that gives life to the thought. As you glance through your newspaper, you will find that some of the headlines, advertisements, and editorials have a far greater pulling power than some of the other items. What is it that draws your attention like a magnet to these features? In almost every case, you will observe that *the secret of their power is a verb or a group of verbs.*

Here, for example, are a number of such newspaper items, with all the verbs in italics:

Headlines

Ryan *Vows* He'll *Crush* Strike
Judge *Fells* Thief
Bus *Plunges* Off Ramp
Police *Seize* Man Who *Shot* Girl
Wife *Dashes* Water in Husband's
    Face at Divorce Trial
Victory *Catapults* Bears Into First Place

Advertisements

How many times a day do you *inhale?*
Check this list. *Hurry* to *make* your
    purchase while quantities *last.*

> *Take* out insurance. *Extend* the support
> of your family beyond your lifetime.
> *Go* light. *Choose* right.
> When you *buy, specify.*
> *Come* now and *save.*

The following is a section of an editorial in the New York *Herald Tribune* that referred to Rocky Marciano's victory over Joe Louis. It began with the outline of a story. This outline, quoted here only in part, will show you the importance of the verb:

> "Many years ago, Jack London *wrote* a story called 'A Piece of Steak' about an aged boxer *named* Tom King who *was fighting* one last fight because if he *won* it he would *get* some desperately *needed* money. It *was* a truthful story and, like most true stories, a sad one. For despite his experience and guile, Tom King *lost* his fight to an opponent who *was armed* with nothing more than the strength and endurance of youth. Afterward, the fighter *wept*, and as he *did* so he *thought* of his own young days and how Old Stowsher Bill, the man he *had beaten* in his first fight years before, *had* also *sat* in his dressing room and *wept* . . ."

In the above story, as you may have noticed, the verbs have carried almost the entire plot. *Needed* money, *fought* last fight, *lost, wept, thought* of another fighter who *had lost* and *wept*.

One of the most famous messages in history, Caesar's report of his triumph on the battlefield, consisted of three verbs: *Veni, vidi, vici*—I *came*, I *saw*, I *conquered*.

It was this message, probably, that inspired the magnificent verb-picture of a victory won in World War II: *Sighted* sub, *sank* same.

The *words* of action are as important in a sentence as the *men* of action are in a city. For it is the dynamic words—the verbs—that keep the wheels of our language on the go.

So here is how you can spot the verb in any sentence. *It is the dynamo that moves the sentence.* For example:

Jesus *whipped* the money lenders out of the temple.
The halfback *threw* a forward pass for a touchdown.
The allied powers *defeated* the Nazis in World War II.

The important thing to remember about the verb is that *it keeps the sentence on the move*. Your effective use of good

English will depend to a great extent upon your ability to choose living, moving, attention-compelling verbs.

Do you get the *feel* of the verb now? Try to see for yourself. Underline all the verbs in the following little story:

A few years ago, a Chinese student came to New York to enter Columbia University. The dean accepted his credentials, and told him that he would be admitted to the college as soon as he had learned the language of the country. This, thought the dean, would take about half a year.

The student got a job on the East Side and returned to Columbia—not half a year but a year later. It had taken him longer than he had anticipated to learn the language of the country. But now, at last, the student was ready for his interview with the dean.

Much to his amazement, however, the dean couldn't understand a word of what the young fellow was saying.

Turning to his secretary, the dean asked, "Are you able to make him out?"

"Sure," said the secretary. "This isn't English he's talking. It's Yiddish!"

—Answers—

1. *came*	13. *to learn*
2. *to enter*	14. *was*
3. *accepted*	15. *couldn't understand*
4. *told*	16. *was saying*
5. *would be admitted*	17. *turning*
6. *had learned*	18. *asked*
7. *thought*	19. *are*
8. *would take*	20. *to make . . . out*
9. *got*	21. *said*
10. *returned*	22. *is (isn't)*
11. *had taken*	23. *is talking*
12. *had anticipated*	24. *is (it's)*

How many of the above verbs have you been able to spot? Less than eighteen? In that case, you're still a bit shaky on the key words of your sentences.

But don't worry. Before you are through with this book, you will become much better acquainted with the verb.

SOME COMMON ERRORS

Now, let's take another look at the two words *effect* and *censor,* with which we began this chapter. Be careful not to confuse them with *affect* and *censer.*

The words *affect* and *effect* are among the most troublesome in the English language. Here are just a few of the many ways in which they are constantly misused:

1. What was the *affect* of the new plan he adopted?
2. How did the speech *effect* you?
3. The *affect* of the speech was tremendous.
4. The prisoner *affected* his escape.
5. Mr. Smith *effected* a sadness he didn't feel.

Do you know how to correct these errors? In your school days you may have learned that *affect* is a verb and *effect* is a noun. And then your teacher may have explained that there are exceptions to this rule; that *affect* may *sometimes* be used as a noun, and *effect* may *on occasion* be used as a verb. And so on and on.

Don't bother about all this. The technical discussion of the various uses of *affect* and *effect* is so complicated that it only tends to confuse the student instead of enlightening him.

A HELPFUL FORMULA

There is a simple formula that will guide you to the correct usage of these two words for all practical purposes. Here it is:

1. Use *effect* if you can substitute the meaning of *bring about,* or *result,* for the required word.
2. Use *affect* if you can't substitute the meaning of *bring about,* or *result.*
3. Never use *effect* before a word denoting a person, such as *me, you, him, man, woman, Jerry, Joan.*

For example:

1. What was the _____ of the new plan he adopted?

In this sentence, you can substitute *result* for the word you want. Hence the word is *effect.*

2. How did the speech _____ you?

You must never use *effect* before *you,* which denotes a person. The correct word therefore is *affect,* which in this sentence means *to impress* (the mind or the feelings).

31

3. The _____ of the speech was tremendous.

Here you can substitute *result* for your required word. Hence the word is *effect*.

4. The prisoner _____ his escape.

In this sentence, can you substitute *brought about* for the missing word? You certainly can. The correct word, therefore, is *effected*.

5. Mr. Smith _____ a sadness he didn't feel.

Neither *brought about* nor *resulted* can fit into the blank space. And so the required word is *affected*, which here means *pretended*, or *assumed*.

There are times when you can use both affect and effect in sentences which may otherwise look exactly alike. But in such sentences, too, you can apply the formula for the correct usage of these two words. For example:

1. This medicine may *affect* (alter the chances for) his recovery.
2. This medicine may *effect* (bring about) his recovery.

As you may have noticed from the various examples in this chapter, both *affect* and *effect* can be used either as verbs or as nouns. But whatever their function, you are not likely to go wrong if you remember the three steps of the formula mentioned a little earlier.

So much, then, for the usage of *affect* and *effect*. As for *censor* and *censer*, the difference in their usage is very simple.

Censor, as we have noted at the beginning of this chapter, can be used either as a verb or as a noun.

Censer can be used only as a noun. A *censer* is a *vessel in which incense is burned*.

AN EASY TEST

Are you ready for your test in the correct usage of *affect, effect, censor* and *censer*? Check the required word in each of the following parentheses. If you remember the simple formula, you should get a high score in this test:

1. The new laws will (effect, affect) all the people.
2. Did the doctor positively promise to (effect, affect) the desired cure?

32

3. His plea produced the desired (affect, effect) and the prisoner was set free.

4. The damp climate seriously (affected, effected) him.

5. Your tears may fail to (affect, effect) his stubborn heart.

6. Don't try to (effect, affect) a boorish mannerism so foreign to your character.

7. A general war (affects, effects) civilians as well as soldiers.

8. The appointment of the new commander may have far-reaching (effects, affects).

9. I hope you can (effect, affect) a reconciliation between Mr. and Mrs. Brown.

10. The offer of a fight for the heavyweight title (effected, affected) him almost to tears.

—*Answers*—
(*Remember your formula*)

1-affect, 2-effect, 3-effect, 4-affected, 5-affect, 6-affect, 7-affects, 8-effects, 9-both may be correct; use *effect* if you mean *bring about*, and *affect* if you mean *alter* or *improve the chances for*, 10-affected.

Later on, you will learn much more about the verb and the noun—their abuses as well as their uses. For a breather at present, let us turn to the second word game.

Time out for the Second Word Game
TWENTY POWER-PACKED VERBS

A

In this game we are going to play with 20 verbs that end in -*ate*. See how many of them you can spot.

Again, as a help for a starter, I will give you the initial of each of the words you are to guess, and a dash for each of the letters you are to fill in.

1. Those who unreasonably assume power   a__o_ate

2. Those who artificially water a field   i__i_ate

3. Those who punish   c__t__ate
4. Those who goad on   i__t__ate
5. Those who make things easier for you   f_c_l__ate
6. Those who wish you happiness   f_l_c__ate
7. Those who are the first to do something   i__t_ate
8. Those who try to appease you   p_o_i__ate
9. Those who stay for a time in the country   r_s___ate
10. Those who weaken you   e__r_ate
11. Those who assume a false appearance   s_m__ate
12. Those who make a quarrel more bitter   ex_c_r_ate
13. Those who talk with a purpose to deceive   e_u_v__ate
14. Those who connect someone with a crime   i_c__m__ate
15. Those who fully satisfy your hunger   s_t_ate
16. Those who sparkle in conversation   s__n___l_ate
17. Those who turn bad impulses into worthy acts   s_b___ate
18. Those who hint at something   i_t__ate
19. Those who can't make up their minds   v_c_l_ate
20. Those who live a stagnant life, like a plant   v_g__ate

—Answers—

1-arrogate, 2-irrigate, 3-castigate, 4-instigate, 5-facilitate, 6-felicitate, 7-initiate, 8-propitiate, 9-rusticate, 10-enervate, 11-simulate, 12-exacerbate, 13-equivocate, 14-incriminate, 15-satiate, 16-scintillate, 17-sublimate, 18-intimate, 19-vacillate, 20-vegetate

B

How many of these words did you get? Only a few? Cheer up! We have just begun the game. You will be familiar with every one of them before we are through. And they will all become a part of your working vocabulary.

Let's now reshuffle the words, so that you can become better acquainted with them in a new setting and different arrangement:

1. Psychoanalysis teaches people to s_____ their baser desires into socially acceptable activities.

2. The witness tried to i_____ an innocent man who had seen the killing.

3. Don't allow yourself to become physically and intellectually dull; don't v_____.

4. A great general never v_____ when called upon to make a decision.

5. The dictators a_____ to themselves the power of life and death over their subjects.

6. He never overate, but always left the table s_____ and happy.

7. The dictator e_____ the quarrel between himself and his people by his inflammatory speech.

8. The wit of Bernard Shaw s_____ like a precious jewel.

9. Many savages think they can p_____ the gods with human sacrifices.

10. The ringleader i_____ a riot among the prisoners.

11. The warden thought the ringleader ought to be c_____ for his insubordination.

12. "Let me f_____ you on landing the job," said John to Henry.

13. "I never would have landed it," replied Henry, "if you hadn't f_____ my interview with the manager."

14. He i_____ that there had been a tacit understanding between them.

15. Some day the Sahara Desert may be i_____ and become fertile.

16. He who wants to be believed never lies or

e_____ or utters anything to arouse suspicion.

17. The Wright brothers i_____ the human conquest of the air.

18. To deceive the judges, he s_____ an ignorant boor.

19. The doctor advised Mr. Brown to r_____ at his brother's farm until he got well.

20. The tropical heat of Panama e_____ the visitor from a colder climate.

—*Answers*—

1-sublimate, 2-incriminate, 3-vegetate, 4-vacillates, 5-arrogate, 6-satiated, 7-exacerbated, 8-scintillates, 9-propitiate, 10-instigated, 11-castigated, 12-felicitate, 13-facilitated, 14-intimated, 15-irrigated, 16-equivocates, 17-initiated, 18-simulated, 19-rusticate, 20-enervates

C

Are the words getting a little more familiar now? Here they are, reshuffled once more. See what you can do with them in this new setting. Match the words in the first column with the definitions in the second column:

1. vacillate	a.	to sparkle
2. satiate	b.	to appease someone to kindness
3. scintillate	c.	to lead a passive life, like a plant
4. facilitate	d.	to waver in mind
5. sublimate	e.	to make more bitter, to irritate
6. incriminate	f.	to satisfy the appetite fully
7. enervate	g.	to weaken
8. equivocate	h.	to water artificially
9. propitiate	i.	to claim for oneself, with pride or arrogance
10. initiate	j.	to charge with a crime
11. felicitate	k.	to make easier
12. vegetate	l.	to stay in the country
13. arrogate	m.	to hint
14. exacerbate	n.	to use deceptive language
15. instigate	o.	to pretend
16. castigate	p.	to congratulate
17. intimate	q.	to punish severely
18. irrigate	r.	to incite someone to a bad action
19. simulate	s.	to start
20. rusticate	t.	to refine lower impulses into higher acts

—*Answers*—

1-d, 2-f, 3-a, 4-k, 5-t, 6-j, 7-g, 8-n, 9-b, 10-s, 11-p, 12-c, 13-i, 14-e, 15-r, 16-q, 17-m, 18-h, 19-o, 20-l

D

The final round in this game is to get the correct pronunciation of the twenty verbs:

arrogate: AR-roe-gate
castigate: CAS-ti-gate
enervate: EN-er-vate
equivocate: e-QUIV-o-cate

exacerbate: egz-ASS-er-bate
facilitate: fa-SIL-i-tate
felicitate: fe-LISS-i-tate
incriminate: in-CRIM-in-ate
initiate: in-ISH-i-ate
instigate: IN-sti-gate
intimate: IN-ti-mate
irrigate: IR-ri-gate
propitiate: pro-PISH-ee-ate
rusticate: RUS-ti-cate
satiate: SAY-she-ate
scintillate: SIN-ti-late
simulate: SIM-you-late
sublimate: SUB-li-mate
vacillate: VASS-il-ate
vegetate: VEJ-e-tate

Now that you have added a number of new words to your vocabulary, try them on your friends. See how many of these words will trip them up. Word games with your friends, you will find, are a fascinating pastime. And these, unlike poker or canasta, are games in which *everybody wins*—in the currency of more words, wider ideas, and greater power.

5

CAN *LAY* AND *LIE* MAKE GOOD BEDFELLOWS?

TWO KINDS OF VERBS

Which, if any, of the following sentences are incorrect?

1. The snow glittered as it *lay* on the ground.
2. He *laid* the book on the table.
3. *Lay* quietly while the doctor examines your ankle.
4. She finds her purse *lying* on the dresser.
5. The baby *laid* in its crib.
6. It's wise to be *lying in* your winter's supply of coal before it's too cold.
7. We have *lain* down our burdens.
8. Having *laid* on the counter for some time, the goods were sold at half price.
9. She has *laid* in bed for two hours.
10. Having *lain* an egg, the hen cackled loudly.

Sentences 3, 5, 6, 7, 8, 9, and 10 are incorrect. And in every case the error is due to a confusion between transitive and intransitive verbs.

But what are *transitive* and *intransitive verbs?*

A *transitive* verb is a word that can *transfer* its action to some person or thing called the *object* of the verb. For example:

The lightning *struck* the house.

Or, simply:

The lightning *struck.*

In the first sentence, the object of the verb *struck* is *the house.* In the second sentence, the object is not expressed but understood. A verb that can take an object, whether expressed or understood, is a *transitive* verb.

But there are some verbs that can not take an object. For example:

Come into my house.
Will you *sleep* late tomorrow?
Don't *walk* so fast.

These verbs—*come, sleep, walk*—are *intransitive.*

And so a *transitive* verb can take an object, and an *intransitive* verb can not take an object.
So far, simple enough.
The next point to be considered is just as simple.

VERBS HAVE VOICES

Notice the difference between the two following sentences:

1. The lightning *struck* the house.
2. The house *was struck* by the lightning.

In the first sentence, the verb *struck* is said to be in the *active* voice. In the second sentence, the verb *was struck* is said to be in the *passive* voice.

When a verb is in the *active* voice, some person or thing *performs* the action.

When it is in the *passive* voice, the action *is performed by* some person or some thing.

This is much easier than it sounds, as you will see from the following examples:

1. *Active:* Mark Twain *wrote* humorous novels.
   Passive: Humorous novels *were written* by Mark Twain.
2. *Active:* His books *have pleased* millions of readers.
   Passive: Millions of readers *have been pleased* by his books.
3. *Active:* Several generations *will remember* his genius.
   Passive: His genius *will be remembered* by several generations.

Transitive verbs can be used in the *passive* as well as in the *active* voice.
Thus:

1. *Active:* Toscanini *conducted* the orchestra.
   Passive: The orchestra *was conducted* by Toscanini.
2. *Active:* The President *will make* an important speech.
   Passive: An important speech *will be made* by the President.

39

3. *Active:* The manager *has fired* the inefficient workers.
   Passive: The inefficient workers *have been fired* by the
   manager.

Intransitive verbs can be used only in the *active* but not in
the *passive* voice.

Thus you can say:

John *arrived* at ten o'clock.

But you can't say:

It *was arrived* by John at ten o'clock.

This, too, as you see, is simple enough. A *transitive* verb
can take an object and can be used in the *passive* as well
as in the *active* voice. An *intransitive* verb *can not take an
object* and can be used only in the *active* voice.

And here is another interesting thing about transitive verbs.
When they change from the active to the passive, the *object*
of the verb becomes the *subject.*

Thus:

Active: Toscanini conducted *the orchestra* (object).
Passive: The orchestra (subject) was conducted by Toscanini.

You already know what the *object* of a verb is. It is the
person or thing upon which the verb *acts.*

And the *subject* of a verb is the person or thing that *performs the action* in the active, or *receives the action* in the
passive.

With these facts in mind we can return to *lay* and *lie* and
straighten out their usage and their meaning.

TWO HARD VERBS MADE EASY

To *lay* means to *place.* It is a *transitive* verb; it can *transfer*
its action to an *object,* and it can be used *either* in the *active*
or in the *passive* voice.

To *lie* means to *recline.* It is an *intransitive* verb; it can *not*
transfer its action to an *object,* and it can be used *only* in the
active voice.

A recent test showed that only one out of a hundred adults
knew how to use these two verbs correctly. Let's take these
verbs apart and put them together again. And then you will
realize how easy it is to understand their proper use.

Like all other verbs, *lay* and *lie* have different forms to express different times for their actions.

Thus, the *transitive* verb *lay* has the following basic forms, known as its *principal parts:*

Present $\begin{cases} \text{I } lay \\ \text{I } am\ laying \end{cases}$

Past $\begin{cases} \text{I } laid \\ \text{I } have\ laid \end{cases}$

Examples:

> John *lays* a carpet.
> John *is laying* a carpet.
> John *laid* a carpet.
> John *has laid* a carpet.

And the *intransitive* verb *lie* has the following basic forms, or *principal parts:*

Present $\begin{cases} \text{I } lie \\ \text{I } am\ lying \end{cases}$

Past $\begin{cases} \text{I } lay \\ \text{I } have\ lain \end{cases}$

Examples:

> The cat *lies* on the carpet.
> The cat *is lying* on the carpet.
> The cat *lay* on the carpet.
> The cat *has lain* on the carpet.

And that is all there is to it. Apply the above forms to the sentences at the beginning of this chapter, remember that *lay* is *transitive* and *lie* is *intransitive,* and you can't go wrong.

Let's see, then, how the idea works out in each of the ten sentences printed at the beginning of this chapter:

1. The snow glittered as it *lay* (past intransitive) on the ground.
2. He *laid* (past transitive) the book on the table.
3. *Lie* (present intransitive) quietly while the doctor examines your ankle.
4. She finds her purse *lying* (intransitive) on the dresser.
5. The baby *lay* (past intransitive) in its crib.
6. It's wise to be *laying in* (transitive) your winter's supply of coal before it's too cold.
7. We have *laid* down (past transitive) our burdens.

8. Having *lain* (past intransitive) on the counter for some time, the goods were sold at half price.

9. She has *lain* (past intransitive) in bed for two hours.

10. Having *laid* (past transitive) an egg, the hen cackled loudly.

Simple enough, isn't it? But before we leave this chapter, let's look at another verb that resembles the above. This verb is to *lie*, meaning to *tell an untruth*. The construction of this verb, however, should give you no trouble:

> The prisoner *lies*.
> The prisoner is *lying*.
> The prisoner *lied*.
> The prisoner *has lied*.

This habit of lying on every possible occasion may sometimes follow a man even into the grave. Such was the case of a certain lawyer, whose tombstone bore the following inscription:

HERE LIES ATTORNEY JOHN RUSSELL.
HE LIES STILL

Have you fully grasped the ideas of this chapter? If so, you will find it easy to determine which is the correct word inside the parentheses in each of the following sentences:

1. Don't (lay, lie) too long in the sun.
2. I hope you have (laid, lain) away enough money for a rainy day.
3. He believes in letting sleeping dogs (lay, lie).
4. The book (lay, laid) on the table where he had put it.
5. The body was (laying, lying) on the ground.
6. Every afternoon he (lies, lays) down for a nap.
7. Get up! You have (lain, laid) in bed too long.
8. We have been (laying, lying) a new carpet on our living room floor.
9. You have now (laid, lain) the foundation for a better understanding of transitive and intransitive verbs.
10. The sick man must (lay, lie) quietly on his back.

—Answers—

1-lie, 2-laid, 3-lie, 4-lay, 5-lying, 6-lies, 7-lain, 8-laying, 9-laid, 10-lie

Still a bit uncertain? Just be patient, and go over the chapter again if necessary. It's not a hard chapter, I repeat, but it does need concentration. And when you are completely through with it, take a deep breath and relax with the next word game.

Time out for the Third Word Game
WORDS THAT DESCRIBE PEOPLE
YOU MAY KNOW

All of us are creatures compounded of many characteristics. Yet many of us have one outstanding trait, by which we are generally classified in the circle of our acquaintances. Thus, Jenny Blake may be known as a gadabout, Johnny Brown as a go-getter, Florence Finch as a celebrity chaser, and so on.

A

In this game, try to get the fifteen words that describe the following types of people. In each case, only one of the three given words is correct.

1. He's had an unhappy love affair, and he hates all women as a result.

> He's a *convivialist*
> He's a *dilettante*
> He's a *misogynist*

2. He despises all people, men and women alike.

> He's an *altruist*
> He's a *misanthrope*
> He's a *virtuoso*

3. He questions everything, even the existence of God.

> He's a *skeptic*
> He's a *devotee*
> He's a *hypochondriac*

4. She likes to abuse everybody and is always looking for a quarrel.

> She's an *introvert*
> She's an *extrovert*
> She's a *termagant*

5. She has an uncontrollable urge to set fires.

> She's a *kleptomaniac*
> She's a *pyromaniac*
> She's a *monomaniac*

6. He loves to attend banquets, especially where they serve plenty of drinks.

> He's a *virtuoso*
> He's a *convivialist*
> He's a *dilettante*

7. He's obsessed by a single dangerous idea that everybody is trying to harm him.

> He's a *devotee*
> He's a *misogynist*
> He's a *monomaniac*

8. She steals everything she lays her hands on—she just can't help herself.

> She's a *kleptomaniac*
> She's a *termagant*
> She's a *hypochondriac*

9. He plays the violin with superb technique.

> He's an *extrovert*
> He's a *virtuoso*
> He's a *dilettante*

10. She imagines she has all sorts of diseases.

> She's a *hypochondriac*
> She's a *termagant*
> She's an *introvert*

11. He is zealously attached to his religious duties and his love for God.

> He's a *convivialist*
> He's an *altruist*
> He's a *devotee*

12. He is self-centered, though not selfish—just likes to be alone with his dreams and his thoughts.

> He's a *dilettante*
> He's an *introvert*
> He's a *misogynist*

13. He loves his follow men and always tries to promote their happiness.

> He's an *altruist*
> He's a *dilettante*
> He's a *virtuoso*

14. He is a superficial dabbler in music, painting, literature, and general culture.

> He's a *devotee*
> He's an *extrovert*
> He's a *dilettante*

15. He gets his greatest satisfaction from his business and social contacts with other people.

> He's an *extrovert*
> He's a *virtuoso*
> He's a *termagant*

— *Answers* —

1-misogynist, 2-misanthrope, 3-skeptic, 4-termagant, 5-pyromaniac, 6-convivialist, 7-monomaniac, 8-kleptomaniac, 9-virtuoso, 10-hypochondriac, 11-devotee, 12-introvert, 13-altruist, 14-dilettante, 15-extrovert

B

Check the correct answer to each of the following questions:

1. Is a *termagant* a person who mostly hates women?   Yes No

2. Does a *convivialist* like especially to dabble in the arts?   Yes No

3. Would a *misanthrope* be likely to refuse a favor?   Yes No

4. Would you expect an extreme *introvert* to be a social success?   Yes No

5. Is it unwise to leave a *kleptomaniac* alone in a department store?   Yes No

6. Is a *hypochondriac* a person guilty of hypocrisy?   Yes No

7. Is an *extrovert* likely to make valuable contacts?   Yes No

8. Would you expect a *dilettante* to play the piano with superb skill?   Yes No

9. Is a *misogynist* a man who does not enjoy female companionship?   Yes No

10. Would you be wise to choose a *skeptic* as the minister of your church?   Yes No

11. Does a *pyromaniac* love to see fires?   Yes No

12. Would you necessarily expect a *virtuoso* to be unusually virtuous?   Yes No

13. Would a *monomaniac* be likely to be arrested for stealing?   Yes No

14. Would you call Carnegie's endowment of libraries the work of an *altruist?*   Yes No

15. Is a *devotee* a person who does not vote?   Yes No

—Answers—

1-no, 2-no, 3-yes, 4-no, 5-yes, 6-no, 7-yes, 8-no, 9-yes, 10-no, 11-yes, 12-no, 13-no, 14-yes, 15-no

C

Give the correct word after each of the following definitions:

1. A jovial person, fond of festivals _____
2. One who suffers from imaginary symptoms of illness

   _____
3. An amateur dabbler in the arts _____
4. A person interested in the welfare of other people

   _____
5. A hater of his fellow men _____
6. A hater of women _____
7. A doubter, especially in religious matters _____
8. A zealous observer of religious rites or an ardent partisan _____
9. A person who turns his thoughts inward _____
10. A person who enjoys his social contacts _____
11. A scolding woman _____
12. A person with a propensity for stealing _____
13. A person crazed by a single morbid idea _____
14. A person with a propensity for setting fires

   _____
15. A master of technique _____

—Answers—

1-convivialist, 2-hypochondriac, 3-dilettante, 4-altruist, 5-misanthrope, 6-misogynist, 7-skeptic, 8-devotee, 9-introvert, 10-extrovert, 11-termagant, 12-kleptomaniac, 13-monomaniac, 14-pyromaniac, 15-virtuoso

D

And now try to recall the meaning of each of these words as you learn their correct pronunciation:

46

convivialist: con-VIV-ee-al-ist
devotee: DEV-o-tee
dilettante: dil-et-TAN-tee
extrovert: EX-tro-vert
hypochondriac: high-po-KON-dree-ac
introvert: IN-tro-vert
kleptomaniac: klep-to-MAY-nee-ac
misanthrope: MISS-an-thrope
misogynist: miss-OJ-in-ist
monomaniac: mo-no-MAY-nee-ac
philanthropist: phil-AN-thro-pist
pyromaniac: pie-ro-MAY-nee-ac
skeptic (also spelled *sceptic*): SKEP-tic
termagant: TER-muh-gant
virtuoso: ver-tew-OWE-so, or ver-too-OWE-so

For a final fling in this game, try to think of two synonyms for each of the above words. If you can't think of them readily, look the words up in the dictionary. Or in Roget's *Thesaurus*. You will find this treasury of English synonyms an excellent aid in the building of your vocabulary.

6

TRICKY VERBS—HANDLE WITH CARE

A SCHOOLBOY'S AMUSING ERROR
There is a story about a schoolboy who was in the habit of saying "I have went" instead of "I have gone." One day his teacher ordered him to stay after school and to write "I have gone" three hundred times on the blackboard.

The boy faithfully completed his task, and then left the following note for his teacher:

"Dear Teacher—I have finished my work and I have went home."

Watch out for bad habits in the usage of your verbs. Such habits are not easy to break. You have learned, in Chapter 5, how to avoid confusion in *lay* and *lie*. In addition to these, there are many other verbs that can play various tricks with our language. This is what makes English so fascinating a study to natives and to foreigners alike.

WHERE LOGIC IS MISLEADING
A German refugee recently prepared a list of parallel verbs whose principal parts he constructed, as he said, in accordance with the "rules of logic." Here are just a few of these words:

I eat	I ate	I have eaten
I treat	I treat	I have treaten
I steal	I stole	I have stolen
I heal	I hole	I have holen
I drink	I drank	I have drunk
I think	I thank	I have thunk
I see	I saw	I have seen
I flee	I flaw	I have fleen
I take	I took	I have taken
I make	I mook	I have maken

I teach	I taught	I have taught
I bleach	I blaught	I have blaught

You can devise for yourself any number of equally absurd principal parts that might appear to be based upon the "rules of logic." Our language, however, is not always logical. Words are not hammered out like pieces of iron on a machine. They grow and change over the centuries, and many of them have assumed forms that are quite irregular. Thus we have, in addition to *regular verbs*, a number of *irregular verbs*.

The principal parts of the *regular verbs* are easy enough to remember. For example:

I help	I helped	I have helped
I miss	I missed	I have missed
I pray	I prayed	I have prayed

It is the *irregular verbs* that are troublesome. Each of them is a law unto itself. Many errors are made in the daily usage of these verbs.

Some of these errors are to be found in several of the following sentences. See if you can spot them in those sentences that are incorrect.

FIND THE ERRORS

1. Now you have gone to work and have did it again.
2. She has broke her promise a number of times.
3. They have froze their toes in the blizzard.
4. The artist has drawn a good likeness of the model.
5. A serious crisis has arisen in the world as a result of the splitting of the atom.
6. Very few people have swam the English Channel.
7. Johnny is sorry he has tore his sweater.
8. I have never drove such a comfortable car.
9. The choir has sung the *Messiah*.
10. They have spoke very well of you.

—*Answers*—

Sentences 4, 5 and 9 are correct. The others should be corrected as follows:

1. Now you have gone to work and have *done* it again.
2. She has *broken* her promise a number of times.
3. They have *frozen* their toes in the blizzard.
6. Very few people have *swum* the English Channel.

7. Johnny is sorry he has *torn* his sweater.
8. I have never *driven* such a comfortable car.
10. They have *spoken* very well of you.

SIMPLE WORDS WITH SURPRISING TWISTS

To avoid such errors as the above, learn the principal parts of these tricky verbs:

Present	Past	Present-Perfect
I arise	I arose	I have arisen
I bear	I bore	I have borne
I beat	I beat	I have beaten
I become	I became	I have become
I begin	I began	I have begun
I bid (*in buying*)	I bid	I have bid
I bid (command)	I bade	I have bidden
I bite	I bit	I have bitten
I blow	I blew	I have blown
I break	I broke	I have broken
I burst	I burst	I have burst
I choose	I chose	I have chosen
I come	I came	I have come
I deal	I dealt	I have dealt
I do	I did	I have done
I draw	I drew	I have drawn
I drive	I drove	I have driven
I eat	I ate	I have eaten
I fall	I fell	I have fallen
I fly	I flew	I have flown
I forbid	I forbade	I have forbidden
I forsake	I forsook	I have forsaken
I freeze	I froze	I have frozen
I get	I got	I have got, gotten
I give	I gave	I have given
I go	I went	I have gone
I grow	I grew	I have grown
I hurt	I hurt	I have hurt
I lead	I led	I have led
I ride	I rode	I have ridden
I run	I ran	I have run
I see	I saw	I have seen
I set	I set	I have set
I sing	I sang	I have sung
I sit	I sat	I have sat

I slay	I slew	I have slain
I sling	I slung	I have slung
I speak	I spoke	I have spoken
I spin	I spun	I have spun
I string	I strung	I have strung
I strive	I strove	I have striven
I swim	I swam	I have swum
I tear	I tore	I have torn
I wring	I wrung	I have wrung
I write	I wrote	I have written

And please note the following verb:

I hang	I hung, or I hanged	I have hung, or I have hanged

When a criminal is executed by hanging, he is *hanged*.
When a thing is suspended, it is *hung*.

QUIZ TIME

Now for a round-up to see how well you've learned these principal parts. Check those of the following sentences that are wrong, and correct the errors:

1. "You shouldn't of did it," said Mrs. Smith to Jerry.
2. The dancers spinned around in a circle.
3. She is sorry she has broken the pitcher.
4. I'm afraid I have bited off more than I can chew.
5. "I have hurted my toe!" cried little Peter.
6. They have ridden 400 miles between sunrise and sunset.
7. He begun the job with the greatest enthusiasm.
8. "You have run an excellent race," said the coach.
9. "I have strove to do my best," replied the captain of the track team.
10. I seen a suspicious character on the street corner.

CORRECTIONS

1. "You shouldn't have done it," said Mrs. Smith to Jerry.
2. The dancers spun around in a circle.
4. I'm afraid I have bitten off more than I can chew.
5. "I have hurt my toe!" cried little Peter.
7. He began the job with the greatest enthusiasm.
9. "I have striven to do my best," replied the captain of the track team.

51

10. I saw a suspicious character on the street corner. The other sentences are correct.

Are you sufficiently familiar now with the principal parts of these irregular verbs? Then take it easy for a while and relax for another word game.

Time out for the Fourth Word Game
WORDS THAT HAVE A COMMON BEGINNING

Words are not isolated things existing by themselves. Many of them are related because they have a common prefix—that is, one or more letters or syllables placed at the beginning of the word to modify its meaning. All the words that have the same prefix—such as con or com, for example—are definitely allied to one another.

A

In the following game you are to guess fifteen such words, and to find out their common relationship. Every dash in the required words represents one letter.

1. Those who feel sorry for, or suffer along with, other people are said to com___er__e with them.
2. When we combine ideas in such a way as to make them more intricate or more difficult, we com__i_a__ them.
3. He brought a number of magazine articles together and c_m__l_d them into a book.
4. A student who can bring his faculties together to bear upon his lesson is able to con___tr___.
5. When you reason with an enemy to win him over, you may be able to con__l_a__ him.
6. By mixing her ingredients skilfully together, she was able to con_o_t a very good dish.
7. The members of the jury agreed with the lawyer for the defense; that is, they con_u_r__ with him.
8. The king used to con__s_e_d to speak to the commoners.

9. "Let me con_ro__ my accuser and talk face to face with him," said the prisoner.

10. When several of the Romans plotted together to assassinate Caesar, they con_p__e_ against him.

11. The general decided to surrender and to com__y with the terms of the enemy.

12. The cold in his chest seemed to pull his muscles together, and to con_t_i_t them with pain.

13. You con__m_n__e food when you allow the good to be mixed with the bad.

14. The infantry and the cavalry drew closely together and tried to con____g_ upon a single objective.

15. He con__k__ the assembly by calling the delegates together.

—*Answers*—

1-commiserate, 2-complicate, 3-compiled, 4-concentrate, 5-conciliate, 6-concoct, 7-concurred, 8-condescend, 9-confront, 10-conspired, 11-comply, 12-constrict, 13-contaminate, 14-converge, 15-convoked

All the above words, as you may have noticed, have one thing in common. They denote an idea that can be expressed by the word *with,* or *together.* The prefix *con*—changed to *com* before the letters *b, m,* or *p* for easier pronunciation—comes from the Latin *cum,* which means *with.* Whenever you see a word with this prefix, you will know at once that it contains the idea of *accompaniment* in its meaning.

B

To fix the fifteen verbs more firmly in your mind, write the proper word after each of the following definitions. The order is *not* the same as in the above sentences.

1. To win someone over _____

2. To collect literary material into a volume _____

3. To sympathize or condole _____

4. To hold the same opinion with another _____

5. To make things difficult or complex _____

6. To come nearer together from different directions

_____

7. To stoop to others in a patronizing manner

_____

8. To prepare by mixing different ingredients together

_____

53

9. To fix your undivided attention upon a problem

_____

10. To call an assembly together _____

11. To spoil the good by mixing it with the bad

_____

12. To bind tightly together _____

13. To plot secretly together _____

14. To come face to face with a person or a problem

_____

15. To act in accordance (with) _____

—*Answers*—

1-conciliate, 2-compile, 3-commiserate, 4-concur, 5-complicate, 6-converge, 7-condescend, 8-concoct, 9-concentrate, 10-convoke, 11-contaminate, 12-constrict, 13-conspire, 14-confront, 15-comply

C

And now, to review these words from still another angle, characterize each of the following persons or situations with the right verb:

1. He gives his entire attention to his lessons.   He _____

2. He agrees with somebody else's opinion.   He _____

3. He pities you when you're in trouble.   He _____

4. He likes to turn his enemies into friends.   He _____

5. He makes things more difficult.   He _____

6. He patronizes his inferiors.   He _____

7. He cooks up all sorts of ingredients into fancy dishes.   He _____

8. A cold in the lungs tightens the chest.   It _____

9. He collects his lectures into a book.   He _____

10. He calls people to a meeting.   He _____

11. He boldly faces people or situations.   He _____

12. He plots with others to overthrow the government.   He _____

13. He gives in to your desires.   He _____
14. Troubles from different directions seem to come together upon you.   They _____
15. One bad apple spoils a whole barrel.   It _____

—Answers—

1-concentrates, 2-concurs, 3-commiserates, 4-conciliates, 5-complicates, 6-condescends, 7-concocts, 8-constricts, 9-compiles, 10-convokes, 11-confronts, 12-conspires, 13-complies, 14-converge, 15-contaminates.

You have just considered fifteen verbs that should belong to your vocabulary if you want to use better English. These words are related in that the idea of *togetherness* is inherent in every one of them. And this idea is expressed by the letters *com* or *con*.

D

Most of the words in this game are easy to pronounce. Here are the more difficult ones:

commiserate: com-MIZ-er-ate
concentrate: CON-cen-trate
conciliate: con-SIL-ee-ate
contaminate: con-TAM-in-ate

Have you added the fifteen verbs of this game to your permanent word-stock? They will introduce you to the entire family-group of words that have this common prefix—*con* or *com*—and share in the common idea of *togetherness*. Try, as you go along, to think of as many of these words as possible. It is an excellent way to expand your vocabulary.

And don't forget your synonyms and antonyms. Try to think of a few similar and opposite words for each of the above fifteen verbs. You can always turn to your dictionary and thesaurus as your unfailing guide.

7

LOOK OUT—YOUR PARTICIPLE IS DANGLING

SPOT THE ERRORS

Here is a list of sentences, some of which are grammatically wrong. See if you can spot the wrong sentences and correct the errors.

1. Looking through the window, I saw my friend across the street.
2. Watching a mystery drama on my television set, the murdered man lay crumpled on the sidewalk.
3. Arriving on my bicycle just in time, the elephants began their act at the circus.
4. The *Queen Mary* greeted my eyes, walking along Riverside Drive.
5. His beard streaked with gray, the little boy was playing with his grandfather.
6. Glittering in the sun, the airship looked like a silver bird.
7. Answering the door bell, I was glad to see my friends.
8. Reading my book, the cat sat on my lap.
9. While taking a shower, the telephone rang.
10. The Princess met the President, wearing a red dress.

How many of the above sentences are wrong? And what is the trouble with them?

The answer to the first question is, *seven;* and to the second question, *dangling participles.*

But what is a dangling participle?

It is the part of a verb that becomes grammatically untied from the rest of the sentence. Every verb has a present participle and a past participle.

For example:

I am *writing*	I have *written*
I am *helping*	I have *helped*
I am *walking*	I have *walked*

The *present participles* are *writing, helping,* and *walking.* The *past participles* are *written, helped,* and *walked.*

These participles must never be left hanging in the air. A dangling participle is as troublesome as a dangling shoelace. If you don't tie your participles up properly, they may cause your English to sprawl in a most ridiculous manner.

CORRECTING THE ERRORS

Let us now return to the sentences at the beginning of this chapter:

The first sentence is correct.

2. From the wording of this sentence, you might infer that the murdered man was watching the drama as he lay crumpled on the sidewalk. Revise the construction to read: *Watching* a mystery drama on my television set, *I saw* the murdered man lying crumpled on the sidewalk.

3. This sentence certainly couldn't mean that the elephants arrived on the bicycle. Yet this is what it says. Revise it to read: *Arriving* on my bicycle just in time, *I watched* the elephants begin their act at the circus.

4. Were my eyes, or was the *Queen Mary,* walking along Riverside Drive? Correct the sentence as follows: The *Queen Mary* greeted my eyes, *as I was walking* along Riverside Drive.

5. This sentence, in its present form, might imply that the little boy had a beard streaked with gray. Change the sentence to read: The little boy was playing with his grandfather, *whose beard was streaked with gray.*

The sixth and the seventh sentences are correct.

8. Was the cat reading my book? That's what the sentence says. Correct it as follows: *As I was reading* my book, the cat sat on my lap.

9. It wasn't the telephone, but some person, who was under the shower. Make this clear: *While he* (or *she*) *was taking* a shower, the telephone rang.

10. Wouldn't the President look lovely in a red dress? What the sentence means to say is: The *Princess, wearing* a red dress, met the President.

THREE EASY RULES

From the above corrections you see that you can avoid a dangling participle by remembering three simple rules:

First, *the participle must be logically related to the person or thing to which it refers.*

Second, *both sides of the relationship must be expressed.*

Third, *the words of the sentence must be so arranged that there can be no doubt about the relationship.*

Look at the following statement now, and see how simple it is to tie your participle firmly up to the rest of the sentence:

Mary first saw *Helen Hayes playing* at the Majestic Theater.

Playing is logically related to Helen Hayes.
Both *Helen Hayes* and *playing* are expressed.

The arrangement of the sentence makes it clear that *playing* refers to Helen Hayes, and not to Mary. Otherwise the sentence would read: Mary, playing at the Majestic Theater, first saw Helen Hayes there.

Rather easy, isn't it, once you know the trick? See now if you can correct the dangling participles in the following sentences.

QUIZ TIME

1. Elected, many reforms will be introduced.
2. Lying on his back, he floated safely to the shore.
3. Surrounded by the enemy, the surrender was inevitable.
4. Having been built for one family, the house had to be remodeled into two apartments.
5. Suffering from a nervous ailment, she twitched her eyebrows.
6. Talking in his sleep, she found out many of his secrets.
7. Shouting these words, the bullet hit him in the temple.
8. Easily earned, money is easily spent.
9. Missing the bus, he came home late.
10. Though coming late, the dinner was waiting for him on the table.

—*Answers*—

Sentences 2, 4, 5, 8 and 9 are correct. The other sentences can be corrected as follows:

58

1. When he is elected, many reforms will be introduced.
3. Since the regiment was surrounded by the enemy, the surrender was inevitable.
6. As he was talking in his sleep, she found out many of his secrets.
7. While he was shouting these words, the bullet hit him in the temple.
10. Though he came late, the dinner was waiting for him on the table.

Avoid similar errors when you use the *infinitive* form of the verb—that is, the *verb* preceded by the word *to*.

Wrong form: To appreciate these dresses, they must be seen.
Correct form: To appreciate these dresses, you must see them.
Or: To be appreciated, these dresses must be seen.

And now that our participles and infinitives have been snugly tucked into their proper places, we can go on to the next word game.

Time out for the Fifth Word Game
SOME MORE WORDS THAT HAVE
A COMMON BEGINNING

In the fourth word game we considered several words that began with the prefix *com* or *con*. The fifth game consists of a number of words that begin with the prefix *sym* or *syn*.

How many of the following words beginning with this prefix can you spot?

A

1. The two sides of your face, like the two sides of a leaf, are in sym__t__with each other.
2. The headmasters held a sym__s__m on the value of teaching history in the high schools.
3. The Jewish congregation met in the syn_g__u_ for the Sabbath services.

4. Your television set is so designed that there is syn_ _r_n_ _m between the picture and the sound.

5. William Randolph Hearst organized a syn_ _c_ _e under his own management.

6. The Lutheran clergymen decided to hold their general assembly, or syn_ _, in Milwaukee.

7. The *Reader's Digest* published a good syn_p_ _ _ of the latest best seller.

8. Artificial rubber can be made by the syn_ _e_ _s of certain chemical elements.

—*Answers*—

1-symmetry, 2-symposium, 3-synagogue, 4-synchronism, 5-syndicate, 6-synod, 7-synopsis, 8-synthesis

As you may have noticed from the above words, the prefix *syn*—spelled *sym* before b, m, or p—means the same as the Latin prefix *con*. All words that begin with this syllable are related in their common meaning of *togetherness*.

B

Here are several other words that have the same relationship of *togetherness*. See if you can guess these words:

1. During Lent, they enjoyed a col_ _t_ _ _n of light food in the evening.

2. The writing of a book is known as a col_ _b_ _a_ _ _ _n when two or more people do it together.

3. A husband and a wife are guilty of col_ _s_ _ _ _ if they coöperate fraudulently to get a divorce.

4. Professor Smith was the col_ _a_ _ _ _ of Professor Jones at Wellesley.

5. Through your cor_ _b_ _a_ _ _ _n of a man's testimony, you may help to inspire confidence in his statements.

6. Little by little, as the acid ate into the meal, cor_ _ s_ _n took place.

7. You form a syl_ _b_ _ by combining letters into a single sounding unit.

8. And you prepare a syl_ _ _ _u_ by bringing together into an outline the principal features of a subject or a course of study.

—*Answers*—

1-collation, 2-collaboration, 3-collusion, 4-colleague, 5-corroboration, 6-corrosion, 7-syllable, 8-syllabus

As you may have observed from the above sentences, the Latin prefix *com* and the Greek prefix *syn* have other forms —*col* and *syl* before the letter *l*, and *cor* before the letter *r*. And all these forms have the selfsame meaning—*together*, or *with*.

C

And now try your mental gymnastics on the words of Sections A and B as you approach them from another angle.

1. It is a formal conference for an exchange of ideas.   s_____

2. It is the product of a job done by several people working together.   c_____

3. It tells the contents of a book in abbreviated form.   s_____

4. It strengthens your own testimony through somebody else's assertion.   c_____

5. It's the combination of several letters into a single sound.   s_____

6. It denotes the simultaneous occurrence of several events.   s_____

7. It's the easy but dishonest way to divorce.   c_____

8. It is a meeting of Christian ministers.   s_____

9. It denotes the harmony of corresponding parts.   s_____

10. It is a meeting place for Jewish worship.   s_____

11. It is a light meal (particularly on a fast day).   c_____

12. It is a group of newspapers under one head.   s_____

13. It denotes a person who is professionally associated with another person.   c_____

14. It is the combining of various elements to produce new chemicals.   s_____

15. It denotes gradual decay.   c_____

16. Teachers often prepare it to outline their courses.   s_____

1-symposium, 2-collaboration, 3-synopsis, 4-corroboration, 5-syllable, 6-synchronism, 7-collusion, 8-synod, 9-symmetry, 10-synagogue, 11-collation, 12-syndicate, 13-colleague, 14-synthesis, 15-corrosion, 16-syllabus

D

The words of this game should be pretty familiar to you by now. So try your final check-up on them. Match the words in the first column with the meanings in the second column.

1. symmetry	a.	an associated group of newspapers
2. symposium	b.	a Jewish place of worship
3. synagogue	c.	a meeting of Christian ministers
4. synchronism	d.	occurrence at the same time
5. syndicate	e.	a formal discussion
6. synod	f.	a professional associate
7. synopsis	g.	the outline of a course of study
8. synthesis	h.	gradual decay
9. collation	i.	the assembling of different things into a new form
10. collaboration	j.	a confirmation of testimony
11. collusion	k.	the brief summary of a book
12. colleague	l.	a job done together
13. corroboration	m.	a light meal
14. corrosion	n.	coöperation in fraud
15. syllable	o.	the harmonious balance of different parts
16. syllabus	p.	a group of letters with a single sound

1-o, 2-e, 3-b, 4-d, 5-a, 6-c, 7-k, 8-i, 9-m, 10-l, 11-n, 12-f, 13-j, 14-h, 15-p, 16-g

E

Here is the pronunciation of the more difficult words in this game:

colloquy: KOL-lo-kwee
symposium: sim-POE-zee-um
synchronism: SIN-kron-ism
synopsis: sin-OP-sis
synod: SIN-ud
synthesis: SIN-the-sis

As you play these word games, you not only increase your vocabulary, but you add to your mental power and general understanding of the world.

You now have a pretty good idea of the relationship of words beginning with *com* or *syn*. But this is only a sample. You will learn much more about the meanings of words and their relationships as you go on with these games. And, in the chapters on grammar, you will learn how to bring your words together into a more effective expression of your ambitions, desires, and ideas.

So let's go ahead to further learning and more fun!

8

HOW TO USE YOUR VERBS

TO TELL THE TIME

Some of the following sentences are incorrect. See if you can spot the errors and make the necessary corrections.

1. When I arrived, I found that they have gone.
2. Galileo discovered that the earth revolved around the sun.
3. Hitler has started World War II in 1939.
4. They all agreed that honesty is the best policy.
5. No sooner had he entered the house than the dog barks at him.
6. They were surprised to hear that Albany was the capital of New York.
7. Come what may, he was determined to tell the truth.
8. It had rained for five days before the river overflowed its banks.
9. I never thought he will have the nerve to do it.
10. He had told them the truth, that they may be prepared for the worst.

Before we discuss the errors in the above sentences, let us glance at the various points of time in which the action of a verb may take place.

The times of all verbal actions, as you will recall from your school days, are grammatically known as *tenses*. There are three principal times, or tenses, to denote the action of a verb:

Present: I *eat* a juicy steak.
Past: I *ate* a juicy steak.
Future: I *shall eat* a juicy steak.

But the time of an action can be expressed even more exactly, by a subtle variation of the three principal tenses:
Present-Perfect: I *have eaten* a juicy steak. This sentence

means that I *have recently finished eating* the steak. The *present-perfect* denotes *a past action that has occurred just before*, or *has continued up to, the present time*. It also indicates something that happened at an indefinite time in the past: *I have been* to London, but not recently.

Past-Perfect. I *had eaten* a juicy steak before my friends arrived. This sentence means that *the eating of the steak had taken place before the arrival of my friends*. The *past-perfect* denotes a *past action that happened prior to another past action.*

Future-Perfect: I *shall have eaten* a juicy steak by the time the dessert is brought. This tense means that *the eating of the steak will be completed before the bringing of the dessert*. And thus the *future-perfect* denotes *a future action that will take place prior to another future action.*

KEEPING TIMES IN LINE

In addition to the above, there are several other tenses that express still subtler variations of time, but here we need not bother ourselves with them. The six main tenses—*Present, Past, Future, Present-Perfect, Past-Perfect*, and *Future-Perfect*—will steer you through most of the difficulties in the ordinary timing of your verbs.

That is, provided you watch your *sequence of tenses*—the agreement between the main verb and the dependent verb in a sentence. These verbs must be made to *harmonize* with each other in time.

This idea is much simpler than it sounds. Look at the following sentences, for example:

He *knows* where you *live* now. (Here the present, *live*, denotes the same time or harmonizes with the present, *knows*.)

He *listened* when you *spoke*. (Here the past, *spoke*, harmonizes with the past, *listened*.)

He *will be* happy if you *will come*. (Here the two verbs harmonize because they are both future.)

But watch out for this one:

The ancient prophets declared that war *is* evil. (Here the present, *is*, follows the past, *declared*. It was not merely an idea of the past, but it is a permanent truth, that war is evil. When you express an axiom, or a permanent fact or truth, use the present tense even after a past verb.)

PICKING UP THE SLIPS

And now we are ready to correct the errors in the sentences at the beginning of this chapter.

1. This sentence should read: When I arrived, I found that they *had gone*. The past-perfect, *had gone*, denotes an action prior to the past, *arrived*.

2. This sentence should read: Galileo discovered that the earth *revolves* around the sun. The revolution of the earth is a permanent fact; hence you use the present, *revolves*, after the past, *discovered*.

3. This should read: Hitler *started* World War II in 1939. The tense to be used here is the simple past, and not the present-perfect, which generally denotes an action that began in the past and continued into, or almost into, the present.

4. This sentence is correct. They agreed that honesty, as a general principle, always *is* the best policy.

5. This sentence should read: No sooner had he entered the house than the dog *barked* at him. Use the past, *barked*, to harmonize with the past-perfect, *had entered*.

6. This sentence should be corrected as follows: They were surprised to hear that Albany *is* (a present fact) the capital of New York.

7. Change the sentence to read: Come what might, he was determined to tell the truth. The past, *might*, harmonizes with the past, *was determined*.

8. This sentence is correct. The action indicated by the past-perfect, *had rained*, is prior to the action indicated by the simple past, *overflowed*.

9. This should read: I never thought he *would* have the nerve to do it. Harmonize *would*, the past of *will*, with the past tense, *thought*.

10. Correct the sentence as follows: He had told them the truth, that they *might* be prepared for the worst. Use the past, *might*, after the past-perfect, *had told*.

HAVE YOU HAD TROUBLE WITH "SHALL" AND "WILL"?

When you went to school, you probably spent many hours trying to learn the difference between *shall* and *will*. As for myself, I still have nightmares about those two little demons that haunted my grammar-school days.

But here is good news. In the progressive streamlining of

our language, much of the distinction between these two words has been abolished in informal usage. Indeed, some of the modern grammarians insist that *shall* is nowadays a "practically obsolete" word, except in questions. Yet, on the other hand, there are quite a few authorities who still insist upon the "logical difference" between *shall* and *will* in formal usage.

In view of this controversy, the safest thing is to steer a middle course. The chances are that you will sound "modern" and "correct" if you observe the following simple rules:

1. To denote *mere future time*, use *shall* in the first person (with *I* and *we*), and *will* in the second and third persons (with *you, he, she, it, they*).

For example:

> *I shall go.*
> *You will go.*
> *He will go.*

These sentences express simple futurity, and no sense of determination.

2. But to denote the exercise of will power or authority or determination, just reverse the above process. Use *will* in the first person (with *I* and *we*), and *shall* in the second and third persons (with *you, he, she, it, they*).

For example:

> *I will learn* means *I am determined to learn.*
> *You shall not kill* means *You are commanded not to kill.*
> *They shall not pass* means *They are not permitted to pass.*

These two rules are easy enough to remember. Do you want to express a simple future idea? Say I *shall*, you *will*, he *will*. Do you want to express a future determination? Say I *will*, you *shall*, he *shall*.

3. The third rule is just as simple as the other two. In questions, use *shall* with the first person, *will* with the second and third persons. In the negative, *won't* is generally used.

For example:

> Shall I open the door?
> Will you open the door?
> Won't I have a good time?

The foregoing three rules satisfy the requirements of good

67

English, according to many of the leading authorities.

These, then, are the distinctions between *shall* and *will*, reduced to a practical minimum. In some of the following sentences, *shall* and *will* are used incorrectly. Are you able, with the above rules in mind, to make the necessary corrections?

QUIZ TIME

1. I think that I shall never see a poem lovely as a tree.
2. "Nobody shall save me," shouted the drowning man in his terror, "and I will die!"
3. "If you can kindly spare the time," wrote Jennie to the opera director, "will I come for an audition next Tuesday?"
4. Shall I take Mrs. Smith along to the party?
5. Don't forget the Commandment: "Thou wilt not kill!"

—Answers—

1. Correct—no changes necessary. Informally, however, *will* is just as good.
2. This sentence sounds a bit ridiculous, as it expresses the exact opposite of what the drowning man is thinking. What he means to say is, "Nobody will save me, and I shall die!" (He could also say, "I will die," and would most naturally say "I'll die," since the occasion is hardly one for formal usage.)
3. Change *will* to *shall*, since this is a question in the first person.
4. Correct.
5. The proper Commandment is, "Thou *shalt* not kill."

Time out for the Sixth Word Game
WORDS ABOUT YOURSELF

Suppose we become personal for a change. How about yourself? What sort of temperament or characteristics do you have? And are you able to describe your temperament or characteristics with the proper words?

Let's see.

A

1. If you like to talk a great deal, you are l___a__o_s.

2. If you prefer to keep silent as a rule, you are t_c_t__n.

3. If you are expert in using your hands, you are d__t__o_s.

4. If you are clumsy with your hands, you are m_l_d___t.

5. If you have a red-blooded and buoyant disposition, you are s__g_i_e.

6. If you have a gloomy disposition, you are d__p__d__t.

7. If you never get tired, you are in____at_g___e.

8. If you are lazy and like to avoid exertion, you are i_d__e_t.

9. If you have a sweet and friendly temper, you are a_i_b_e.

10. If you are easily angered, you are i__s__b_e.

11. If you have extensive knowledge, you are e__d__e.

12. If you have too little learning (which I hope is not true), you are i_l_t_r__e.

13. If you are very formal in your etiquette, you are p_n_t_l___s.

14. If you are rather informal, you are un__r_m__i__s.

15. If you are inclined to make peace with people, you are p_c___c_l.

16. If you are always looking for a fight, you are b__l__o_e.

17. If you feel sorry for a wrong you have done, you are c__p___t_o_s.

18. If you are too stubborn to admit your errors, you are o_d_r__e.

19. If you have an exalted and unselfish soul, you are m__n___m__s.

20. If you have a mean and cowardly soul, you are p_s_l__n__o_s.

—Answers—

1-loquacious, 2-taciturn, 3-dexterous (also spelled *dextrous*), 4-maladroit, 5-sanguine, 6-despondent, 7-indefatigable, 8-indolent, 9-amiable, 10-irascible, 11-erudite, 12-illiterate, 13-punctilious, 14-unceremonious, 15-pacifical, 16-bellicose, 17-compunctious, 18-obdurate, 19-magnanimous, 20-pusillanimous

B

Let's reshuffle these words, and look at them under different surroundings.

In each of the following sentences, point out whether the statement is true or false.

1. You are an *obdurate* person if you are ready to admit your mistakes.   True   False

2. If you couldn't read, you would be *illiterate*.   True   False

3. You are *punctilious* when you are careless about your punctuation.   True   False

4. If you are too *loquacious*, people may call you a chatterbox.   True   False

5. When the day is overcast, you are likely to feel *despondent*.   True   False

6. You are *maladroit* if you are good at playing a melody on the piano.   True   False

7. You would be *pusillanimous* if you were afraid to fight for the right.   True   False

8. You're likely to get into trouble if you're *bellicose*.   True   False

9. You are *irascible* if you lose your temper too easily.   True   False

10. You are very sad when you feel *sanguine*.   True   False

11. It's wise to be *taciturn* when you have something helpful to say.   True   False

12. You are all fagged out when you are *indefatigable*.   True   False

13. It's nice to be *dexterous* when your house needs repairs.   True   False

14. When you're *amiable*, your friends are likely to dislike you.   True   False

15. If you like to dole out your money, you are *indolent*.   True   False

16. It gives you an exalted feeling to be *magnanimous*.   True   False

17. If you are *pacifical*, you will avoid quarreling.   True   False

18. When you're *unceremonious*, you're not

70

likely to follow Emily Post.   True   False
    19. You show the right spirit when you are
compunctious after you have done an injury.   True   False
    20. The study of scholarly books is likely to
make you *erudite*.   True   False

—Answers—

1-false, 2-true, 3-false, 4-true, 5-true, 6-false, 7-true, 8-true,
9-true, 10-false, 11-false, 12-false, 13-true, 14-false, 15-false,
16-true, 17-true, 18-true, 19-true, 20-true

C

For the next round in this game, match the words of the
first column with the definitions of the second column:

1. amiable	a. dejected, disheartened
2. bellicose	b. very learned
3. compunctious	c. clumsy
4. despondent	d. disinclined to talk
5. dexterous	e. tireless
6. erudite	f. given to continual talking
7. illiterate	g. friendly
8. indefatigable	h. lazy
9. irascible	i. high-minded, unselfish
10. indolent	j. hopeful
11. loquacious	k. warlike, aggressive
12. magnanimous	l. very ignorant
13. maladroit	m. remorseful
14. obdurate	n. easily angered
15. pacifical	o. skilful
16. punctilious	p. mean-spirited, cowardly
17. pusillanimous	q. unyielding, stubborn
18. sanguine	r. inclined to make peace
19. taciturn	s. precise in the observance of etiquette
20. unceremonious	t. informal

—Answers—

1-g, 2-k, 3-m, 4-a, 5-o, 6-b, 7-l, 8-e, 9-n, 10-h, 11-f, 12-i,
13-c, 14-q, 15-r, 16-s, 17-p, 18-j, 19-d, 20-t

D

For the next round, pair off each word in the first column
with its antonym in the second column by writing the letter

of the second word next to the first one. An *antonym*, you will recall, is *a word directly opposite to another word in meaning*.

1.	amiable	a.	maladroit
2.	compunctious	b.	bellicose
3.	dexterous	c.	magnanimous
4.	illiterate	d.	indefatigable
5.	loquacious	e.	irascible
6.	pacifical	f.	punctilious
7.	pusillanimous	g.	sanguine
8.	despondent	h.	erudite
9.	unceremonious	i.	obdurate
10.	indolent	j.	taciturn

—Answers—

1-e (or b), 2-i, 3-a, 4-h, 5-j, 6-b (or e), 7-c (or b), 8-g, 9-f, 10-d

E

And now, before you add the above words to your permanent vocabulary, get the correct pronunciation of those among them that are most frequently mispronounced:

bellicose: BEL-li-kose
erudite: ER-oo-dite, or ER-you-dite
illiterate: il-LIT-er-it
indefatigable: in-de-FAT-i-ga-bl
irascible: eye-RASS-i-bl
indolent: IN-doe-lent
loquacious: lo-KWAY-shus
magnanimous: mag-NAN-i-mus
maladroit: mal-a-DROIT
obdurate: AB-dew-rate
punctilious: punk-TIL-ee-us
pusillanimous: pew-sil-AN-i-mus
taciturn: TASS-it-ern

Try this game, like the others, on your friends. They, too, will be interested in checking their personalities and in finding the correct words to express their various moods. It is not only a builder of vocabulary, it is also an interesting little journey into human psychology.

9

VERBS ARE SUBJECT TO MOODS

LET'S INDICATE SOME FACTS

In Chapter 8 you noticed how the tenses of a verb are used to express various points of time. In this chapter you will observe the verb in its various moods.

As you may recall from your school days, the grammatical term *mood* or *mode* means *manner*. And since there are various manners in which an action may be expressed, the English verb has several different moods.

The commonest of these is the *indicative*. This mood, as the term implies, *indicates* a fact or something assumed to be a fact.

For example:

> There *was* an atom bomb explosion in Nevada.
>
> I understand that only a few officials *were* present at the experiment.
>
> I am sure the results of the experiment *will be* of the greatest importance.

This mood, as you can see, offers practically no difficulties to the student. But the English verb has other moods—the *subjunctive*, the *imperative*, and the *infinitive*—which may have caused you some trouble in the past. So let's see how you can avoid the more important pitfalls in their usage.

WHEN TO USE THE SUBJUNCTIVE

An educated waiter was serving an ill-bred customer and taking considerable abuse from him. Unable to snap back at the customer for fear that he might lose his job, he finally made the quiet but perfect retort:

"My position, sir, doesn't allow me to fight you. But if the choice of weapons were mine, I would choose grammar."

The waiter, knowing his grammar, said "*were* mine" instead of "*was* mine." And he was correct. He was using the subjunctive to express a condition that was contrary-to-fact.

Verbs that denote wishes, demands, contrary-to-fact conditions, or the like, are in the *subjunctive mood*. Note, for example, the following five sentences:

1. If I *were* as rich as you, I would be happy.
2. If he *were* honest, he would be trusted.
3. I wish I *were* in Florida this winter.
4. I insist that he *come* to see me.
5. Monkeys sometimes act as if they *were* human.

The italicized words in the above sentences are all in the *subjunctive*.

The first sentence gives a condition contrary-to-fact. The fact is that I am not as rich as you, and therefore I am not happy.

The second sentence is also contrary-to-fact. He is *not* honest; hence he is *not* trusted.

The third sentence, as you see, denotes a wish.

The fourth sentence indicates a demand.

The fifth sentence is a contrary-to-fact statement. Monkeys are *not human*.

The *subjunctive*, then, is used:

1. To express a wish or a command.
2. To indicate a contrary-to-fact condition after *if*.
3. To indicate a condition after *as if* or *as though*, since every condition introduced by these two words is contrary-to-fact.
4. To denote other similar ideas of condition or supposition or doubt.

WATCH YOUR FORM

You must be careful about the *form* of the verb when you use the subjunctive:

1. Use the *plural* form of the verb, even when the subject is *singular*.

He insisted that she *keep* her promise.
He acts as if he *were* the boss.

2. Use the form *be*, instead of *is* or *are*.

I prefer that she *be* there alone.
He ordered that they *be* examined one by one.

74

3. Use the *past* form of the subjunctive to express a *present* or *future* contrary-to-fact condition.

If he *repented* now, it would be too late.
If only we *knew* the future possibilities of the atom bomb!

4. In the passive voice, use *be* plus the *past participle.*

He demands that the job *be done* at once.
He desired that his request *be granted.*
It was suggested that he *be invited* to the conference.

The *subjunctive mood* is becoming less and less important in modern English. In informal usage it is often disregarded. But you had better stick to the usage as indicated in this chapter, for formal purposes at least. In the judgment of many authorities, the subjunctive is still necessary when you want to say exactly what you mean.

TEST YOUR SKILL

Are you ready now to test your own skill in the uses of the subjunctive? Check the right word in the parentheses in each of the following sentences:

1. He pretends a limp as if he (is, was, were) lame.
2. I wish that my sick friend (were, was) out of danger.
3. It is desirable that you (are, be) there when we arrive.
4. He requests that she (listen, listens) when he talks.
5. The doctor advised that she (goes, go) to the hospital.
6. I am sure he would do it if he (has, had) the time.
7. The general ordered that the enemy (is, was, be) stopped.
8. Don't act as if you (are, were) the only pebble on the beach.
9. In the coming election it is necessary that every citizen (expresses, express) his own opinion.
10. The judge insisted that the witness (tells, tell) the truth.

—Answers—

1-were, 2-were, 3-be, 4-listen, 5-go, 6-had, 7-be, 8-were, 9-express, 10-tell

75

DO YOU FEEL LIKE GIVING ORDERS?

If you do, you will have occasion to use the *imperative*. It is the mood in which an officer speaks to a private. *Turn right; present arms; forward march.* This may be called the "short-cut" method to communicate your thoughts. It saves words. When you meet somebody who is walking ahead of you and you want to catch up to him, you say, "Wait!" What you actually mean is, "I want you to stop or slow down until I reach you."

There are times when this mood can be very effective. A long-winded lecturer had come to speak at a boys' club in the slums. He looked at the youngsters with a patronizing smile and said: "Now what in the world shall I talk about? School? Sports? The evils of smoking? The behavior of children in the presence of their elders? There are so many subjects to choose from. Can you," pointing to one of the boys, "tell me what to talk about?"

"Yes, sir," said the boy. "Talk about five minutes, and sit down."

Talk and *sit down* are in the *imperative mood.*

IS IT RIGHT TO SPLIT AN INFINITIVE?

The *infinitive mood* is the form of the verb introduced by the word *to: to go, to see, to read, to have gone, to have seen, to have read.*

And this brings us to one of the most controversial points among teachers of English: what about the use of the *split infinitive?*

The *split infinitive* is a construction in which a word, or a group of words, is thrust in between the two parts of the infinitive. For example: *to* swiftly *run, to* faithfully *obey, to* clearly and carefully *observe.*

Some teachers and text books forbid this practice as almost a crime. The proper way to express an infinitive, they insist, is as follows: "*to run* swiftly," or "swiftly *to run.*"

Yet, actually, this irregular construction is not wrong. At times, it is even preferable to the regular form. Those who frown upon the split infinitive are the pedants who belong to the horse-and-buggy period of English. They forget that a living language keeps growing and changing all the time. The split infinitive—like any other unconventional arrangement—may be properly used *to particularly emphasize* a point. The best writers—Shakespeare, Franklin, Washington

Irving, Hawthorne, Walt Whitman, Herbert Spencer, Theodore Roosevelt and Woodrow Wilson, to mention only a few—have never hesitated to use it.

The famous British biographer Philip Guedalla made a humorous proposal to organize a society called *Friends of the Infinitive*. The wording of the suggestion is an exaggerated caricature of the idea. But it proves the point. "We propose," said Mr. Guedalla, "*to* zealously and ruthlessly, in season and out of season, day by day, week by week, and year by year, in Great Britain and (weather permitting) in the Irish Free State, *proceed* with our objectives until they are achieved."

In the above sentence, there is a gap of thirty words between *to* and *proceed*. This is carrying a good idea too far. A narrow split infinitive may emphasize your thought. But too wide a split will cause a spill. *To* successfully *lay* a carpet, you mustn't allow it *to* loosely, with edges all turned up, with lumps in the middle, and with various tables and chairs and sofas sprawled over it, *lie* on the floor. A carpet so laid is almost sure to trip you.

But, under ordinary circumstances, a split infinitive is perfectly correct. That is, if you know how to use it effectively at the right time.

AVOID THESE PITFALLS

When you use the infinitive, be careful to avoid such expressions as the following:

1. He was discovered to embezzle ten thousand dollars.
2. It has always been my desire to have seen you.
3. I hadn't ought to have done it.

Correct these sentences to read:

1. He was discovered to have embezzled ten thousand dollars. (The embezzlement was prior to the discovery.)
2. It has always been my desire to see you.
3. I ought not to have done it.

The incorrect phrases *had ought* and *hadn't ought* are heard too frequently in everyday conversation. This common error tripped up even the mother who was trying to teach her little boy how to speak better English. "Mother," said Johnny, "which of the two expressions is right—*I had ought to have gone*, or *I hadn't ought to have gone?*"

77

"Neither is right, Johnny," replied his mother. "Any one who says *had ought to have gone* hadn't ought to have been allowed to graduate from high school."

Here are the corrections for Johnny's and for his mother's errors:

> I ought to have gone.
> I ought not to have gone.
> Any one . . . ought not to have been allowed to graduate, etc.

And now for a change of mood—or, rather, for a change of pace—as we relax to play our next word game.

Time out for the Seventh Word Game
WORDS ABOUT DOCTORS AND THEIR SPECIALTIES

This game consists of a number of words that concern everybody. For they deal with our physical welfare, the ills that afflict us, and the various physicians who, in this age of specialization, try to keep us in good health.

A

Some of these words look so much alike that we often confuse them. See if you can get them straight. Here are twenty-one specialists with brief descriptions of their specialties. Check the one correct title that fits the description in each case.

1. He takes care of your corns.
> He's a *podiatrist*
> He's a *pediatrician*
> He's an *orthopedist*

2. He treats children's diseases.
> He's a *roentgenologist*
> He's an *orthopedist*
> He's a *pediatrician*

3. He corrects deformities of the body.
> He's a *podiatrist*
> He's an *orthopedist*
> He's a *gynecologist*

4. He treats disease by manipulating the spinal column.

> He's a *chiropractor*
> He's an *orthopedist*
> He's a *dermatologist*

5. He straightens crooked teeth.

> He's a *chiropodist*
> He's an *osteopath*
> He's an *orthodontist*

6. He is also known, correctly, as a podiatrist.

> He's a *pediatrician*
> He's a *chiropodist*
> He's an *orthopedist*

7. He measures your vision.

> He's an *oculist*
> He's an *optician*
> He's an *optometrist*

8. He's a doctor of medicine who specializes in the diseases of the eyes.

> He's an *optician*
> He's an *oculist*
> He's an *optometrist*

9. He makes your eyeglasses.

> He's an *optician*
> He's an *oculist*
> He's an *ophthalmologist*

10. He is also known as an oculist.

> He's an *ophthalmologist*
> He's an *optometrist*
> He's an *optician*

11. He specializes in the disorders of the mind.

> He's a *psychiatrist*
> He's a *physiotherapist*
> He's an *internist*

12. He treats diseases by electricity.

> He's a *pathologist*
> He's a *chiropractor*
> He's a *physiotherapist*

13. His specialty is taking and interpreting X rays.

> He's a *neurologist*
> He's a *gynecologist*
> He's a *roentgenologist*

14. He specializes in the diseases of the nervous system.

> He's a *cardiologist*
> He's a *dermatologist*
> He's a *neurologist*

15. He treats the diseases of old age.

> He's a *pediatrician*
> He's a *geriatrician*
> He's a *gynecologist*

16. He specializes in skin diseases.

> He's a *podiatrist*
> He's a *neurologist*
> He's a *dermatologist*

17. He treats women's diseases.

> He's a *chiropractor*
> He's a *gynecologist*
> He's an *orthopedist*

18. He brings children into the world.

> He's an *obstetrician*
> He's a *chiropractor*
> He's a *pediatrician*

19. He takes medical training as a resident in a hospital.

> He's an *internist*
> He's an *intern*
> He's a *neophyte*

20. He specializes in the diseases of the internal organs.

> He's an *internist*
> He's an *intern*
> He's a *gynecologist*

21. He helps you to adjust or to get rid of your suppressed desires by bringing them into the open.

> He's a *dermatologist*
> He's a *pathologist*
> He's a *psychoanalyst*

—*Answers*—

1-podiatrist, 2-pediatrician, 3-orthopedist, 4-chiropractor, 5-orthodontist, 6-chiropodist (*podiatrist* and *chiropodist* are synonyms), 7-optometrist, 8-oculist, 9-optician, 10-ophthalmologist (*oculist* and *ophthalmologist* are synonyms), 11-psychiatrist, 12-physiotherapist, 13-roentgenologist, 14-neurologist, 15-geriatrician, 16-dermatologist, 17-gynecologist, 18-obstetrician, 19-intern, 20-internist, 21-psychoanalyst

B

In this round of the game, imagine you are looking at an office directory in the lobby of a medical building. You see all sorts of specialists listed in this directory. Would you know which is which?

To find out for yourself, try to match the titles in the first column with the definitions in the second:

1. chiropodist	a. specializes in correcting bodily deformities
2. chiropractor	b. man who treats foot trouble
3. dermatologist	c. specialist in women's diseases
4. geriatrician	d. dentist who straightens teeth
5. gynecologist	e. one who treats disease through massage, electricity, etc.
6. intern	f. specialist in diseases of internal organs
7. internist	g. one who gets medical training in a hospital
8. neurologist	h. specialist in skin diseases
9. obstetrician	i. maker of eyeglasses
10. oculist	j. one who measures vision for glasses
11. ophthalmologist	k. X-ray specialist
12. optician	l. eye specialist
13. optometrist	m. doctor who manipulates spinal column
14. orthodontist	n. specialist in childbirth
15. orthopedist	o. nerve specialist
16. pediatrician	p. specialist in children's diseases
17. physiotherapist	q. specialist in mental diseases
18. podiatrist	r. specialist in old people's diseases
19. psychiatrist	s. doctor who treats motorcycle accidents
20. psychoanalyst	t. specialist in kidney diseases
21. roentgenologist	u. specialist who treats the mind through the analysis of the patient's dreams, suppressed desires, etc.

81

1-b, 2-m, 3-h, 4-r, 5-c, 6-g, 7-f, 8-o, 9-n, 10-l, 11-l, 12-i, 13-j, 14-d, 15-a, 16-p, 17-e, 18-b, 19-q, 20-u, 21-k

Please note again that you can use two titles—*chiropodist* and *podiatrist*—for a man who cuts corns and treats other minor foot troubles, and two titles—*oculist* and *ophthalmologist*—for a doctor who specializes in eye diseases.

But don't confuse the terms *psychiatrist* and *psychoanalyst*. Both of them deal with mental disorders. But the psychiatrist treats mental diseases in general, while the psychoanalyst bases his practice largely upon the method developed by Sigmund Freud. He specializes in analyzing the patient's dreams and in helping him to discover his unconscious memories and repressed desires—such as infantile sexuality, for example—in order to resolve his mental conflicts. The psychoanalyst, therefore, confines his practice to one branch of psychiatric treatment.

C

Are you getting these words clearly in mind? Try them again, in this new setting of three columns. The first column contains the doctors' titles, the second column consists of brief hints about their jobs, and the third column is blank. Fill in the *name* of the job, or specialty, in each case; the first one has already been done for you.

The Doctor	What He Does	Name of His Specialty
1. chiropodist	cuts corns	chiropody
2. chiropractor	manipulates muscles	
3. dermatologist	treats skin diseases	
4. geriatrician	treats diseases of old people	
5. gynecologist	specialist in women's diseases	
6. intern	undergoes hospital training	
7. internist	treats diseases inside the body	
8. neurologist	treats nerve diseases	
9. obstetrician	helps mothers give birth to babies	
10. oculist	eye specialist	
11. ophthalmologist	" "	

12. optician	makes optical instruments
13. optometrist	measures your eyesight
14. orthodontist	straightens children's teeth
15. orthopedist	corrects bodily deformities
16. pediatrician	treats babies' diseases
17. physiotherapist	treats by electricity
18. podiatrist	treats foot-trouble
19. psychiatrist	specializes in diseases of the mind
20. psychoanalyst	specializes in diseases due to suppressed conflicts, subconscious memories, etc.
21. roentgenologist	takes and studies X-rays

—*Answers*—

2-chiropractic, 3-dermatology, 4-geriatrics, 5-gynecology, 6-internship, 7-internal medicine, 8-neurology (don't confuse this with *neuralgia*, which means *a nerve pain*), 9-obstetrics, 10 & 11-ophthalmology, 12-the making of optical instruments, 13-optometry, 14-orthodontia, 15-orthopedics, 16-pediatrics, 17-physiotherapy, 18-podiatry, 19-psychiatry, 20-psychoanalysis, 21-roentgenology

D

Which of the professionals would you consult in each of of the following cases?

1. To treat a bunion _____
2. To operate on an eye cataract _____
3. To cure little Johnny's measles _____
4. To make your new glasses _____
5. To deliver a baby _____
6. To test your eyesight _____
7. To straighten little Mary's teeth _____
8. To cure a rash on the skin _____
9. To give you electrical treatment for a stiff shoulder _____
10. To treat a sick mind _____

11. To take an X-ray _____
12. To cure a nervous disorder _____
13. To examine your lungs, liver, and kidneys _____
14. To examine the old-age complaints of your grandfather

_____
15. To treat the ailments of your womenfolk _____
16. To massage your spinal column _____
17. To treat Billy's deformed hip _____
18. To recommend the best doctor among those who are training him at the hospital _____
19. To analyze your dreams _____

—Answers—

1-chiropodist (or podiatrist), 2-oculist (or ophthalmologist), 3-pediatrician, 4-optician, 5-obstetrician, 6-optometrist, 7-orthodontist, 8-dermatologist, 9-physiotherapist, 10-psychiatrist, 11-roentgenologist, 12-neurologist, 13-internist, 14-geriatrician, 15-gynecologist, 16-chiropractor, 17-orthopedist, 18-intern, 19-psychoanalyst

E

And now that you know the titles of the various doctors, specialists, and medical trainees, you will want to know how to pronounce the words so you can talk about them to your friends. Here are the pronunciations:

1. chiropodist: kigh-ROP-o-dist
2. chiropractor: kigh-ro-PRAK-ter
3. dermatologist: dur-ma-TOL-o-jist
4. geriatrician: jer-ee-at-RISH-un; he specializes in geriatrics: jer-ee-AT-rix
5. gynecologist: jin-i-KOL-o-jist or jigh-ni-KOL-o-jist, or guy-ni-KOL-o-jist
6. intern: IN-turn; and he serves his internship: IN-turn-ship
7. internist: in-TURN-ist
8. neurologist: new-ROL-o-jist
9. orthodontist: or-tho-DON-tist; he specializes in orthodontia: or-tho-DON-shuh
10. obstetrician: ob-stet-RISH-un; he specializes in obstetrics: ob-STET-rix
11. oculist: OK-you-list
12. ophthalmologist: off-thal-MOL-o-jist
13. optician: op-TISH-un

14. optometrist: op-TOM-et-rist
15. orthopedist: or-tho-PEE-dist
16. pediatrician: pee-dee-at-RISH-un; he specializes in pediatrics: pee-dee-AT-riks
17. physiotherapist: fiz-ee-oh-THER-uh-pist
18. podiatrist: po-DIE-at-rist
19. psychiatrist: sigh-KIGH-at-rist; he specializes in psychiatry: sigh-KIGH-at-ree; but the treatment he gives you is
   psychiatric: sigh-kee-AT-rik
20. psychoanalyst: sigh-ko-AN-a-list; he specializes in psychoanalysis: sigh-ko-an-AL-i-sis; and his method is psychoanalytic: sigh-ko-an-al-IT-ik
21. roentgenologist: rent-gen-OL-o-jist, hard g, or rent-yen-OL-o-jist

And thus you have added another group of important words to your vocabulary. And you can now think and talk intelligently—with the proper pronunciation of the various medical terms—about one of the most fascinating subjects in the world: the people who keep us healthy, and the work in which they specialize.

10

VERBS AND NUMBERS

ANYTHING WRONG HERE?

Can you check the errors, if any, in the following sentences?

1. Two and two is four.
2. Two and two are four.
3. Three times three is nine.
4. Three times three are nine.

Answer: There are no errors in the above sentences. All are correct. You can regard "two and two" as a single idea, and therefore you can use the *singular* verb *is*. But you can also regard "two and two" as separate units, and therefore you can use the *plural* verb *are*.

The same holds true of "three times three" or of any similar mathematical computation. In all such computations, it is equally correct to use either the singular or the plural form of the verb.

NOT SO SINGULAR

But what is the meaning of *singular* and *plural* as applied to verbs?

A verb is *singular,* as you may have already noted, when its subject consists of *only one* idea or person or thing. For example:

The tree *grows.*
The boy *runs.*
The beauty of this landscape *is* superb.

A verb is *plural* when its subject consists of *two or more* ideas or persons or things. For example:

The trees *grow.*
The boys *run.*
The beauties of this landscape *are* many and varied.

So far, so good. But here are a few subjects that are a little different. See if you can check the correct form of the verb in each of the following sentences:

1. A scholar and poet (was, were) what they called their friend who had just died.
2. A scholar and a poet—two of my best friends—(has, have) just arrived in town.
3. Either Jerry or Edith (is, are) the oldest in the family.
4. Neither Jerry nor Edith (likes, like) bananas.
5. Orange juice and coffee (makes, make) a good breakfast.
6. The scissors (has, have) a sharp edge.
7. The eyeglasses (is, are) on the table.

—*Answers*—

1-was, 2-have, 3-is, 4-likes, 5-makes or make, 6-have, 7-are

The reason for the answer in every instance is easy to understand:

1. They were talking about *one* individual when they referred to the man as a scholar and poet. A compound subject referring to *one* person or idea or thing takes a *singular* verb.
2. In this sentence "a scholar and a poet" are *two different* individuals. A compound subject referring to *two or more* persons or ideas or things takes a *plural* verb.
3. "*Either* Jerry *or* Edith" is regarded as a singular subject —one *or* the other, not both, is the oldest—and therefore it takes a singular verb. You can readily understand this point if you recast the sentence as follows: "Either Jerry is the oldest in the family, or Edith (is)."
4. "*Neither* Jerry *nor* Edith" is likewise regarded as a singular subject which requires a singular verb. You can rewrite this sentence, also, as follows: "Neither Jerry likes bananas, nor (does) Edith."
5. Both forms of the verb are correct. If you regard "orange juice and coffee" as a breakfast *unit*, you will use the *singular* verb. But if you regard them as *two separate* items of food, you can use the *plural*.

The same principle holds true of other common food combinations—such as *ham and eggs, bread and butter, lettuce and tomato*, and the like. You can use either the *singular* or the *plural* with any such combination, depending on whether you think of the words as *separate items* or as *a food unit*.

6. It takes *two* blades to make a pair of scissors. When we use the word, therefore, we think of it as plural, to be followed by a plural verb.

7. You must use the plural because it takes *two* lenses to make a pair of eyeglasses.

TO BE OR NOT TO BE SINGULAR

There are a few easy rules that govern the number of all the verbs in the above sentences:

1. With a *singular* subject, use a *singular* verb.
2. With a *plural* subject, use a *plural* verb.
3. With two or more singular subjects referring to the *same* person or thing, use a *singular* verb.
4. With two or more singular subjects referring to *different* persons or things, use a *plural* verb.
5. With two or more singular subjects connected by *either —or*, or *neither—nor*, use a *singular* verb.
6. With such words as *scissors, eyeglasses, tongs, trousers, pants, pincers, goods*—things made up of two or more parts—use a *plural* verb.

TEST YOUR SKILL

If you bear the foregoing simple rules in mind, you will have no trouble in checking the following sentences. Point out, in each case, whether the verb is right or wrong:

1. Either your carburetor or your battery are out of order.   Right   Wrong
2. We was happy to see you come home.   Right   Wrong
3. Neither John nor Mary is eligible for the prize.   Right   Wrong
4. Billy's pants was soiled when he fell in the mud.   Right   Wrong
5. Here are the book, paper, and pencil I bought for you at the store.   Right   Wrong
6. My shirt and my suit was bought in the same store.   Right   Wrong
7. Neither America nor England desires to be aggressive.   Right   Wrong
8. The coat, shirt and vest is ready for you to take home.   Right   Wrong
9. He and I was always good friends.   Right   Wrong
10. The goods were spoiled in transit.   Right   Wrong

11. The pincers was made too tight.   Right Wrong
12. A soldier, statesman, and scholar is a combination rarely to be found in one person.   Right Wrong
13. Every soldier on both sides want to come home alive.   Right Wrong
14. A large shipment of logs has been floated down the river.   Right Wrong
15. Meet Mr. and Mrs. Smith, both of whom wants to go to Florida.   Right Wrong

—*Answers*—

1-wrong, 2-wrong, 3-right, 4-wrong, 5-right, 6-wrong, 7-right, 8-wrong, 9-wrong, 10-right, 11-wrong, 12-right, 13-wrong, 14-right, 15-wrong

DO'S AND DONT'S

Don't use *don't* with the third person singular. The word is a contraction for the plural *do not*. The proper form for the third person is *doesn't*, the contraction for *does not*.
Examples:

Wrong: Harry complains that his razor don't work.
Right: Harry complains that his razor doesn't work.
Wrong: If he don't come soon, he will miss the train.
Right: If he doesn't come soon, he will miss the train.
Wrong: She tells me that she don't expect to go.
Right: She tells me that she doesn't expect to go.
Wrong: To use *don't* for *doesn't*—an expression frequently heard in conversation—don't sound right.
Right: To use *don't* for *doesn't*—an expression frequently heard in conversation—doesn't sound right.

And please note the following incorrect usage:

Wrong: Don't let's go.
Right: Let's not go.

Time out for the Eighth Word Game
A SCORE OF *ISMS*

Almost everybody nowadays seems to be attached to some sort of *ism*—capitalism, socialism, idealism, radicalism, skepticism, liberalism, and so on. You hear and read about such *isms* practically every day. But are you sure you thoroughly understand the meanings of these words? Try this game and see for yourself.

A

1. He thinks largely of his own selfish interests; he is prone to   e_ _ism

2. He denies the existence of God; he advocates   a_ _ _ism

3. He questions, but neither denies nor accepts, the doctrines of religion; he professes   s_ _p_ _ _ism

4. He tells you frankly that he doesn't know whether or not God exists; he admits his   a_n_ _t_ _ism

5. He believes in one God; he practices   m_ _ _t_ _ism

6. He believes in many gods; he practices   p_ _y_ _ _ism

7. He advocates the public ownership of the means of production; he believes in   s_c_ _ _ism

8. He is opposed to every form of government; he believes in   a_ _r_ _ism

9. He supports a system of private wealth, lawfully acquired through private enterprise; he advocates   c_ _ _t_ _ism

10. He adheres to the existing order of things, and opposes any political changes; he believes in   c_n_ _r_ _ _ism

11. He advocates extreme changes in government; he believes in   r_d_c_ _ism

12. His is a middle-of-the-road attitude in politics, leaning neither too much to the right nor too much to the left; he believes in   l_b_ _ _lism

13. He has learned to be indifferent to pleasure and pain; he practices   s_ _i_ism

14. He forms his opinions by following his reason; he practices   r_t_o_ _ _ism

15. He is carried away by unreasonable enthusiasm; he yields to   f_ _a_ _ _ism

16. He asserts his beliefs without sufficient evidence; he is inclined to

d_g___ism

17. He insists upon the independence of his action without any outside interference; he maintains his

i___v__u__ism

18. He maintains that the most important thing in life is pleasure; he believes in

e__c___a_ism

19. He shows favoritism to his relatives regardless of their merits; he practices

n_p__ism

20. He has an exaggerated sense of patriotism; he practices

ch_u_i_ism

—Answers—

1-egoism, 2-atheism, 3-skepticism, 4-agnosticism, 5-monotheism, 6-polytheism, 7-socialism, 8-anarchism, 9-capitalism, 10-conservatism, 11-radicalism, 12-liberalism, 13-stoicism, 14-rationalism, 15-fanaticism, 16-dogmatism, 17-individualism, 18-epicureanism, 19-nepotism, 20-chauvinism

B

In this round, try to get the nouns for the people who practice or represent or advocate the twenty different *isms* listed above:

1. The n_p__ist promoted his undeserving nephew to the vice presidency of the firm.

2. The e_o__t is willing to sacrifice everybody for himself.

3. The c_a_v____t will probably tell you that his country is never in the wrong.

4. The a__e__t has no proof for his assertion that God doesn't exist.

5. The e__c_____n enjoys food and drink.

6. The s__p__c, in questions of religion, asserts that he "wants to be shown."

7. The i___v__u____t thinks he can stand on his own feet.

8. The m____t_____t asserts that God is One.

9. The a__o___c is honest in professing his ignorance about God.

10. The d__m_____t asserts his belief without proof.

11. The c__s____a____e likes the good old laws and the good old times.

12. The r__i__l prefers to take a chance on "new lamps for old."

13. The l__e__l favors greater freedom in political and religious matters.

14. The c____t_____t is proud of the big business he has built up through his own enterprise.

15. The a__r____t believes that all government is evil.

16. The p____t_____t sees gods in many objects of nature.

17. The f__a__c is sometimes ready to kill for his beliefs.

18. The r____o__l__t accepts only what he sees clearly with his mind.

19. The s_o_c is very brave in the face of pain.

20. The s__i_____t is opposed to the private ownership of big business.

—*Answers*—

1-nepotist, 2-egoist, 3-chauvinist, 4-atheist, 5-epicurean, 6-skeptic, 7-individualist, 8-monotheist, 9-agnostic, 10-dogmatist, 11-conservative, 12-radical, 13-liberal, 14-capitalist, 15-anarchist, 16-polytheist, 17-fanatic, 18-rationalist, 19-stoic, 20-socialist

C

Next round: Match the words on the left with the definitions on the right:

1. agnosticism	a. assertion of belief without proof
2. anarchism	b. the philosophy of pleasure
3. atheism	c. belief in one God
4. capitalism	d. advocacy of extreme political changes
5. chauvinism	e. unreasonable zeal
6. conservatism	f. the theory that the truth about God is beyond our knowledge
7. dogmatism	g. extreme selfishness
8. egoism	h. belief in many gods
9. epicureanism	i. aversion to political change
10. fanaticism	j. the belief that all government is unnecessary
11. individualism	k. advocacy of public ownership

92

12. liberalism	l. disbelief in God
13. monotheism	m. the system of private ownership
14. nepotism	n. a progressive attitude in politics
15. polytheism	o. the practice of personal freedom from restraint
16. radicalism	p. reliance upon reason
17. rationalism	q. an attitude of doubt, with a willingness to be shown
18. skepticism	r. indifference to pleasure and pain
19. socialism	s. favoritism to relatives
20. stoicism	t. exaggerated patriotism

—Answers—

1-f, 2-j, 3-l, 4-m, 5-t, 6-i, 7-a, 8-g, 9-b, 10-e, 11-o, 12-n, 13-c, 14-s, 15-h, 16-d, 17-p, 18-q, 19-k, 20-r

D

And now see how many of the more difficult of these words you can pronounce:

agnosticism: ag-NOS-ti-sizm
chauvinism: SHOW-vin-izm
egoism: EE-go-izm
epicureanism: ep-i-kew-REE-an-izm
monotheism: MON-o-thee-izm (*th* as in *thank*)
nepotism: NEP-o-tizm
polytheism: POL-ee-thee-izm
rationalism: RASH-on-al-izm
skepticism: SKEP-ti-sizm
stoicism: STO-i-sizm

In this game you have played with 40 words—20 of them dealing with ideas, and 20 with persons who profess or practice these ideas. Are you sure you are now familiar with the definitions and the pronunciations of these 40 words? Then you are ready to go on with the next chapter.

11

HOW TO NAME PERSONS AND THINGS

THE DIFFERENCE BETWEEN VERBS AND NOUNS

Do you notice any difference in the word *effect* as used in the two following sentences?

1. Penicillin can *effect* a cure in many diseases.
2. The *effect* of penicillin as a cure in many diseases is now generally recognized.

In the first sentence, *effect* is a verb.

In the second sentence, *effect* is a noun.

The verb, as you will recall from Chapter 4, where we discussed these words earlier, is *the* word that makes a sentence move. You are now, I trust, pretty familiar with its various functions.

So let us turn to the noun and become a little better acquainted with it.

What is a noun?

Everything you can see, hear, touch, taste, or smell is a noun.

You see a *house*, hear a *bell*, touch a *book*, taste an *apple*, smell a *flower*. (All these *italic* words are nouns.)

A noun, as was mentioned earlier, is a name.

The names of persons are nouns.

Dwight D. Eisenhower	man
Helen Hayes	woman
Jimmy Jones	boy

The names of places are nouns:

New York	Broadway
Mount Washington	Yellowstone Park
Florida	Times Square

The names of things are nouns:

pencil	cigarette lighter
glass	refrigerator
airplane	window

The names of actions, ideas, qualities, concepts and emotions are also nouns:

prize fight	goodness
politics	friendship
philosophy	revenge

Let us at this point clear up a confusion about the word *action*. You will find this word in the grammatical definitions of the verb as well as of the noun. But note this important difference:

A verb *shows* action.

A noun is the *name* of an action.

Thus, in the following three sentences, the *italic* words are verbs:

1. They *will run* a good race.
2. He *will deal* fairly with the prisoner.
3. It's good to *play* now and then.

These are verbs because they *show* action.

But in the next three sentences, the *italic* words are nouns:

1. They will make a good *run* of it.
2. He will give the prisoner a fair *deal*.
3. It's good to inject a little *play* into our daily activities.

These words are nouns because they are the *names* of actions.

CHECK THEM OFF

As you have noted from the above six sentences, the same word may sometimes be used either as a verb or as a noun. But the distinction is always clear. A verb *denotes* action (among other things). It predicates, or tells something about the subject. But a noun is the *name* of an action, idea, quality, concept, emotion, person, place, or thing.

Do you get the difference? Then try to check the nouns and the verbs in the following passage:

Asked if he could summarize all history in a few chapters, Dr. Charles A. Beard replied that he could do so in four sentences:

1. Whom the gods would destroy, they first make mad with power.
2. The mills of God grind slowly, yet they grind exceeding small.
3. The bee fertilizes the flower it robs.
4. When it is dark enough, you can see the stars in the sky.

But Anatole France, somewhat more cynically, condensed the entire story of man's life on earth into a single sentence:

Men are born, they suffer and cause suffering, then they are sentenced to die.

In the above passage there are twenty nouns—that is, names of persons, things, places, ideas, activities, qualities, concepts, or emotions:

history	stars
chapters	sky
Dr. Charles A. Beard	Anatole France
sentences	story
gods	man's
power	life
mills	earth
God	sentence
bee	men
flower	suffering

In the same passage, there are eighteen verbs:

asked	robs
could summarize	is
replied	can see
could do	condensed
would destroy	are born
make	suffer
grind	cause
grind	are sentenced
fertilizes	to die

Please note also, in the above passage, such words as *he, whom, they, it*. These and similar words are not nouns, but pronouns—words used in place of nouns. We shall take up the pronoun in a later chapter. For the present, let us return to the noun as distinguished from the verb.

The following section will help you to fix the distinction a little more clearly in your mind.

BOY MEETS GIRL

Take the simple sentence at the head of this section: *Boy* and *girl* are the nouns. *Meets* is the verb.

The verb *meets*, in this title, puts the sentence into action.

As for the nouns, *boy* is the *subject*, and *girl* is the *object* of the verb.

Two of the main functions of a noun, in other words, are to serve either as the subject (the doer) or as the object (the receiver) of an action.

You can reduce almost the entire plot of any story to the simple formula of two nouns and a verb—noun subject + verb action + noun object:

Boy meets girl. Boy loses girl. Boy finds girl.

Some stories become a little more complicated after the finding of the girl. But the formula still holds true. For example:

Husband betrays wife. Wife discovers husband. Wife shoots husband.

And so on.

Leonard Merrick tells an interesting story based upon the subject + verb + object formula. Two strangers meet in a café. Outside, a hurdy-gurdy is playing an old-time popular song. A tear trickles down the face of one of the two strangers.

"What's the trouble? Sad memories?"

"Yes."

"Do you mind telling me about it?"

"Not at all . . . Many years ago I met a beautiful young lady at this very same café. And on that occasion, we heard this very same song . . . I fell in love with the lady . . . And now, whenever I hear this song, my heart is oppressed with sorrow, and the tears come to my eyes."

"Poor fellow, so she jilted you."

"No, my friend, she married me."

Boy loves girl. Boy marries girl. Boy hates girl. This is but another variation on the self-same theme. But, in every case, you find the basic part of the sentence—*of every sentence*—in the verbs and the nouns. The verbs *denote the action;* and the nouns indicate *what person or thing performs the action,* and *upon what person or thing the action is performed.*

We shall consider the further uses of the noun in Chapter 12, right after the intermission for the next word game.

Time out for the Ninth Word Game
WORDS ABOUT TEACHERS AND STUDIES

A

Suppose you wanted to decide upon a course of education —for yourself or for some member of your family. You have just received a catalog listing all sorts of studies, from Advertising to Zoology. Do you know the meanings of the words that indicate the various studies and the experts who teach them?

Let's see. Which of the three given definitions most nearly describes each of the following subjects?

1. Agronomy, taught by an agronomist, is
    a. the study of primitive races
    b. the survey of human emotions
    c. scientific farming

2. Anthropology, taught by an anthropologist, is
    a. the science of anthracite
    b. the study of man
    c. the art of poetry

3. Archeology, taught by an archeologist, is
    a. the study of history through ancient relics
    b. the study of archangels
    c. the science of animal breeding

4. Biology, taught by a biologist, is
    a. the art of story telling
    b. the study of poisons
    c. the science of life

5. Botany, taught by a botanist, is
    a. the study of plants
    b. the art of buying and selling
    c. the study of navigation

6. Embryology, taught by an embryologist, is
    a. the study of coals and ashes
    b. the study of the development of living creatures before their birth
    c. the study of amber

7. Entomology, taught by an entomologist, is
    a. the study of insects
    b. the study of the derivation of words
    c. the study of tombs and monuments

8. Etymology, taught by an etymologist, is
    a. the study of insects
    b. the study of the derivation of words
    c. the science of atomic energy

9. Geology, taught by a geologist, is
    a. a branch of mathematics dealing with lines and angles
    b. the study of the earth
    c. the study of fishes

10. Graphology, taught by a graphologist, is
    a. the analysis of handwriting
    b. the study of maps
    c. the making of phonographs

11. Linguistics, taught by a linguist, is
    a. the science of language
    b. the making of lingerie
    c. the study of linking chains together

12. Meteorology, taught by a meteorologist, is
    a. the study of motor vehicles
    b. the study of the weather
    c. the adjustment of meters

13. Penology, taught by a penologist, is
    a. the art of good penmanship
    b. the study of old-age pensions
    c. the study of prison management

14. Philology, taught by a philologist, is
    a. the art of wisdom
    b. literary scholarship, the scientific study of written records
    c. the study of timber

15. Physics, taught by a physicist, is
    a. the study of medicine

b. the science of matter and energy
c. physical education

16. Physiology, taught by a physiologist, is
  a. the study of the functions of the body
  b. the study of the functions of the mind
  c. the splitting of the atom

17. Seismology, taught by a seismologist, is
  a. the tailoring of small-sized dresses
  b. the science of earthquake phenomena
  c. the changes of fashions in clothes

18. Theology, taught by a theologian, is
  a. the study of religion
  b. the science of heat
  c. the art of the theater

19. Typography, taught by a typographer, is
  a. the making of maps
  b. secretarial work
  c. the art of printing

20. Zoology, taught by a zoologist, is
  a. the study of the animal kingdom
  b. the history of Zululand
  c. the study of the twelve zodiacs

—Answers—

1-c, 2-b, 3-a, 4-c, 5-a, 6-b, 7-a, 8-b, 9-b, 10-a, 11-a, 12-b, 13-c, 14-b, 15-b, 16-a, 17-b, 18-a, 19-c, 20-a

B

Combine each group of words in column I with the most appropriate word or group of words in column II:

I	II
1. The zoologist tells about	a. languages
2. The typographer teaches	b. "books in running brooks, and sermons in stones"
3. The theologian teaches	c. agriculture
4. The seismologist teaches	d. the mystery of life
5. The physiologist explains	e. the weather
6. The physicist describes	f. the derivation of words
7. The philologist explains	g. the science of handwriting
8. The penologist is interested in	h. plants

9. The meteorologist forecasts	i. printing
10. The linguist is an expert in	j. the science of earthquake phenomena
11. The graphologist specializes in	k. the human race
12. The geologist deciphers	l. the reformatory treatment of prisoners
13. The etymologist explains	m. the forms of living things before birth
14. The entomologist tells about	n. religion
15. The embryologist studies	o. the functions of the muscles
16. The botanist examines	p. the texts of ancient manuscripts
17. The biologist is interested in	q. the nature of matter and motion
18. The archeologist digs up	r. ancient ruins
19. The anthropologist studies	s. insects
20. The agronomist teaches	t. the different animals of the world

—*Answers*—

1-t, 2-i, 3-n, 4-j, 5-o, 6-q, 7-p (or a or f), 8-l, 9-e, 10-a, 11-g, 12-b, 13-f (or a), 14-s, 15-m, 16-h, 17-d, 18-r, 19-k, 20-c

C

Give the correct word for each of the following definitions:

1. The study of religion   t_____
2. The study of manuscripts   p_____
3. The study of languages   l_____
4. The study of the earth   g_____
5. The study of energy   p_____
6. The study of printing   t_____
7. The study of handwriting   g_____
8. The study of animals   z_____
9. The study of prison reform   p_____
10. The study of the weather   m_____
11. The study of farming   a_____
12. The study of life   b_____
13. The study of earthquakes   s_____

14. The study of the functions of
the body   p_____
15. The study of man   a_____
16. The study of unborn babies   e_____
17. The study of plants   b_____
18. The study of words   e_____
19. The study of ancient ruins   a_____
20. The study of insects   e_____

—*Answers*—

1-theology, 2-philology, 3-linguistics, 4-geology, 5-physics,
6-typography, 7-graphology, 8-zoology, 9-penology, 10-me-
teorology, 11-agronomy, 12-biology, 13-seismology, 14-physi-
ology, 15-anthropology, 16-embryology, 17-botany, 18-ety-
mology, 19-archeology, 20-entomology

D

In the following table, note the pronunciation of the three
forms—the idea-noun, the person-noun, and the adjective that
refers to each of the nouns in this game:

1. agronomy: a-GRON-o-mee
   agronomist: a-GRON-o-mist
   agronomical: ag-ro-NOM-i-kul
2. anthropology: an-thro-POL-o-jee
   anthropologist: an-thro-POL-o-jist
   anthropological: an-thro-po-LOJ-i-kul
3. archeology: ar-kee-OL-o-jee
   archeologist: ar-kee-OL-o-jist
   archeological: ar-kee-o-LOJ-i-kul
4. biology: by-OL-o-jee
   biologist: by-OL-o-jist
   biological: by-o-LOJ-i-kul
5. botany: BOT-an-ee
   botanist: BOT-an-ist
   botanical: bo-TAN-i-kul
6. embryology: em-bree-OL-o-jee
   embryologist: em-bree-OL-o-jist
   embryological: em-bree-o-LOJ-i-kul
7. entomology: en-to-MOL-o-jee
   entomologist: en-to-MOL-o-jist
   entomological: en-to-mo-LOJ-i-kul
8. etymology: et-i-MOL-o-jee
   etymologist: et-i-MOL-o-jist
   etymological: et-i-mo-LOJ-i-kul

9. geology: jee-OL-o-jee
   geologist: jee-OL-o-jist
   geological: jee-o-LOJ-i-kul
10. graphology: graf-OL-o-jee
    graphologist: graf-OL-o-jist
    graphological: graf-o-LOJ-i-kul
11. linguistics: lin-GWIS-tiks
    linguist: LIN-guist
    linguistical: lin-GWIS-ti-kul
12. meteorology: mee-tee-ur-OL-o-jee
    meteorologist: mee-tee-ur-OL-o-jist
    meteorological: mee-tee-ur-o-LOJ-i-kul
13. penology: pee-NOL-o-jee
    penologist: pee-NOL-o-jist
    penological: pee-no-LOJ-i-kul
14. philology: fil-OL-o-jee
    philologist: fil-OL-o-jist
    philological: fil-o-LOJ-i-kul
15. physics: FIZ-iks
    physicist: FIZ-i-sist
    physical: FIZ-i-kul
16. physiology: fiz-ee-OL-o-jee
    physiologist: fiz-ee-OL-o-jist
    physiological: fiz-ee-o-LOJ-i-kul
17. seismology: size (or sice)-MOL-o-jee
    seismologist: size (or sice)-MOL-o-jist
    seismological: size (or sice)-mo-LOJ-i-kul
18. theology: thee-OL-o-ji (*th* as in *thank*)
    theologian: thee-o-LOW-jun
    theological: thee-o-LOJ-i-kul
19. typography: tie-POG-raf-ee
    typographer: tie-POG-raf-ur
    typographical: tie-po-GRAF-i-kul
20. zoology: zo-OL-o-jee
    zoologist: zo-OL-o-jist
    zoological: zo-ol-OJ-i-kul

With these 60 words firmly fixed in your mind, you will be able to identify quite a few of the educational courses, the teachers of such courses, and some of the important adjectives that describe them.

But before you leave this game, make sure that you don't confuse the meanings of the words in each of the following groups:

1. astronomy —the science that treats of the heavenly bodies

   astrology —the study of the imagined influence of the stars upon the destinies of men

2. anatomy —the science of the *structure* of organisms

   physiology —the science of the *functions* of organisms

3. geology —the science that treats of the origin, history, constitution, and structure of the earth

   geodesy —the measurement of vast areas of the earth's surface

   geography —the science that describes the surface of the earth—its climates, peoples, animals, and products

4. meteorology —the science dealing with the weather

   metrology —the science dealing with the system of weights and measures

5. topography —the description of the physical features of a region

   typography —the art of composing and printing from type

And by the way, suppose a person specialized in speleology; would he be regarded as an expert in spelling? Not at all. Speleology (spee-lee-OL-o-jee) is the scientific study of caves.

HOW TO MAKE TWO OR MORE OUT OF ONE

SPOONSFUL OR SPOONFULS?

This chapter will show you how to change singular nouns into plural nouns. It is easy to get mixed up on this point—unless you know a few simple rules.

What, for example, is the plural of *spoonful?* Is it *spoonsful, poonsfull,* or *spoonfuls?*

What is the plural of *court-martial?* Is it *courts-martial,* or *court-martials?*

Is *brother-in-laws* the plural of *brother-in-law?*

Would you use, in your writing, such words as *potatoes, octavos, heroes, echos, curioes, ponchoes,* as the plurals for *potato, octavo, hero, echo, curio, poncho?*

Which of the following plurals is correct: (a) the two *Miss Whites,* or (b) the two *Misses White,* or (c) the two *Misses Whites?*

Is the expression, "he saw a strange *phenomena,*" correct?

The above, as well as most other English nouns, form their plural in accordance with a few simple principles. Fix these principles in your mind, and you will rarely go wrong:

1. You can form the plural of the great majority of nouns by adding *s* to the singular: *table, tables; floor, floors; park, parks; book, books; window, windows; house, houses.*

2. It will help you to memorize the next rule if you listen to the advice that Mary gave her husband when he was shining his shoes: "Put your *brush* in the *box* on the *porch,* and come in for a *kiss* and a *waltz.*" You notice that the five nouns in the quotation end in *sh, x, ch, s,* and *z.* Most nouns with these endings add *es,* instead of *s,* to the singular: *brush, brushes; box, boxes; porch, porches; kiss, kisses; waltz, waltzes.*

3. Nouns ending in *f* or *fe* generally change *f* to *v* and add

es or *s*: *leaf, leaves; wolf, wolves; shelf, shelves; wharf, wharves; life, lives; knife, knives.*

But be careful about such exceptions as *chief, chiefs; grief, griefs; proof, proofs; safe, safes.*

4. Nouns ending in a *consonant* + *y* change the *y* to *i* and add *es: city, cities; country, countries; sky, skies.*

5. Nouns ending in a *vowel* + *y* simply add *s: journey, journeys; monkey, monkeys; turkey, turkeys; play, plays.*

6. Hyphenated words form their plurals by adding *s* to the *principal*—that is, the *most important*—part: *brother-in-law, brothers-in-law; court-martial, courts-martial; editor-in-chief, editors-in-chief; passer-by, passers-by; notary-public, notaries-public; maid-of-honor, maids-of-honor.*

When the name of a person is preceded by a title, it is customary to pluralize the title rather than the name. Thus, it is better to say the *Misses White* than the *Miss Whites* or the *Misses Whites.*

7. Figures, signs, and letters form their plurals by adding *'s:*

There are two *x's* in Foxx, the name of a baseball player who was famous several years ago.

There are three *7's* in my telephone number.

There are four *s's* and four *i's* in Mississippi.

8. The plurals of nouns ending in *o* may cause you some trouble. But there are two fairly accurate rules that govern such plurals:

a. Nouns ending in *o* preceded by a vowel generally add *s* to the singular: *cameo, cameos; curio, curios; radio, radios; ratio, ratios; rodeo, rodeos.* This principle applies also to nouns ending in double *o: bamboo, bamboos; hoodoo, hoodoos; kangaroo, kangaroos; shampoo, shampoos; zoo, zoos.*

b. Nouns ending in *o* preceded by a consonant generally add *es: echo, echoes; hero, heroes; mosquito, mosquitoes; potato, potatoes; tomato, tomatoes; torpedo, torpedoes.*

But here comes the trouble. There are several nouns that end in *o* preceded by a consonant, and yet form the plural by adding *s* instead of *es.* How are you going to pluralize them when you have occasion to use them?

Well, here's a simple guide for you to follow. If the noun has been borrowed from a foreign language and has not yet become "fully naturalized" as an English word, the chances are that its plural ends in *s* instead of *es.* For example: *banjo, banjos; bolero, boleros; cello, cellos; chromo, chromos; octavo,* ctavos; poncho, ponchos; rancho, ranchos; virtuoso, virtu-sos; sombrero, sombreros.

As a general rule, you will be correct if you follow the instructions as given under a and b. But whenever you are in doubt, look the word up in a good modern dictionary. Get into the habit of using your dictionary frequently.

9. Many words derived from the Latin and the Greek keep their original plurals; *alumnus* (male), *alumni; alumna* (female), *alumnae; axis, axes; criterion, criteria; crisis, crises; datum, data; phenomenon, phenomena.*

But here, too, the tendency is to gradually "naturalize" the Latin and the Greek words by giving them an English plural. Thus, there are two possible plurals—the foreign and the English—for many words: *formula—formulae* or *formulas; radius—radii* or *radiuses; syllabus—syllabi* or *syllabuses; vertex—vertices* or *vertexes.*

Here, too, consult a standard modern dictionary to be on the safe side.

10. Several nouns have irregular plurals: *woman, women; child, children; ox, oxen; mouse, mice; louse, lice; tooth, teeth; foot, feet; goose, geese.*

But the plural for the *goose* which is *a tailor's smoothing iron* is *gooses.*

Sometimes, when you're in doubt and no dictionary is available, you can avoid the difficulty by substituting another word or phrase for the required word. This is what the tailor did when he wanted to send an order for two irons. He didn't know whether to order "two gooses" or "two geese." But he got out of the difficulty by asking for one goose, and by adding the following postscript:

"Please send me another one also."

11. And, finally, here is that troublesome group of words—*cupful, glassful, handful, spoonful.*

You will have no trouble if you remember that each of these nouns is a *single word,* and forms its plural in the regular way—*cupfuls, glassfuls, handfuls, spoonfuls.*

To fix this idea in your mind, look at the difference between the two following sentences:

1. She poured three cupfuls of water into her cake mixture.
2. She placed three cups full of water upon the table.

In the first sentence, you have *one* cup for the measures. Hence, *three cupfuls.*

In the second sentence, you have *three* cups for three portions. Hence, *three cups full*.

And thus the correct forms for measuring ingredients in your recipes are: *spoonfuls, cupfuls, glassfuls* and *handfuls*.

WHEN NOUNS ARE POSSESSIVE

It is a simple matter to form the possessive of an English noun.

1. When a noun, whether singular or plural, *does not* end in s, x, z, or j, add apostrophe s (*'s*): *week's* pay; *children's* books; *men's* hats; *Arthur's* shoes.

2. When a singular noun of *one* syllable ends in s, x, z, or j, likewise add *'s*: *fox's* tail; *James's* car; *Wells's* novels; *boss's* office.

3. When a singular noun of *more than one* syllable ends in s, x, z, or j, the more common practice is to add *'s*: *Dickens's* biography; *Thomas's* house; *Gladys's* hat.

4. But when the last syllable of a noun ending in s is preceded by an s or another sibilant (hissing) sound, the preferable form is to add only the apostrophe. This avoids the disagreeable excessive repetition of the s sound. Thus, *Moses'* story, *Jesus'* Sermon, *Xerxes'* defeat, sound better than *Moses's* story, *Jesus's* Sermon, *Xerxes's* defeat.

5. When a name ending in s is long, it is better to add an apostrophe only: *Demosthenes'* orations, *Diogenes'* lamp.

6. When a plural noun ends in s, just add the apostrophe: *girls'* schools, *workers'* wages, *printers'* ink.

You can also indicate the possessive by the preposition *of* placed before the noun: the vicissitudes *of life*, the adventures *of Ulysses*, the death *of a salesman*. This form of possessive is sometimes more effective than the other—especially when you want to *emphasize* the noun.

PUT IT TO THE TEST

Have you done this chapter carefully? Suppose you put it to the test.

A

Check the correct plural for each of the following nouns:

1. sombrero: (a) sombreroes, (b) sombreros
2. monkey: (a) monkeys, (b) monkies
3. ox: (a) oxes, (b) oxen
4. housefly: (a) houseflys, (b) houseflies

108

5. the letter *m:* (a) *m's,* (b) *ems*
6. court-martial: (a) court-martials, (b) courts-martial
7. hanger-on: (a) hanger-ons, (b) hangers-on
8. jack-in-the-box: (a) jacks-in-the-box, (b) jack-in-the-boxes
9. goose, meaning a tailor's iron: (a) geese, (b) gooses
10. rancho: (a) ranchoes, (b) ranchos
11. potato: (a) potatoes, (b) potatos
12. mother-in-law: (a) mother-in-laws, (b) mothers-in-law

B

In each of the following phrases, remove the preposition and change the possessor to the possessive case:

1. The plays of Aristophanes (a-ris-TOF-an-eez)
2. The wanderings of Ulysses
3. The tail of the ox
4. The fur of the foxes
5. The altar of the church
6. The enamel of the teeth
7. The salary of the secretaries
8. The cold of the last two winters
9. The traps of the golf links
10. The antlers of the deer (plural)

—Answers—

1-b, 2-a, 3-b, 4-b, 5-a, 6-b, 7-b, 8-a, 9-b, 10-b, 11-a, 12-b

1-Aristophanes' plays, 2-Ulysses' wanderings, 3-ox's tail, foxes' fur, 5-church's altar, 6-teeth's enamel, 7-secretaries' salary, 8-the last two winters' cold, 9-the golf links' traps, 10-the deer's antlers.

Time out for the Tenth Word Game

ARE THERE ANY MISFITS IN YOUR VOCABULARY?

A

The following sentences have been taken from the examination papers of high school students. Each of these papers

contains a "boner"—that is, a misused or misspelled word
See if you can replace the boners with the correct words:

1. The United States and Canada are contagious countries.
2. A merger of several business companies is known as concubine.
3. When a man is married to two women at the same time, he is guilty of bigotry.
4. When a man is married to only one woman, he lives in a state of monotony.
5. The Rialto is the business center of Venus.
6. Napoleon had three sons, not one of whom lived to maternity.
7. My sister is preparing her torso for her wedding.
8. He illuminated all his competitors and won the prize.
9. Birds seem to fly with the utmost felicity.
10. Edmund Spenser wrote an allergy called "The Faerie Queene."
11. Dr. Roberts administered the unesthetic at the operation.
12. Mark Twain told many amusing antidotes in his lectures.
13. Emerson was an octopus who looked at life through rose-colored glasses.
14. People who imagine they are sick are called hypodermics.
15. My father has diabetes, and they are treating him with insolence.
16. The flying saucers are regarded as a celestial progeny.
17. The difference in their languages mitigates against a better understanding between different nations.
18. He suffered from a skeptic infection in the elbow.
19. It sounded like the voracious story of an honest man.
20. Poets often like to illiterate their words.

—*Answers*—

1. *contiguous* should replace *contagious*
   contiguous means *adjoining*
   contagious means *catching a disease by contact*
2. *combine* should replace *concubine*
   a *combine* is *an association of several business companies, a trust.*

110

a *concubine* is *a woman who lives with a man without a marriage bond*
3. *bigamy* should replace *bigotry*
bigamy is *marriage to two persons at the same time; polygamy is marriage to two or more persons at the same time*
bigotry is *obstinate devotion to one's own belief and intolerance toward other people's beliefs.*
4. *monogamy* should replace *monotony*
monogamy means *marriage to one person*
monotony means *boredom caused by the absence of variety*
5. *Venice* should replace *Venus*
Venice is the city
Venus is the goddess.
6. *Maturity* should replace *maternity*
maturity is *the state of being full-grown*
maternity is *the condition of being a mother*
7. *trousseau* should replace *torso*
trousseau means *bridal outfit*
torso means *trunk—the body without the head and the limbs*
8. *eliminated* should replace *illuminated*
to *eliminate* is to *remove*
to *illuminate* is to *supply with light*
9. *facility* should replace *felicity*
facility means *ease*
felicity means *good fortune*
10. *allegory* should replace *allergy*
an *allegory* is *a symbolic poem or story*
an *allergy* is *a susceptibility to sickness from certain foods or plants*
11. *anesthetic* should replace *unesthetic*
an *anesthetic* means *a drug that produces temporary insensitivity to pain*
unesthetic means *unbeautiful, or unable to appreciate beauty*
12. *anecdotes* should replace *antidotes*
an *anecdote* is *a brief, amusing story about a famous character*
an *antidote* is *a remedy against poison*
13. *optimist* should replace *octopus*

an *optimist* is *a person who believes that everything is for the best*

an *octopus* is *an eight-armed sea animal*

14. *hypochondriacs* should replace *hypodermics*
a *hypochondriac* is *a person morbidly anxious about his health*
a *hypodermic* is *an injection of medicine under the skin, or an instrument with which the injection is made*

15. *insulin* should replace *insolence*
insulin is *a drug used in diabetes*
insolence means *offensive impertinence*

16. *prodigy* should replace *progeny*
a *prodigy* is *something out of the ordinary course of nature*
progeny means *offspring—children of human beings or of lower animals*

17. *militates* should replace *mitigates*
to *militate* means *to fight against*
to *mitigate* means *to soften, to make less severe*

18. *septic* should replace *skeptic*
septic means *poisonous to the blood*
skeptic means *doubting*

19. *veracious* should replace *voracious*
veracious means *truthful*
voracious means *eating with greediness*

20. *alliterate* should replace *illiterate*
to *alliterate* means *to begin several successive words with the same letter or sound*
illiterate means *uneducated, unable to read*

B

Are you better acquainted now with these tricky words? Then you are ready for the next round. Match the words in the first column with the definitions in the second column:

1. allegory   a. a humorous story about famous people
2. allergy   b. a pain-deadening drug
3. alliterate   c. a poison-curing drug
4. anecdote   d. good fortune
5. anesthetic   e. intolerance to certain plants or foods
6. antidote   f. fanatical devotion to a cause
7. bigamy   g. a business merger

8. bigotry	h. a symbolical story
9. combine	i. marriage to two women
10. concubine	j. to begin several words with the same sound
11. contagious	k. adjoining
12. contiguous	l. catching, as applied to certain diseases
13. eliminate	m. to light up
14. facility	n. ease
15. felicity	o. an injection under the skin
16. hypochondriac	p. an "unmarried wife"
17. hypodermic	q. one who suffers from imaginary sickness
18. illiterate	r. ignorant
19. illuminate	s. to remove or eject
20. insolence	t. a drug used in diabetes
21. insulin	u. insulting treatment
22. maternity	v. marriage to one woman
23. maturity	w. boredom through lack of variety
24. militate	x. to fight against
25. mitigate	y. poisonous
26. monogamy	z. motherhood
27. monotony	aa. full development, ripeness
28. octopus	bb. a strange phenomenon in nature
29. optimist	cc. a bridal outfit
30. prodigy	dd. to make less painful
31. progeny	ee. a person who looks on the bright side of things
32. septic	ff. not artistic
33. skeptic	gg. an 8-armed sea animal
34. torso	hh. offspring, children
35. trousseau	ii. a city in Italy
36. unesthetic	jj. truthful
37. Venice	kk. a Roman goddess
38. Venus	ll. greedy
39. veracious	mm. a doubter
40. voracious	nn. the human trunk

—*Answers*—

1-h, 2-e, 3-j, 4-a, 5-b, 6-c, 7-i, 8-f, 9-g, 10-p, 11-l, 12-k, 13-s, 14-n, 15-d, 16-q, 17-o, 18-r, 19-m, 20-u, 21-t, 22-z, 23-aa, 24-x, 25-dd, 26-v, 27-w, 28-gg, 29-ee, 30-bb, 31-hh, 32-y, 33-mm, 34-nn, 35-cc, 36-ff, 37-ii, 38-kk, 39-jj, 40-ll

C

And now test your skill on the forty words from another angle. Out of the three endings to each of the following statements, check the one that is most nearly correct.

1. An allegory is
    (a) a state of mind (b) an attitude toward food (c) a symbolic story, like *Pilgrim's Progress*
2. An allergy may make you
    (a) bored (b) sneeze (c) energetic
3. Alliterate is a word used in connection with
    (a) a poet (b) an ignoramus (c) a glutton
4. You are likely to use an anecdote if you want to
    (a) tell a funny story (b) counteract a poison (c) help somebody financially
5. You hear the word anesthetic most frequently
    (a) in art circles (b) in business conferences (c) in hospitals
6. Antidotes serve to
    (a) amuse (b) remove the effects of poison (c) please doting relatives
7. A man is guilty of bigamy if he has
    (a) too many wives (b) too much devotion (c) ideas that are too big for him
8. He is guilty of bigotry if he
    (a) gambles in a lottery (b) has too many wives (c) is too fanatical
9. You are most likely to find a combine in
    (a) business (b) a king's palace (c) people who suffer from diabetes
10. If you heard of a concubine, you would expect to see
    (a) a board of directors (b) a military maneuver (c) a woman
11. If a thing is contagious, it might be
    (a) a neighboring country (b) smallpox (c) a drug
12. You can use the word contiguous of
    (a) The United States and Mexico (b) diphtheria and scarlet fever (c) two mortal enemies
13. Conventions are held to eliminate
    (a) electric bulbs (b) unwanted candidates (c) ignorant voters
14. Facility in a sport comes from
    (a) practice (b) money (c) luck
15. If you have felicity, people are likely to

(a) distrust you (b) envy you (c) pity you

16. You dislike hypochondriacs because
    (a) they grumble (b) they hurt you (c) they cheat you

17. You connect the word hypodermic with
    (a) a needle (b) a person who needles you (c) a needless complaint

18. The word illiterate best describes
    (a) a poet (b) a general (c) a savage

19. Electricity serves to illuminate
    (a) discomfort (b) worry (c) a dark room

20. A man who uses insolence is likely to be
    (a) a doctor (b) a patient (c) a dictator

21. A man who gives insulin is likely to be
    (a) a dictator (b) a boaster (c) a doctor

22. Maternity applies to all
    (a) grownups (b) mothers (c) fathers

23. Maturity is the state of being
    (a) a mother (b) secure (c) grown up

24. To militate is to
    (a) fight (b) cure (c) make

25. You try to mitigate
    (a) success (b) suffering (c) a broken watch

26. A man who enjoys monogamy is
    (a) dull (b) happily married (c) a designer of monograms

27. Monotony is the result of
    (a) too little variety (b) too many wives (c) rebellion against a commanding officer

28. If you saw an octopus, you'd call it
    (a) an optical illusion (b) a pair of rose-tinted glasses (c) a sea animal

29. If you were an optimist, you'd be
    (a) grasping (b) far-sighted (c) cheerful

30. A prodigy occurs
    (a) to every parent (b) to all animals as well as humans (c) only once in a while

31. The progeny of Adam, according to the Bible, consisted of
    (a) the miracle of his creation (b) the visit of the serpent (c) his two sons

32. A septic condition may result in
    (a) acceptance (b) inquiry (c) severe pain

33. A skeptic is a
   (a) spreader of poison (b) doubter (c) high jumper
34. If you saw a torso in a trunk, you'd suspect a
   (a) bullfight (b) murder (c) wedding
35. If you saw a trousseau in a trunk, you'd suspect a
   (a) wedding (b) murder (c) bullfight
36. An unesthetic person
   (a) loves art (b) doesn't care about art (c) makes
   you indifferent to pain
37. Venice is famous as
   (a) an Italian city (b) the goddess of beauty (c) a
   waltz by Strauss
38. We are likely to associate Venus with
   (a) gondolas (b) beautiful features (c) canals and
   palaces
39. A veracious person is found of
   (a) steaks and chops (b) the truth (c) cruelty
40. A voracious person
   (a) can always be trusted (b) eats a lot (c) looks for
   quarrels

—*Answers*—

1-c, 2-b, 3-a, 4-a, 5-c, 6-b, 7-a, 8-c, 9-a, 10-c, 11-b, 12-a,
13-b, 14-a, 15-b, 16-a, 17-a, 18-c, 19-c, 20-c, 21-c, 22-b, 23-c,
24-a, 25-b, 26-b, 27-a, 28-c, 29-c, 30-c, 31-c, 32-c, 33-b, 34-b,
35-a, 36-b, 37-a, 38-b, 39-b, 40-b

D

And here is the pronunciation of the more difficult words
in this game:

allergy, noun: AL-ur-jee
allergic, adjective: al-UR-jik
combine, noun: COM-bine; but note the same word
combine, verb: com-BINE
concubine: CONK-you-bine
contiguous: con-TIG-you-us
monogamy: mon-OG-am-ee
prodigy: PROD-ij-ee
progeny: PROJ-en-ee

SLIPS OF THE TONGUE

The boners we have played with in this game are due to
poor spelling or to slips of the mind. There are also a number

of errors we make through slips of the tongue. These errors are called *spoonerisms*, after a famous Oxford professor, Dr. William A. Spooner, who had a nervous habit of transposing the initial letters of his words. Among his most amusing slips of the tongue were the following:

He struck a blushing crow, for *He struck a crushing blow.*
He harbored in his bosom a half-warmed fish, for *He harbored in his bosom a half-formed wish.*
He tasted a whole worm, for *He wasted a whole term.*
He rode on a well-boiled icicle, for *He rode on a well-oiled bicycle.*
They hissed the mystery lecture, for *They missed the history lecture.*
It is kisstomary to cuss the bride, for *It is customary to kiss the bride.*

Avoid slips of the mind and slips of the tongue. Know what you are about to say, and be careful how you say it.

13

HOW TO DESCRIBE PERSONS
AND THINGS

WHEN ADJECTIVES GO WRONG

Can you tell what is wrong with the following sentences?

1. One of the principle buildings in Washington is the White House.
2. Murder is a capitol crime in many states.
3. John had a chronicle heart ailment.
4. He made an abortion attempt to fight back, but he was too weak.
5. The gardener had course manners but a kindly disposition.
6. Don't be such a truculence witness.
7. Some of the oldest species of animals are still extent.
8. His sickness remained stationery for some time.

In each of the above sentences, a noun is incorrectly used where an adjective is required. But before we go on with the correction, let us look at the functions of the adjective.

We have already discussed the noun, with its various uses and abuses. The adjective, it has been aptly observed, dances attendance upon the noun. Grammatically speaking, it is "a word used to modify a noun." It describes a noun, qualifies it, limits or restricts it, explains it, gives it color, and helps to shape its meaning. There is a tendency among some writers to belittle the value of the adjective. Mark Twain, for example, has observed: "As for the adjective . . . strike it out." And Voltaire has referred to it as "the enemy of the noun." Yet even these writers have made excellent use of the adjective which they so flippantly dismiss. Look at the following passage from Mark Twain, for example:

> "The holy passion of friendship is of so sweet and steady and loyal and enduring a nature that it will last through a whole lifetime, if not asked to lend money."

In this single sentence there are no fewer than six adjectives: *holy, sweet, steady, loyal, enduring, whole.*

YOU CAN'T GET ALONG WITHOUT ADJECTIVES

You can't get along without the adjective. It is "the versatile and colorful servant of the noun." Sometimes a single adjective may enable you to condense a long and involved thought into a few syllables.

Take, for example, the adjective *versatile*—derived from the Latin *versatilis*, which means *capable of being turned around.* A versatile person is so many-sided that he can easily turn from one activity to another; he is therefore a person of many capabilities and interests and thoughts.

Or take the adjective *plebeian.* This word, derived from the Latin *plebs*, meaning the *common people*, describes a person, or an action performed by a person, of no distinction or refinement or imagination—a member of the "common herd." There's a lot of meaning in this simple word.

Adjectives, you can see, are handy words, especially if you have a wide knowledge of them. When properly used, they are an important element in the speaking and writing of good English.

CORRECTING SOME COMMON ERRORS

Don't ever confuse the adjective with the noun. Look once more at the incorrect sentences at the start of this chapter. These sentences should be corrected as follows:

1. One of the *principal* buildings in Washington is the White House.
2. Murder is a *capital* crime in many states.
3. John had a *chronic* heart ailment.
4. He made an *abortive* attempt to fight back, but he was too weak.
5. The gardener had *coarse* manners but a kindly disposition.
6. Don't be such a *truculent* witness.
7. Some of the oldest species of animals are still *extant.*
8. His sickness appeared *stationary* for some time.

In Sentence 1, *principal* is an adjective; it means *main*, and it modifies—that is, it limits or restricts the meaning of —the noun *buildings*. The word *principal*, as we shall soon see, can also be used as a noun.

But the word *principle* is always a noun, and it means *a general truth, a settled rule of conduct*.

In Sentence 2, *capital* is an adjective. This word also, as we shall see, can sometimes be used as a noun. In this sentence, *capital* means *punishable by death* and it modifies the noun *crime*.

The word *capitol* is a noun, and it denotes *a state house, or the official building of the United States Congress in Washington*.

In Sentence 3, *chronic* is an adjective; it means *lingering, lasting for a long period*, and it modifies the noun *ailment*.

The word *chronicle*, a noun, means *a historical record arranged chronologically*—that is, in the order of time.

In Sentence 4, *abortive* is an adjective; it means *prematurely born*, and therefore *coming to naught, failing*. Here the adjective modifies the noun *attempt*.

The word *abortion* is a noun, and it means *the act of bringing about*, or *the result of, a premature birth*.

In Sentence 5, *coarse* is an adjective meaning *low, vulgar, indelicate;* it modifies the noun *manners*.

The word *course* is a noun.

In Sentence 6, *truculent* is an adjective which means *harsh, violent, cruel*. It modifies the noun *witness*.

The word *truculence* is a noun.

In Sentence 7, *extant* is an adjective; it means *still existing and known, still alive*, and it modifies the noun *species*. (This adjective is pronounced *EX-tant*, or *ex-TANT*.)

The word *extent* is a noun.

In Sentence 8, *stationary* is an adjective which means *remaining in one place, exhibiting no change*. Here it qualifies the noun *sickness*.

The word *stationery* is a noun which denotes writing materials.

IS A PRINCIPAL A MAN OF PRINCIPLE?

As already suggested, some words can be used either as nouns or as adjectives. Thus:

Principal is a noun when it refers to

1. *a sum of money:* He gets a good interest on his *principal*.

2. *the leader of a school:* The *principal* dismissed the head of the English Department.

It is an adjective when it is used as a modifier meaning *main, leading, first in rank:* The *principal* subject for debate was the question of peace or war.

But the word *principle* should never be used as an adjective. It is always a noun.

Capital is another word that can be used either as a noun or as an adjective. For example:

Noun: Their business has a *capital* of $5,000,000.
Adjective: Washington is the *capital* city of the United States.

But *capitol* should always be used as a noun.

There are some words that can be used either as verbs, as nouns, or as adjectives. Such words as *advance* and *net*, for example, belong to this category. Thus:

The captain ordered the company to *advance* (*verb*).
The public objected to a further *advance* in prices (*noun*).
He made an *advance* payment on the house (*adjective*).

He tried to *net* a big profit (*verb*).
He caught many fishes in his *net* (*noun*).
His *net* income was $10,000 a year (*adjective*).

In many cases, however, the *form* of the word changes along with the change in its *function*. Thus:

Verb	*Noun*	*Adjective*
to signify	significance	significant
to differ	difference	different
to observe	observation	observant

IN A NUTSHELL

To summarize:

Does a word express action or occurrence or state of existence? Then it is a verb.

Does it denote a thing, a place, a person, a quality, or an idea? Then it is a noun.

Does it modify or limit or qualify or explain or describe a noun? Then it is an adjective.

TEST YOUR SKILL

Do you get the "feel" of the adjective as distinguished from the other parts of speech? Try to spot the adjectives in the following passages, and see for yourself:

1. Enrico Caruso, the great tenor, told this experience, which would seem to prove that no man is as famous as he thinks he is.

"As I was motoring over the Catskill Mountains, my auto broke down and I sought refuge in a lonely farmhouse while the car was being repaired at a nearby garage. The farmer and I got into conversation and after a while he asked my name. I told him it was Caruso.

"The astounded farmer jumped to his feet and, grabbing my hand, exclaimed, 'I never expected to see *you* in my humble home! Caruso! The famous traveler! Robinson Caruso!'"

2. An English lady, self-appointed supervisor of village morals, accused a workman of drunkenness because "with her own eyes" she had seen his wheelbarrow outside a public house.

The accused man made no verbal defense, but the same evening he placed his wheelbarrow outside her door and left it there all night.

—*The Countryman*

—Answers—

Here are the adjectives in the first passage, together with the nouns they "modify." Please remember that the verb *to modify*, grammatically speaking, means *to limit* or *to restrict the meaning of, to qualify*:

great	modifies	*tenor*
this	modifies	*experience*
no	modifies	*man*
famous	modifies	*man*
Catskill	modifies	*Mountains*
my	modifies	*auto*
lonely	modifies	*farmhouse*
nearby	modifies	*garage*
my	modifies	*name*
astounded	modifies	*farmer*
my	modifies	*hand*
humble	modifies	*home*
famous	modifies	*traveler*

And here are the adjectives, with the nouns they modify, in the second passage:

English	modifies *lady*
self-appointed	modifies *supervisor*
village	modifies *morals*
her	modifies *eyes*
own	modifies *eyes*
his	modifies *wheelbarrow*
public	modifies *house*
accused	modifies *man*
verbal	modifies *defense*
same	modifies *evening*
his	modifies *wheelbarrow*
her	modifies *door*
all	modifies *night*

Note that the words *village* and *public* can be used either s adjectives or as nouns, depending upon their construction 1 a given sentence. In the above anecdote they are used as djectives. But in the following examples these same words re used as nouns:

The village is rapidly growing into a town. (*Village* is the subject of *is . . . growing*.)

The speaker respected his public. (*Public* is the object of *respected*.)

Thus, as you see, it is generally easy to distinguish between he adjective and the noun. But the correct usage of the adective presents a number of other problems. We shall conider some of these problems in Chapter 14—right after the ntermission for our next word game.

Time out for the Eleventh Word Game
TWENTY PICTURESQUE ADJECTIVES

In this game you are going to play with twenty adjectives hat end in *ic*. When you have added these colorful words to our stockpile, you will possess a richer vocabulary and a reater power for the expression of your various thoughts.

A

After each of the following adjectives, check the definition that fits it best:

1. phlegmatic
   (a) scholarly, (b) not easily excited, (c) very friendly, (d) self-satisfied
2. sycophantic
   (a) suffering from a dog bite, (b) cooled by a fan, (c) addicted to giving false flattery, (d) dull
3. sardonic
   (a) cynical, (b) packed like a sardine, (c) talkative, (d) reserved
4. enigmatic
   (a) artistic, (b) vicious, (c) fragrant, (d) puzzling
5. dogmatic
   (a) pertaining to the care of dogs, (b) used as a mat, (c) too authoritative, (d) sweet
6. sadistic
   (a) inclined to sadness, (b) inflicting cruelty, (c) fond of beauty, (d) untiring
7. masochistic
   (a) inflicting cruelty, (b) immature, (c) enjoying cruel treatment, (d) gracious
8. eccentric
   (a) hostile, (b) fond of being in the midst of things, (c) easily deceived, (d) queer
9. spasmodic
   (a) convulsive, (b) foolish, (c) traveling through space, (d) delicious
10. seismic
    (a) swanky, (b) pertaining to earthquakes, (c) small-sized, (d) pompous
11. myopic
    (a) nearsighted, (b) selfish, (c) childlike, (d) farsighted
12. presbyopic
    (a) farsighted, (b) religious, (c) pertaining to newspapers, (d) nearsighted
13. quixotic
    (a) speedy, (b) contented, (c) poisonous, (d) impractically idealistic
14. toxic

124

(a) pertaining to taxes, (b) poisonous, (c) dressed in a tuxedo, (d) delicious

15. antiseptic
    (a) germ-killing, (b) dealing with the number 7, (c) fermented, (d) sour
16. ascetic
    (a) practicing self-denial, (b) climbing upward, (c) inquisitive, (d) fond of beauty
17. esthetic
    (a) practicing self-denial, (b) fond of beauty, (c) argumentative, (d) lazy
18. soporific
    (a) soapy, (b) sleep-producing, (c) having large pores, (d) wide awake
19. Teutonic
    (a) huge, (b) made up of two tonics, (c) German, (d) very heavy
20. titanic
    (a) huge, (b) sunburnt, (c) very firm, (d) appreciative

—Answers—

1-b, 2-c, 3-a, 4-d, 5-c, 6-b, 7-c, 8-d, 9-a, 10-b, 11-a, 12-a, 13-d, 14-b, 15-a, 16-a, 17-b, 18-b, 19-c, 20-a

B

In this round, put the proper adjective after each defini-tion:

1.	nearsighted	m__p__
2.	pertaining to earthquakes	s___s___
3.	farsighted	p__s_____
4.	convulsive	s____m_____
5.	impractically idealistic	q__x_____
6.	queer	e___n_____
7.	poisonous	t_x__
8.	enjoying cruel treatment	m___c__s___
9.	germ-killing	a__is_____
10.	inflicting cruelty	s_d_____
11.	practicing self-denial	a_c_____
12.	too authoritative	d__m_____
13.	fond of beauty	e_t_____
14.	puzzling	e__g_____
15.	sleep-producing	s____r_____

16. cynical	s___d_____
17. German	T__t_____
18. addicted to giving false flattery	s_c__h_____
19. huge	t_t_____
20. not easily excited	p___g_____

C

This round of the game is somewhat different. In each of the following sentences, put the correct word into the blank space:

1. Saint Francis, denying himself the luxuries of the world, was a man with an a_____ disposition.

2. The doctor prescribed iodine as an a_____ measure for the accidental cut.

3. A teacher becomes d_____ when he asserts his personal opinions as actual facts.

4. The composer Johannes Brahms was so e_____ that he often came to his recital without any socks or necktie.

5. The origin of the universe may remain e_____ for many centuries to come.

6. He enjoyed music and painting and the other e_____ pleasures of life.

7. She was so m_____ that she enjoyed being flogged by her husband.

8. He was rejected by the Army because of his m_____ vision.

9. It takes a p_____ personality to be indifferent to the dangers of battle.

10. He was so p_____ that he could see the smallest objects on the horizon.

11. The q_____ type of person, like the hero of Cervantes' novel, sees a palace in a pigsty.

12. Bluebeard, in the treatment of his wives, was a vicious and s_____ monster.

13. The Devil, in Goethe's *Faust*, answered the cries of his victims with s_____ laughter.

14. There was a s_____ disturbance that rocked the tallest buildings of the city.

15. The doctor gave him a s_____ drug to help him to fall asleep.

16. She cried out at intervals because of her convulsive, s_____ pains.

17. I don't believe his s_____ smiles, because they are false.

18. Goliath was a man of t_____ size.

19. Hitler believed in the supremacy of the T_____ people.

20. The t_____ effects of certain diseases can be overcome by an antitoxin.

—*Answers*—

1-ascetic, 2-antiseptic, 3-dogmatic, 4-eccentric, 5-enigmatic, 6-esthetic, 7-masochistic, 8-myopic, 9-phlegmatic, 10-presbyopic, 11-quixotic, 12-sadistic, 13-sardonic, 14-seismic, 15-soporific, 16-spasmodic, 17-sycophantic, 18-titanic, 19-Teutonic, 20-toxic

D

Try to change each of the following adjectives to a noun. I shall give you the answer to the first, as a starter:

Adjective	Noun
1. ascetic	asceticism
2. antiseptic	_____
3. dogmatic	_____
4. eccentric	_____
5. enigmatic	_____
6. esthetic	_____
7. masochistic	_____
8. myopic	_____
9. phlegmatic	_____
10. presbyopic	_____
11. quixotic	_____
12. sadistic	_____
13. sardonic	_____
14. seismic	_____
15. soporific	_____
16. spasmodic	_____
17. sycophantic	_____
18. titanic	_____

127

19. Teutonic   _____
20. toxic   _____

1-asceticism, 2-antisepsis, 3-dogmatism, dogma, dogmatist, 4-eccentricity, 5-enigma, 6-estheticism, esthete, 7-masochism, masochist, 8-myopia, 9-phlegm, 10-presbyopia, 11-quixotism, 12-sadism, sadist, 13-sardonicism, 14-seismography, seismograph, 15-soporific, 16-spasm, 17-sycophancy, sycophant, 18-titan, 19-Teuton, 20-toxin

E

Now for the correct pronunciations:

1. ascetic: as-SET-ik; this form can also be used as a noun
   asceticism: as-SET-i-sizm
2. antiseptic: an-ti-SEP-tic; this form can also be used as a noun
   antisepsis: an-ti-SEP-sis
3. dogmatic: dog-MAT-ik
   dogmatism: DOG-ma-tizm
   dogma: DOG-ma
   dogmatist: DOG-ma-tist, a person who is dogmatic
4. eccentric: ek-SEN-trik; this form can also be used as a noun
   eccentricity: ek-sen-TRISS-i-tee
5. enigmatic: enig-MAT-ik
   enigma: e-NIG-ma
6. esthetic: es-THET-ik
   estheticism: es-THET-i-sizm
   esthete: ES-theet, a person devoted to beauty
7. masochistic: mass-o-KIS-tic
   masochism: MASS-o-kizm
   masochist: MASS-o-kist, a person who is masochistic
8. myopic: my-OP-ik
   myopia: my-OWE-pee-a
9. phlegmatic: fleg-MAT-ik
   phlegm: FLEM
10. presbyopic: press-bee-OP-ik
    presbyopia: press-bee-OWE-pee-a
11. quixotic: kwix-OT-ik
    quixotism: KWIX-o-tizm
12. sadistic: sa-DIS-tik

sadism: SAD-izm

sadist: SAD-ist, a person who inflicts cruelty

13. sardonic: sar-DON-ic

    sardonicism: sar-DON-i-sizm

14. seismic: SIZE-mik or SICE-mic ("SICE" may be used in the following two words also)

    seismography: size-MOG-ra-fee, the science of earthquakes

    seismograph: SIZE-mo-graff, the instrument that records earthquakes

15. soporific: so-po-RIFF-ik, the same form for the adjective and the noun

16. spasmodic: spaz-MOD-ik

    spasm: SPAZM

17. sycophantic: sik-o-FAN-tik

    sycophancy: SIK-o-fan-see

    sycophant: SIK-o-fant, a sycophantic person

18. titanic: ti-TAN-ik

    titan: TIE-tun

19. Teutonic: tew-TON-ik

    Teuton: TEW-tun

20. toxic: TOKS-ik

    toxin: TOKS-in

The words used in this game—and in all the other games—are not the only possible words that can express similar ideas. Don't forget that our language is rich in synonyms. Whenever you come to a new word, be sure to look up several of its synonyms. This is one of the best ways to keep enlarging your vocabulary.

14

WHEN ADJECTIVES GO WRONG

COMPARATIVELY SPEAKING

What is wrong with the following sentences?

1. He was the most fastest runner on the team.
2. I am more happier than I can tell you.
3. The more, the merriest.
4. John is taller than any member of his class.
5. His father is the richest of all the other men in the town.
6. Shakespeare was greater than any English poet.
7. Johnny has less dimes than Sally.
8. The sooner you do it, the best.
9. If the police were more alert, there would be less crimes in this country.
10. There is no question about the greater usefulness of our broiler.

The above errors in the usage of comparisons are more or less common. Before we correct them, however, let us briefly glance at the comparison of adjectives.

As you will recall from your school days, the rules of comparison are few and simple:

1. Adjectives of one syllable, and many adjectives of two syllables, add *-er* for the *comparative* degree, and *-est* for the superlative degree:

Positive	Comparative	Superlative
cold	colder	coldest
fair	fairer	fairest
clever	cleverer	cleverest
sallow	sallower	sallowest
polite	politer	politest

2. Adjectives of two syllables ending in *-y* preceded by a consonant change the *-y* to *i* and add *-er* and *-est*:

Positive	Comparative	Superlative
hungry	hungrier	hungriest
sorry	sorrier	sorriest
chilly	chillier	chilliest
funny	funnier	funniest

3. Adjectives of more than two syllables generally use *more* for the comparative, and *most* for the superlative:

Positive	Comparative	Superlative
turbulent	more turbulent	most turbulent
studious	more studious	most studious
obedient	more obedient	most obedient
interesting	more interesting	most interesting

4. Don't use double comparatives like *more happier*, or double superlatives like *most speediest*. It is true that some of our greatest writers have used such expressions. Thus, in *Julius Caesar*, Shakespeare refers to the blow struck by Brutus as "the *most unkindest* cut of all." In his day, the present rule had not yet become firmly established; but in modern English, according to the best authorities, this sort of construction is downright wrong.

5. Watch out for such expressions as: "New York is bigger than any city in the United States." This sentence is incorrect. For the expression "any city" includes New York along with all the other cities. The sentence therefore means that New York is bigger than New York—a statement that is obviously absurd.

Here is the proper way to express the idea: "New York is bigger than *any other* city in the United States."

6. On the other hand, watch out for the opposite error: "New York is the biggest of all the other cities in the United States." This sentence, too, is absurd. To provide a *biggest* city, all cities must be included. But New York is not included in the *other cities,* and therefore it cannot be the biggest of them *all.* Restate the sentence to read: "New York is the *biggest of all the cities* (or, the *biggest city*) in the United States."

7. When each of two comparatives is preceded by the word *the,* be careful to keep both terms uniform.

Right: the *more* the *merrier*
the *later* the *better*

Wrong: the *more* the *merriest*
the *later* the *best*

8. When there is a comparison, the standard for the comparison should be made clear. For example, it doesn't make complete sense to say: "Caruso's voice was superior." The sentence should read: "Caruso's voice was superior to most other operatic voices of his day."

9. Finally, there are a few adjectives with irregular comparisons that may have tripped you up in the past. Study them carefully, to avoid any future errors in their usage:

far	farther, further	farthest, furthest
little	less	least
few	fewer	fewest

CORRECTING THE ERRORS

With the above rules in mind, you should have no difficulty in correcting the sentences at the start of this chapter. Here are the corrections:

1. He was the *fastest* runner on the team. (Rule 4)
2. I am *happier* than I can tell you. (Rule 4)
3. The more, the *merrier*. (Rule 7)
4. John is *taller than any other* member of his class. (Rule 5)
5. His father is the *richest man* in the town. (Rule 6)
6. Shakespeare was *greater than any other English poet.* (Rule 5)
7. Johnny has *fewer* dimes than Sally.

Less refers to quantity, measure, or degree; *fewer* refers to numbers. The proper expression is *less* money, but *fewer* coins. (Rule 9)

8. The sooner you do it, the *better*. (Rule 7)
9. If the police were more alert, there would be *fewer* crimes in this country. (The correct expression is *less* crime, but *fewer* crimes, as shown in Rule 9.)
10. There is no question about the *greater* usefulness of our broiler *compared to others*. (Rule 8)

ARTICLES ARE ADJECTIVES

The words *a, an,* and *the,* generally called *articles,* are really adjectives. A book means *any* book or *one* book; *the* book means *this* book.

Use *a* before consonant sounds: *a street, a job, a historical novel, a unique event.*

In the above examples, the *h* in *historical* and the *u* in *unique* are pronounced as consonants.

Yet note the following expressions: *an hour, an honor, an heirloom.* In these expressions you use *an* because the *h* is silent in *hour, honor,* and *heirloom.*

So your choice of *a* or *an* depends not upon the *spelling* but upon the *sound* of the word that comes after it.

DISPLACED ADJECTIVES

I once overheard the following conversation between a college teacher and one of his students:

> *Student:* "I have a friend with a clubfoot named Jack Smith."
> *Teacher:* "That's an interesting name for a clubfoot. Now tell me the name of your friend."

This displacement of an adjective is a common error, and it sometimes leads to ridiculous results.

For example:

> The fish was taken out of the icebox and handed to Mary stiff as a board.
> The lamb chop was a welcome sight to Harry sizzling in the electric broiler.

To avoid such errors, keep your adjectives close to the words they modify.

Rewrite the above sentences as follows:

> I have a friend named Jack Smith who has a clubfoot.
> The fish, stiff as a board, was taken out of the icebox and handed to Mary.
> The lamb chop, sizzling in the electric broiler, was a welcome sight to Harry.

SOMETHING ABOUT THIS AND THAT

Many of the common errors made in our everyday English are due to the misuse of the demonstrative adjectives—*this, these, that,* and *those.* See whether you can spot the errors in the following sentences.

1. He dislikes those kind of people.
2. I have performed that sort of experiment quite often.

3. Why don't you like these sort of dishes?
4. He spoke about baseball and other sports of those kind.
5. The Hindus are quite clever at these sort of tricks.
6. This sort of sandwiches is the most appetizing.
7. He always raced in those sort of cars.
8. He likes to wear these kinds of hats.
9. A good knowledge of English will enable you to correct these kind of errors.
10. I refuse to listen to them kinds of arguments.

To correct the errors in the above sentences, bear in mind the following facts:

1. The demonstrative adjectives are the only English adjectives that agree in number with the nouns they modify.

2. Therefore, you must never use the plural adjectives *these* or *those* with the singular nouns *kind* or *sort*. And vice versa. The correct forms are *this kind, this sort, that kind, that sort, these kinds, these sorts, those kinds, those sorts*. This rule holds true even when such phrases are followed by plural nouns: *this kind of books, that sort of overcoats*.

3. The word *them* is not an adjective, but a pronoun. We shall discuss the pronoun in a later chapter. But, for the present, it is sufficient to remember that a pronoun can not be used to modify a noun.

CORRECTING THE ERRORS

Following the above three formulas, you should have no trouble in correcting the errors in our quiz:

1. Change *those* to *that* (*singular*, to agree with *kind*).
2. This sentence is correct.
3. Change *these* to *this*.
4. Change *those* to *that*.
5. Change *these* to *this*.
6. This sentence is correct.
7. Change *those* to *that*.
8. This sentence is correct (*plural*, to agree with *kinds*).
9. Change *these* to *this*.
10. Change *them* to *these*.

A RAPID-FIRE REVIEW

And now, for an over-all review of the adjective, try to correct the grammatical errors in those of the following sentences that are wrong. Your score should be pretty close to 100:

1. The doctor said the disease had changed from acute to chronicle.

2. He sold stationary, such as paper, pencils and ink, in his store.

3. The extent of the damages will not be known until the flood has receded.

4. There are less people attending baseball games this year than last year.

5. I admire Mantle, Musial, and Williams; but of the three players, the latter is perhaps the best hitter.

6. They have produced these sorts of pictures for many years.

7. Don't bother me with them complaints.

8. Cheerful people are more pleasanter to be with than sad people.

9. He invested his principle at a good interest.

10. Many people consider Lincoln greater than any president.

11. But many other people still regard Washington as the greatest of all the presidents.

12. Mrs. Jackson is an hysterical woman.

13. The body was recognized by John Stevens, the detective, rigid and lifeless and cold.

14. The tide carried away the swimmer foaming over the rocks.

15. These kind of ties are my favorite.

CORRECTIONS

1. The correct word is *chronic*.
2. The correct word is *stationery*.
3. This sentence is correct.
4. The correct word is *fewer*.
5. Change *latter* to *last-named*.
6. This sentence is correct.
7. The correct word is *these*.
8. Omit the word *more*.
9. The correct word is *principal*.
10. Insert *other* between *any* and *president*.
11. This sentence is correct.
12. Change *an* to *a*.
13. Rewrite the sentence to read: The body, rigid and lifeless and cold, was recognized by John Stevens, the detective.

14. Rewrite the sentence to read: Foaming over the rocks, the tide carried away the swimmer.

15. This kind of ties is my favorite.

Are you ready for the next word game? As you will see when you play it, this game may well be entitled *Murder in the Classroom.*

Time out for the Twelfth Word Game
SOME MORE MISFITS

A

A "boner"—as you have noted in the Tenth Word Game— is a misused or misspelled word. In that game the boners were taken from the examination papers of high school students. Here are a number of similar errors taken from the papers of college students. See how many of these errors you can correct:

1. Achilles was venerable only in his heel.
2. King Louis XVI was gelatined in 1793.
3. There is considerable heredity in the Sahara Desert.
4. A pharynx was a compact body of soldiers in ancient Greece.
5. The American statesman Andrew Mellon was a cynosure of art.
6. The angels of the highest order are known as terrapin.
7. A polyglot is a figure having many sides and angles.
8. The ancient oracles frequently gave amphibious answers.
9. Robert Louis Stevenson suffered from congenial tuberculosis.
10. Andrew Carnegie was praised as a philanderer when he founded a number of libraries.
11. Pontius Pilate was the Roman procreator of the Jews.
12. The judge refused the divorce on the ground of collision between the husband and the wife.
13. The arrival of the police brought about the aspersion of the mob.
14. The investigator's conclusions were wrong because of his faulty hypotenuse.

15. The dead man's body was placed in the moratorium.

16. He was not a great sinner, but he committed many armadillos.

17. The thermometer measured 70 degrees centipede.

18. The seconds were ticked off by the osculations of the pendulum.

19. Neutralized citizens are illegible for the Presidency; only those who have been born in the United States can be elected to that high office.

20. Every man who enters the medical profession takes the hypocritical oath.

—*Answers*—

1. *vulnerable* should replace *venerable*
   vulnerable means *susceptible to being wounded*
   venerable means *worthy of honor and respect*, generally applying to advanced age

2. *guillotined* should replace *gelatined*
   guillotined means *executed on the guillotine*—the machine used for beheading people in the French Revolution
   gelatined means *coated with animal jelly*

3. *aridity* should replace *heredity*
   aridity means *dryness, a state of being without rain*
   heredity is *the transmission of the physical and psychical characters of parents to their offspring*

4. *phalanx* should replace *pharynx*
   the *phalanx* was *a Greek body of heavy-armed infantry formed in close ranks*
   the *pharynx* is *the part of the alimentary canal between the mouth and the esophagus*
   (Don't confuse *alimentary*, which means *pertaining to the absorption and digestion of food*, with *elementary*. This sort of confusion would make another boner.)

5. *connoisseur* should replace *cynosure*
   a *connoisseur* is *one who understands a fine art*
   a *cynosure* is *a center of attraction*

6. *seraphim* should replace *terrapin*
   seraphim is the plural for *seraph*, which means a *fiery angel*
   a *terrapin* is a *turtle*

7. *polygon* should replace *polyglot*
   a *polygon* is *a geometric figure containing more than four sides and angles*

a *polyglot* is *a person who speaks or writes many languages*

8. *ambiguous* should replace *amphibious*
   ambiguous means *doubtful, having two or more possible meanings*
   amphibious means *able to live both on land and in water*

9. *congenital* should replace *congenial*
   congenital means *existing from birth*
   congenial means *kindred in spirit, sympathetic*

10. *philanthropist* should replace *philanderer*
    a *philanthropist* is *a person devoted to human welfare*
    a *philanderer* is *a male flirt*

11. *procurator* should replace *procreator*
    a *procurator* was *the governor of a territory conquered by the Romans*
    a *procreator* is *a parent, one who begets children*

12. *collusion* should replace *collision*
    collusion means *a secret agreement to commit fraud*
    collision means *a violent meeting, a clash*

13. *dispersion* should replace *aspersion*
    dispersion means *the act of scattering or being scattered in different directions*
    aspersion means *the act of slandering or defaming*

14. *hypothesis* should replace *hypotenuse*
    hypothesis means *a tentative theory adopted as a basis for a scientific investigation*
    the *hypotenuse* is *the side opposite to the right angle in a right-angled triangle*

15. *mortuary* or *crematorium* should replace *moratorium*
    a *mortuary* is *a deadhouse, a morgue*
    a *crematorium* is *a place for cremating—that is, burning—dead bodies*
    a *moratorium* is *a period in which a person or an institution has a legal right to delay meeting an obligation*

16. *peccadillos* should replace *armadillos*
    a *peccadillo* is *a petty fault*
    an *armadillo* is *a small earth-burrowing animal having a body encased in an armor of bony plates*

17. *centigrade* should replace *centipede*
    centigrade refers to a thermometer in which the interval between the freezing point and the boiling point of water is divided into a hundred equal parts, or degrees

138

a *centipede* is a *small backboneless animal with a large number of legs*

18. *oscillations* should replace *osculations*
    oscillation means a *swinging backward and forward*
    osculation means *the act of kissing*
19. This sentence contains two boners:
    Naturalized should replace *Neutralized*
    to *naturalize* means to *confer the rights of citizenship upon an alien*
    to *neutralize* is to *make neutral, to destroy the effect of*
    ineligible should replace *illegible*
    ineligible means *not qualified to be chosen*
    illegible means *incapable of being read*
20. *Hippocratic* should replace *hypocritical*
    The *Hippocratic Oath,* named after *Hippocrates,* the "Father of Medicine," is an oath embodying a high code of medical ethics; it is administered to young men about to enter the practice of medicine
    hypocritical means *assuming a false appearance of virtue or piety*

B

Most of these words are a little harder than those you have considered in your other word game on boners. Are you sure you know the meanings of these words? Try the next round, and see for yourself. Match the words in the first column with the definitions in the second column:

1. ambiguous   a. the act of kissing
2. amphibious   b. sympathetic
3. aridity   c. a place for burning dead bodies
4. armadillo   d. fiery angels
5. aspersion   e. a scattering
6. centigrade   f. an animal armored with bony plates
7. centipede   g. a turtle
8. collision   h. to turn an alien into a citizen
9. collusion   i. a part of the alimentary canal
10. congenial   j. a person who understands a fine art
11. congenital   k. a male flirt
12. connoisseur   l. a man actively devoted to his fellow men
13. crematorium   m. assuming a false appearance

139

14. cynosure	n. a parent
15. dispersion	o. a swinging to and fro
16. gelatined	p. slander, a slanderous report
17. guillotined	q. a thermometer measurement
18. heredity	r. to destroy the effect of
19. Hippocratic	s. incapable of being read
20. hypocritical	t. a petty fault
21. hypotenuse	u. the line opposite the right angle in a right-angled triangle
22. hypothesis	v. easily wounded
23. illegible	w. an authorized period for suspension of payments
24. ineligible	x. beheaded on the guillotine
25. moratorium	y. a tentative theory
26. mortuary	z. a deadhouse
27. naturalize	aa. inheritance of certain characteristics
28. neutralize	bb. able to live on land and in water
29. oscillation	cc. a clash
30. osculation	dd. dryness
31. peccadillo	ee. a center of attraction
32. phalanx	ff. a fraudulent agreement
33. pharynx	gg. relating to Hippocrates
34. philanderer	hh. worthy of honor, usually because of advanced age
35. philanthropist	ii. not qualified to be chosen
36. polyglot	jj. coated with jelly
37. polygon	kk. a figure of many sides and angles
38. procreator	ll. a speaker of many languages
39. procurator	mm. a 100-footed animal
40. seraphim	nn. the governor of a Roman territory
41. terrapin	oo. a body of Greek infantry
42. venerable	pp. existing from birth
43. vulnerable	qq. doubtful

—*Answers*—

1-qq, 2-bb, 3-dd, 4-f, 5-p, 6-q, 7-mm, 8-cc, 9-ff, 10-b, 11-pp, 12-j, 13-c, 14-ee, 15-e, 16-jj, 17-x, 18-aa, 19-gg, 20-m, 21-u, 22-y, 23-s, 24-ii, 25-w, 26-z, 27-h, 28-r, 29-o, 30-a, 31-t, 32-oo, 33-i, 34-k, 35-l, 36-ll, 37-kk, 38-n, 39-nn, 40-d, 41-g, 42-hh, 43-v

C

In this round, try to fit the correct word into each of the following sentences:

1. Being a professional runner, he is i_____ for the college track team.
2. The h_____ is the longest side of a right-angled triangle.
3. Albert Einstein, born in Germany, became a n_____ citizen of the United States.
4. Any flat figure of more than four sides is called a p_____.
5. Casanova was a famous ph_____.
6. The ph_____ was an important fighting unit in the army of Alexander the Great.
7. Anatole France's famous story about Pontius Pilate is called "The P_____ of Judea."
8. To understand all the foreign languages spoken in New York, one has to be a p_____.
9. The beautiful Helen of Troy was the c_____ of all eyes.
10. It's good to be in the company of con_____ friends.
11. The dis_____ of the Jews took place when the Romans conquered Palestine.
12. The s_____ are supposed to be the highest order of angels.
13. The frog is an am_____ animal.
14. There are two well-known kinds of thermometers: C_____ and Fahrenheit.
15. His enemies have cast as_____ on his character.
16. They attacked the argument at its most v_____ point.
17. The t_____ is an edible North American turtle.
18. According to the Bible, Noah was the pr_____ of Shem, Ham and Japheth.
19. Old and sacred institutions are generally regarded as ven_____.
20. Rockefeller made his money as a capitalist, and gave much of it away as a ph_____.
21. The ph_____, situated between the palate and the esophagus, serves as a passage for food and air.
22. The Nebular H_____ is one of the unproved theories about the origin of the heavenly bodies.

23. Napoleon's handwriting was said to have been so i_____ that it was almost impossible to decipher his letters.

24. The man's weakness for drink was a mere p_____ rather than a serious crime.

25. There was much os_____ at the young people's party.

26. Sodium bicarbonate is said to n_____ the acidity of the stomach.

27. The legislature enacted a m_____ allowing the banks to suspend payments for three months.

28. The os_____ of the tides is due to the attraction of the moon.

29. The high standard of medical ethics is largely due to the H_____ Oath.

30. He spoke in such an am_____ manner that you couldn't make out what he really had in his mind.

31. Many people, disliking burial, prefer to have their bodies taken to a cr_____.

32. It was a summer of practically no rain, great ar_____, and poor crops.

33. Genius, according to some, is a matter of h_____; it is transmitted from father to son.

34. Many nobles were g_____ in the French Revolution.

35. You can sometimes recognize a h_____ person by the insincere sound of his voice.

36. A c_____, with its many legs, is not a pleasant sight.

37. An ar_____, like a turtle, has a bony shield for protection.

38. They were arrested for col_____ in cheating the public.

39. He had a con_____ weakness—at least he had shown it from infancy—and was not expected to live long.

40. He was a wealthy con_____ of the arts.

41. A m_____ is another name for a morgue.

—*Answers*—

1-ineligible, 2-hypotenuse, 3-naturalized, 4-polygon, 5-philanderer, 6-phalanx, 7-Procurator, 8-polyglot, 9-cynosure, 10-congenial, 11-dispersion, 12-seraphim, 13-amphibious, 14-Centigrade, 15-aspersions, 16-vulnerable, 17-terrapin, 18-procreator, 19-venerable, 20-philanthropist, 21-pharynx,

22-Hypothesis, 23-illegible, 24-peccadillo, 25-osculation, 26-neutralize, 27-moratorium, 28-oscillation, 29-Hippocratic, 30-ambiguous, 31-crematorium, 32-aridity, 33-heredity, 34-guillotined, 35-hypocritical, 36-centipede, 37-armadillo, 38-collusion, 39-congenital, 40-connoisseur, 41-mortuary.

D

Here is the correct pronunciation of the more difficult words in this game:

ambiguous: am-BIG-you-us
amphibious: am-FIB-ee-us
aridity: a-RID-i-tee
armadillo: ar-ma-DIL-low; plural armadillos, pronounced ar-ma-DIL-oze
centipede: SEN-ti-peed
congenial: con-JEEN-yal, or con-JEEN-ee-al
congenital: con-JEN-i-tal
connoisseur: kon-i-SIR, or kon-iss-URE (as *ure* in *pure*)
crematorium: kree-ma-TOE-ri-um, or krem-a-TOE-ri-um
cynosure: SIGH-no-shoor, or SIN-o-shoor, or SIGH-no-zhoor, or SIN-o-zhoor
dispersion: dis-PUR-shun, or dis-PUR-zhun
guillotined: GIL-o-teend
Hippocratic: Hip-po-KRAT-ik
Hippocrates: Hip-POK-rat-eez, the Greek physician after whom the oath is named
hypocritical: hip-o-KRIT-i-kul
hypotenuse: high-POT-in-use
hypothesis: high-POTH-e-sis
illegible: il-LEJ-ibl
ineligible: in-EL-i-jibl
peccadillo: pek-a-DIL-low; plural peccadilloes or peccadillos, pronounced pek-a-DIL-oze
phalanx: FAY ' ' s or FAL-lanks
pharynx: FA ' ' s; plural pharynxes or pharynges (pronounce *a* as in *a*)
philanderer: fil-AN-der-er
philanthropist: fil-ANTH-ro-pist (but note the pronunciation of the adjective philanthropic: fil-anth-ROP-ik)
polyglot: POL-ee-glot
polygon: POL-ee-gon
procreator: PRO-kree-ay-ter
procurator: PROK-you-ray-ter

seraphim: SER-a-fim; another form of the plural for seraphim is seraphs, pronounced SER-afs

terrapin: TER-ra-pin

Have you enjoyed this word game? Let's conclude it now with a "boner" which is really a "howler." (A "howler" is an absurd blunder or mistake.)

At the National Dog Show, Bennett Cerf tells us in his *Shake Well Before Using*, a dowager inquired of an attendant, "Do you know the way to the Labradors?"

"Yes'm," he answered. "The gents' is in the basement; the ladies' is down the hall on your right."

15

WORDS THAT PINCH-HIT FOR NOUNS

COUNT THE PRONOUNS

One of the shortest and most striking stories in modern English literature is the following fantasy written by Somerset Maugham:

> Death Speaks: There was a merchant in Bagdad who sent his servant to market to buy provisions, and in a little while the servant came back white and trembling and said, "Master, just now in the market place I was jostled by a man in the crowd, and when I turned I saw it was Death. He looked at me and made a threatening gesture. Now, lend me your horse and I will go to Samarra and there Death will not find me."
>
> The merchant lent his horse, and the servant mounted, and as fast as the horse could gallop he went. Then the merchant went down to the market place and saw me standing in the crowd and came to me and said, "Why did you make a threatening gesture to my servant when you saw him this morning?"
>
> "That was not a threatening gesture," I said. "It was only a start of surprise. I was astonished to see him in Bagdad, for I had an appointment with him tonight in Samarra."

In the above little story, there are twenty-three pronouns:

1. who	9. I	17. That
2. I	10. me	18. I
3. I	11. he	19. it
4. I	12. me	20. I
5. it	13. me	21. him
6. He	14. you	22. I
7. me	15. you	23. him
8. me	16. him	

Every one of the above words stands in place of a noun. Thus:

who stands in place of *merchant*
I stands in place of *servant*
He stands in place of *Death*
me stands in place of *servant*
and so on.

PRONOUNS ARE TIME-SAVERS

Pronouns, as you see, are used as *substitutes for nouns*—to avoid repetition and to save time. Note, for example, the clumsiness of the following passage:

John Brown sold his house. The house had cost John Brown plenty of money, but John Brown was able to make a good profit on the house.

And now see how much better the idea can be expressed by the substitution of pronouns for some of the nouns:

John Brown sold his house. *It* had cost *him* plenty of money, but *he* was able to make a good profit on *it*.

Or, still better:

John Brown bought a house at a high price, but sold *it* at a good profit.

In this final version of the idea, just one little pronoun takes care of all the unnecessary nouns.

AVOIDING AWKWARD REPETITION

Look at the following anecdote, and see how neatly the italicized pronouns avoid the awkward repetition of nouns:

Former Vice-President Garner had lost a ten-dollar bet on a Washington baseball game and the winner asked *him* to autograph the bill *he* was paying with. "*I* will give *it* as a souvenir to my grandson, *who* wants to frame *it* and hang *it* in his room."
"You mean *he* will not spend the money?"
"*That* is correct."
"Well," said Garner, "in that case *I* will just write *you* a check."

Please note: In the last sentence of the above anecdote, the word *that* is not a pronoun but an *adjective* which modifies the noun *case*. Pronouns do not modify, but are used in place of, nouns.

Pronouns are handy words to carry around in the tool-chest of your mind. But they can also be troublesome at times. Many of the common errors in English are due to their incorrect use.

So let's get better acquainted with the pronoun, and learn how to use it properly.

DON'T ABUSE YOUR PRONOUNS

There are several different kinds of pronouns:

Demonstrative Pronouns. Noun-substitutes which *demonstrate,* or *point out,* an object. For example:

> this   that   these   those

The above words, as we saw in Chapter 14, can also be used as adjectives. They are *pronouns* when they *substitute for* nouns, and *adjectives* when they *go with* nouns:

Pronouns:
    I like *this.*
    These are the best.

Adjectives:
    I like *this man.*
    These peaches are the best I have eaten in a long time.

Unlike the *demonstrative adjective,* the *demonstrative pronoun* is very easy to handle. So we can dismiss it without further discussion, and go on to

Personal Pronouns. Noun-substitutes that *indicate a person.* For example:

> I   he   they
> mine   his   them

And now watch out. There are many mistakes made in the use of these simple personal pronouns.

SOME COMMON ERRORS

Here are some of the more common examples of their misuse. See if you can spot the errors:

1. I am fond of my sister. Are you fond of your's?
2. Him and I are partners.
3. Us boys belong to the same club.
4. I expect you and she at my house tomorrow.
5. Did you see her and I at the game?
6. Her's was the prettiest dress at the dance.
7. The baby wriggled it's toes.

To make the corrections in the above sentences, and to avoid all similar errors, we must get down to *cases*.

A *case*, in grammar, is the form given to a noun or a pronoun to indicate its connection with the rest of the sentence. Thus:

The *subjective case* represents the *subject* of a verb: *I* have a watch.

The *possessive case* represents the *owner* or *possessor* of a thing: This car is *mine*.

The *objective case* represents the *object* of a verb: I hope you like *me*.

And now, if you remember the case-forms of the personal pronouns, you will readily see the errors in the seven incorrect sentences. Here are the case-forms:

Subjective	Possessive	Objective
I	mine	me
we	ours	us
you	yours	you
he	his	him
she	hers	her
it	its	it
they	theirs	them

CORRECTING THE ERRORS

Bear the above chart in mind as you follow the corrections:

1. I am fond of my sister. Are you fond of *yours?* (The word *yours* is in the *possessive* case. It does not need an apostrophe.)

2. *He* and I are partners. (*He* is in the *subjective* case.)

3. *We* boys (*subjective*) belong to the same club.

4. I expect you and *her* (*objective*) at my house tomorrow.

5. Did you see her and *me* (*objective*) at the game?

6. *Hers* (*possessive*, without an apostrophe) was the prettiest dress at the dance.

7. The baby wriggled *its* (*possessive,* without an apostrophe) toes.

It's *"its"* that causes the most trouble. In the preceding sentence, the first word stands for the subject *it* and the verb *is.* The apostrophe represents the omission of the letter *i* in the verb. Hence the form *it's.* But the second word stands for the possessive of *it,* which must *always* be written *without* an apostrophe. Hence the form is *its.*

So it's all very simple. Use the subjective form of the personal pronoun for the subject, the objective for the object, the possessive for the thing possessed; don't ever use an apostrophe before the *s* in the possessive forms *ours, yours, his, hers, its,* and *theirs.*

To clinch the point, try to correct the incorrect forms in the following little story:

One day, when Oscar Wilde was walking with a friend, a huge dog obstructed their path. Wilde hesitated, and seemed nervous.

"Don't be afraid, Oscar," said his friend. "This dog is our's. Besides, look at its tail—how it wags. When a dog wags it's tail, it's in a good humor."

"That may well be," replied Oscar. "But look at the ugly glitter in it's eye. How do I know which end to believe?"

In the above story, the incorrect sentences should be corrected as follows:

This dog is *ours.*
When a dog wags *its* tail, etc.
But look at the ugly glitter in *its* eye.

You have just learned how to use the demonstrative and the personal pronouns. In addition to these, there are various other kinds of pronouns. But before we go on to them, let's have another of our word games.

Time out for the Thirteenth Word Game
WORDS ABOUT BANKING AND BUSINESS

All of us are called upon to transact some sort of business at one time or another. Even those of us who are not active in the commercial world have to buy goods, pay bills, keep bank accounts, check our budgets, and watch our assets and liabilities. Yet many of us are not sufficiently clear about the technical terms used in the business world.

A knowledge of these terms will help you to cope more intelligently with the business problems that you may encounter in your daily life.

This word game consists of twenty-four terms used frequently in business and banking transactions. See how many of them you know.

A

Indicate whether each of the following statements is right or wrong:

1. A *lessor* is a person who owns less property than another. — Right Wrong
2. You give your *collateral* when you work together with somebody else. — Right Wrong
3. *Lien* is the opposite of fat. — Right Wrong
4. A *stipend* is a rather small salary. — Right Wrong
5. A man becomes *insolvent* when he's able to solve a business problem. — Right Wrong
6. We all like to have a *remunerative* job. — Right Wrong
7. *Stagnation* in business is a state of standing still. — Right Wrong
8. An *inflation* is a falling in prices. — Right Wrong
9. A *pecuniary* transaction has something strange about it. — Right Wrong
10. A *tycoon* is a tempest that destroys shipping — Right Wrong
11. *Indigence* is chronic dyspepsia from business worries. — Right Wrong

12. The government allows you to pocket your *gross* profit.   Right   Wrong

13. You get your *net* profit after you deduct all expenses.   Right   Wrong

14. Your *surplus* is the excess of your liabilities over your assets.   Right   Wrong

15. A *cartel* is the business of conveying goods.   Right   Wrong

16. *Affluence* is the service of influential friends.   Right   Wrong

17. A person is very careless when he *disburses* his money.   Right   Wrong

18. You *amortize* a debt when you pay it off.   Right   Wrong

19. An *entrepreneur* is usually an enterprising business man.   Right   Wrong

20. A *promissory* note is a promise to pay.   Right   Wrong

21. You accommodate others when you *borrow money*.   Right   Wrong

22. You assume an obligation to pay back when you *lend* it.   Right   Wrong

23. Accounts payable are known as *assets*.   Right   Wrong

24. Accounts receivable are called *liabilities*.   Right   Wrong

—Answers—

1-wrong, 2-wrong, 3-wrong, 4-right, 5-wrong, 6-right, 7-right, 8-wrong, 9-wrong, 10-wrong, 11-wrong, 12-wrong, 13-right, 14-wrong, 15-wrong, 16-wrong, 17-wrong, 18-right, 19-right, 20-right, 21-wrong, 22-wrong, 23-wrong, 24-wrong

B

The questions in Section A have tested your general knowledge about business and banking words. But the answers have not helped you much with the precise meanings. Try now to get these meanings. Match the words on the left with the definitions on the right:

1. affluence
2. amortize
3. assets
4. borrow
5. cartel

a. poverty
b. a legal claim on property
c. debts which you are obliged to pay
d. to receive a loan
e. something deposited as security on a loan

151

6. collateral	f. an international business monopoly
7. disburse	g. to extinguish a debt by periodical payments
8. entrepreneur	h. wealth
9. gross	i. remainder after deducting expenses
10. indigence	j. expressing a promise to pay, as a *promissory note*
11. inflation	k. monetary, relating to money
12. insolvent	l. profitable
13. lend	m. to grant a loan
14. lessor	n. a sluggishness in business
15. liabilities	o. accounts receivable, inventory and business property
16. lien	p. one who undertakes a business enterprise
17. net	q. undiminished by deduction of expenses, as *gross profits*
18. pecuniary	r. bankrupt
19. promissory	s. a powerful business leader
20. remunerative	t. assets in excess of liabilities
21. stagnation	u. a meager salary
22. stipend	v. to pay out for expenses
23. surplus	w. increase in price levels
24. tycoon	x. one who grants a lease

—Answers—

1-h, 2-g, 3-o, 4-d, 5-f, 6-e, 7-v, 8-p, 9-q, 10-a, 11-w, 12-r, 13-m, 14-x, 15-c, 16-b, 17-i, 18-k, 19-j, 20-l, 21-n, 22-u, 23-t, 24-s

C

Do you know most of these terms now? See what you can do with them in a new setting. Point out the word that completes each of the following statements:

1. Most teachers have a small
   (a) inflation, (b) stipend, (c) lien
2. A coolie's job is not
   (a) gross, (b) insolvent, (c) remunerative
3. A business depression may result in
   (a) indigence, (b) affluence, (c) collateral

4. A claim upon a house for the satisfaction of a debt is a
   (a) surplus, (b) tycoon, (c) lien
5. Through a sinking fund, a debt can be gradually
   (a) netted, (b) amortized, (c) grossed
6. You get a rental contract from a
   (a) cartel, (b) surplus, (c) lessor
7. Carnegie was a man of great
   (a) affluence, (b) indigence, (c) inflation
8. A bankrupt business is
   (a) pecuniary, (b) insolvent, (c) disbursed
9. An international business combination aiming at a monopoly would be called a
   (a) collateral, (b) lien, (c) cartel
10. Rockefeller was a famous
    (a) cartel, (b) tycoon, (c) stipend
11. You're lucky if your business has a
    (a) surplus of assets over liabilities, (b) promissory note, (c) stagnation
12. Most commercial transactions are
    (a) gross, (b) net, (c) pecuniary
13. In bad times, many business firms suffer from
    (a) stipend, (b) affluence, (c) stagnation
14. A note for the repayment of a loan is called
    (a) promissory, (b) surplus, (c) stipend
15. The money left after you've paid your taxes is
    (a) gross, (b) net, (c) lien
16. To negotiate a loan, you may have to give
    (a) cartel, (b) collateral, (c) indigence
17. Money paid out for current expenses is
    (a) borrowed, (b) stipend, (c) disbursed
18. Your total income before expense deductions is
    (a) surplus, (b) gross, (c) net
19. The business was launched by an
    (a) inflation, (b) insolvent, (c) entrepreneur
20. High prices may be due to
    (a) amortization, (b) inflation, (c) remuneration
21. When you have too much money, you can afford to
    (a) borrow, (b) lend, (c) stipend
22. When you have too little money, you may have to
    (a) borrow, (b) lend, (c) disburse

—Answers—

1-b, 2-c, 3-a, 4-c, 5-b, 6-c, 7-a, 8-b, 9-c, 10-b, 11-a, 12-c, 13-c, 14-a, 15-b, 16-b, 17-c, 18-b, 19-c, 20-b, 21-b, 22-a

D

Here are the pronunciations of some of the harder words. Try to recall the meanings as you pronounce these words:

affluence: AF-flew-ence
amortize: a-MORE-tize, AM-er-tize, or a-MORE-tiz
cartel: KAR-tel or kar-TEL
entrepreneur: un-truh-prun-ERR
indigence: IN-dij-ence
lessor: LES-sor
lien: LEEN
pecuniary: pe-KEW-nee-a-ree
promissory: PROM-iss-or-ee
remunerative: re-MEW-ner-a-tiv
stipend: STY-pend
tycoon: tie-KOON

16

THE TROUBLE WITH RELATIVES AND THE LIKE

ARE YOU SURE YOU TREAT THEM RIGHT?

Many of the common blunders in English are due to the abuse of our relatives—that is, our relative pronouns *who*, *whom*, *whose* and *which*. These simple little pronouns, to quote the eminent authority H. W. Fowler, "are as troublesome . . . as they are useful." They have tripped up not only the uneducated layman but the professional writer as well. Here, for example, are a number of quotations from newspaper articles and book reviews that contain typical errors in the use of the relative pronoun:

1. Dark Star, whom many people never thought was in the running, won the Kentucky Derby in 1953.
2. To me, who has a copy of this book, it seems a somewhat trivial fragment.
3. There has been some speculation as to whom the next heavyweight champion will be.
4. This was the man who in other days we knew as the Galloping Ghost.
5. Among others whom we hope will attend the party are the two Senators from New York.
6. He is one of the best men who has ever lived.

CORRECTIONS

1. The pronoun *whom* should be changed to *who*, which is the subject of the verb *was*.

2. The word *has* should be changed to *have*. This verb should be in the first person singular to agree with its subject *who*, which here is also in the first person singular to agree with its principal, *me*.

3. The pronoun *whom* should be changed to *who*, the subject of *will be*.

4. The pronoun *who* should be changed to *whom,* the object of the verb *knew.*

5. The word *whom* should be changed to *who.* In this sentence, the relative pronoun is not the object of the verb *hope* but the subject of the verb *will attend.* You will readily see this point if you punctuate the sentence as follows:

Among others who, we hope, will attend the party are the two Senators from New York.

6. The singular *has* should be changed to the plural *have,* since the pronoun *who* in this sentence is plural to agree with its principal, *men.*

THREE SIMPLE RULES

The above corrections, as you may have observed, contain three simple rules which should help you to eliminate many of the errors in the usage of *who* and *whom.*

Here are the rules:

1. Use the *subjective* form of the relative pronoun when the pronoun is the *subject* of a verb—as in Sentences 1, 3 and 5.

2. Use the *objective* form when the pronoun is the *object* of a verb—as in Sentence 4.

3. The pronoun, as well as the verb of which the pronoun may be a subject, must agree in person and number with its principal—as in Sentences 2 and 6.

RELATIVES THAT ARE FAR AWAY

But there are still a few instances in which the relative pronoun may trip you up, if you are not careful.

Take the following sentence, for example:

1. Here is the man *whom,* as you know from our former conversation in which we discussed the matter, was invited to dinner.

In this sentence, the pronoun should be *who* instead of *whom.* For it is the *subject* of the verb *was invited.*

And now look at the next sentence.

2. Here is the man *who,* as I told you in our former conversation about the matter, we invited to dinner.

In this sentence, the pronoun should be *whom.* For it is the *object* of the verb *invited.*

The trouble with each of the two incorrect sentences is

156

that the construction is obscured by an obstacle of several words between the relative pronoun and the verb that goes with it. You will readily see the point if you recast the sentences so as to bring the pronouns closer to their verbs:

1. Here is the man who was invited to dinner, as you know from our former conversation in which we discussed the matter.
2. Here is the man whom we invited to dinner, as I told you in our former conversation about the matter.

So don't allow a confusing accumulation of words to obstruct your view. Get your relatives to stick to their cases—subjective for the subject, objective for the object.

And just one further precaution: Don't allow your relatives to stray too far away from the nouns to which they are related. The following error, which sounds so ridiculous, is much more common than you think:

This house belongs to Mr. Smith, whose attic is full of bats.

Don't ever put bats into the wrong attic, or relatives into the wrong place. Rewrite the sentence to read:

This house, whose attic is full of bats, belongs to Mr. Smith.

WHOEVER AND WHOSOEVER

Sometimes a relative pronoun is used with the word *ever* or *soever* attached to it. The usage of such compounds is exactly the same as that of the simple relatives:

Whoever (or whosoever) is a friend to you is also a friend to me.
I invite whomever (or whomsoever) I like.

And now you should have no further trouble with your relatives.

PRONOUNS THAT ASK QUESTIONS

The relative pronouns—*who, whom, whose,* and *which*—can also be used as interrogative pronouns. Thus:

1. It is a wise son who knows his own father (*relative*).
2. Who is so wise as to know his own friend (*interrogative*)?

The construction of the interrogative pronouns is similar to that of the relative pronouns. As a rule, therefore, you should have little difficulty with them.

But look at the following special instance:

Who did you invite to the theater?

Is this sentence correct?

Grammatically, of course, the answer is *no*. The pronoun *who* is the object of the verb *did . . . invite*, and therefore should be changed to the objective *whom*.

Yet in everyday speech there is a tendency, even among educated people, to use the relative, and especially the interrogative *who* in place of *whom*. This colloquial usage has good authority. In a letter written (March 20, 1953) to the New York *Herald Tribune*, for example, Professor Cormac Philip, Head of the Department of English at Manhattan College, upholds this conversational usage of *who* for *whom*, and cites a number of grammarians, teachers, and even the Oxford Dictionary to support his view.

And thus the colloquial form—"Who do you take me for?" —may be used, at a cultured gathering or in a conversation between two professors, without causing the lifting of too many eyebrows. But some of the best authorities are still opposed to this usage. For you, who are trying to speak *better English*, the grammatical form is preferable, especially in formal use.

So this would be my suggestion. Until you have completely mastered your English, stick to the established grammatical constructions. You can assume a studied carelessness in your attire only after you have learned to dress well. For the present, try to avoid such constructions as the following:

Who do you see across the street?
Who did you call?
Who would you like for our next Senator?

In each of the above sentences, the pronoun should be in the *objective* case, because it is the *object* of a verb.

WHICH AND WHOSE

There are two other pronouns that have often tripped up the unwary. See if you can spot the errors in the following sentences:

1. Here is a salesgirl which knows my style.
2. Let me know who'se house this is.
3. These are the friends which I value the most.
4. Who's argument do you like the best?

CORRECTIONS

1. Substitute *who* for *which*. The word *which* belongs to *things*, and the word *who* to *persons*.
2. Change *who'se* to *whose*. Never use an apostrophe in a possessive pronoun.
3. Substitute *whom* for *which*.
4. Change *who's* to *whose*.

HOW TO USE "WHOSE"

The word *whose* can be used both for persons and for things. In other words, it means *of whom* and *of which*. For example:

> Here is the man *whose* brother is my partner.
> This is the house *whose* roof needs to be repaired.

The use of *whose* for inanimate objects is often better than the use of the expressions *in which* or *of which*. Note, for example, the awkwardness of the following sentences:

1. This book, from the concentrated harvest of wisdom *of which* we get so much delight, is the work of Thomas Mann.
2. The baseball game, with the complicated plays *of which* he was not familiar, held no attraction for him.

See how much clearer the sentences become when you substitute the word *whose* for the phrases *in which* and *of which*:

1. This book, from *whose* concentrated harvest of wisdom we get so much delight, is the work of Thomas Mann.
2. The baseball game, with *whose* complicated plays he was not familiar, held no attraction for him.

It is quite likely that in your school days your teacher prohibited the use of *whose* for non-living objects. But modern authorities are agreed that such a use is all right, if it helps you to avoid clumsiness. "Let us in the name of common sense," declares H. W. Fowler, "prohibit the prohibition of *whose* inanimate."

WILL EVERYBODY GIVE THEIR ATTENTION?

Is the above heading correct? Or should the word *Their* be changed to *His?*

And now look at two more sentences:

1. If anybody calls, tell him I'm out.

But suppose the caller is a woman—what then?

2. When the speaker sat down, everybody stood up and clapped his hands.

Whose hands? The speaker's? And if there were women in the audience, whose hands were *they* clapping?

The confusion in the meaning of these sentences arises because in the English language there is no *singular* pronoun that denotes both the masculine and the feminine gender—*him-or-her, his-or-hers.* In the absence of such a pronoun, there are three possible ways of clearing up the confusion.

A. Use both pronouns:

Will everybody give his or her attention?
If anybody calls, tell him or her I'm out.
When the speaker sat down, everybody stood up and clapped his or her hands.

But this is a rather clumsy makeshift.

B. Use the masculine pronoun—*he, him, his*—with the idea that this pronoun represents a person of either gender instead of a man.

Will everybody give his attention?
If anybody calls, tell him, etc.
. . . everybody stood up and clapped his hands.

But even Fowler, who recommends this usage, admits that perhaps he is influenced by "the arrogant demand on the part of male England"—not to mention male America.

C. Use the colloquial plural *their* with the singular *anybody* or *everybody:*

Will everybody give their attention?
If anybody calls, tell them I'm out.
When the speaker sat down, everybody stood up and clapped their hands.

This use of the *plural* with the *singular* may not seem accurate to the purist. But it is natural enough. For, in the above sentences, and in all similar sentences, the *idea* if not the *form* of the indefinite pronoun is plural. When you say, "If anybody calls," you imply that *more than one person* may call. And when you talk about the clapping of hands at the conclusion of a speech, you are referring to *a number of people*, and not merely to one listener. This usage is sanctioned in the *Oxford English Dictionary* and is not condemned even in Fowler's *Modern English Usage*.

Surveys show that many educated persons use the *plural*. But grammars and teachers have not caught up with this practice. It is probably safer to use the *singular* in formal speech and writing, unless you are not afraid of criticism.

Now for your self-quiz on the pronouns. You should pass this test rather easily.

TEST YOUR SKILL

What, if anything, is wrong with the pronouns in each of the following sentences?

1. You and he and me will always remain good friends.
2. Whom, do you believe, was at Harry's house yesterday?
3. Who, do you expect, will win the prize?
4. I just adore Sally and he. They are an ideal couple.
5. I don't remember whom they were.
6. This is the man whom he expects will be his partner.
7. This is the man whom he expects to take into partnership.
8. Was it her you were admiring?
9. I am going to buy the coat, because I realize it's value.
10. I am going to buy the coat, because I realize it's value that counts.
11. Everybody bowed his knees in prayer at church.
12. I'll mind my own business and you mind yours.
13. I don't believe that you and us can ever quarrel.
14. I admire whomever has an even temper.
15. Was it her whom you blame for all this trouble?
16. Here is the man who'se brilliance we all admire.
17. Let us not praise ourself too much.
18. As for myself, who has never read the book, I can say nothing about it.
19. These are the students which have carried off most of the prizes.
20. They have no reason to blame theirselves.

Here are the corrections for the incorrect sentences in the quiz:

1. You and he and *I* (*subjective*) will always remain good friends. (The three pronouns—you, he, I—are the subjects of the verb, *will remain.*)

2. *Who*, do you believe, was at Harry's house yesterday? (*Who* is the subject of *was.*)

3. This sentence is correct.

4. I just adore Sally and *him*. (*Him* is the object of the verb *adore.*)

5. I don't remember *who* they were. (*Who* is the subject of *were.*)

6. This is the man *who*, he expects, will be his partner. (The commas help to show that *who* is the subject of *will be.*)

7. This sentence is correct.

8. Was it *she* you were admiring? (This sentence is a little more difficult than the others. But you will see the point if you rewrite the sentence: Was it *she whom* you were admiring? In Sentence 8, the objective pronoun *whom* is understood, though not expressed.)

9. Simple enough: *its*, the possessive pronoun, uses no apostrophe.

10. This sentence is correct. The word *it's* stands for *it is.*

11. Everybody bowed *his* knees in prayer. (This expression is perhaps less natural than "Everybody bowed *their* knees in prayer," but it has traditional acceptance among the well-educated. The second use is common, but more colloquial.)

12. Correct.

13. I don't believe that you and *we* (*subjective*) can ever quarrel.

14. I admire (*him*) *whoever* (subjective) has an even temper. (But this sentence, even though correct, is awkward. Rewrite it somewhat as follows: I admire anyone who has an even temper.)

15. Was it *she* (subjective) whom you blame for all this trouble?

16. Here is the man *whose* (no apostrophe) brilliance we all admire.

17. Let us not praise *ourselves* too much. (The correct plural forms are *ourselves, yourselves, themselves.*)

18. As for myself, who *have* (first person) never read the book, I can say nothing about it.

19. These are the students *who* (referring to persons) have carried off most of the prizes.

20. They have no reason to blame *themselves*.

And now for our next interlude—another pleasant word game to relax the tension of your grammatical chores.

Time out for the Fourteenth Word Game
TRICKY WORDS THAT LOOK ALIKE

The words in this game look simple enough, but watch out. They are frequently misused because of the similarity in their appearance.

How many of these words have tripped you up in the past? Well, proceed with this game and you will find out for yourself.

A

In each of the following sentences, check the correct word enclosed by parentheses:

1. He told a very (ingenious, ingenuous) but untrue story.
2. He gladly (accepted, excepted) the nomination for the Senate.
3. They called him (luxurious, uxorious) because he liked to kiss his wife in public.
4. The (imminent, eminent) Doctor Jones cured her of her sickness.
5. Helen, now a schoolteacher, was (formally, formerly) a typist.
6. They danced in a (spacious, specious) hall.
7. The jury believed the witness because his story sounded so (credible, credulous).
8. They had (averse, adverse) winds throughout the voyage.
9. Jesse James was a (noted, notorious) criminal.
10. The sermon was a good (stimulus, stimulant) to noble action.

163

11. All the critics acclaimed the (exceptionable, exceptional) merit of the young painter's landscapes.

12. Did Joan's marriage (proceed, precede) or follow her graduation from Vassar?

13. Dictators are generally (contemptible, contemptuous) of their people's wishes.

14. The prisoner was (indicted, indited) on three counts.

15. The doctor (proscribed, prescribed) a cathartic for the patient.

16. He went up to the tenth floor on the (elevated, elevator).

17. The attorney for the (persecution, prosecution) rested his case.

18. Collecting stamps in his spare time was his (vocation, avocation).

19. Everybody loved him because he was so generous (disinterested, uninterested) and friendly.

20. The bishop summoned the members of the (council, counsel) for an important discussion on religious matters.

—*Answers*—

1. ingenious
   ingenious means *clever*
   ingenuous means *frank, honest*

2. accepted
   to *accept* is to *take something that is offered*
   to *except* is to *leave something out*

3. uxorious
   uxorious means *excessively devoted to one's wife*
   luxurious means *pertaining to luxury, ministering to luxury, or supplied with the conditions of luxury*

4. eminent
   eminent means *outstanding*
   imminent means *threatening*

5. formerly
   formerly means *in the past*
   formally means *conventionally, in accordance with the rules*

6. spacious
   spacious refers to objects of *wide dimensions*
   specious refers to things that are *deceptively beautiful or right, superficially plausible but not so in reality*—as a *specious claim*

7. credible
   credible means *worthy of belief*
   credulous means *ready to believe, easily imposed upon*

8. adverse
   adverse means *acting against, opposed, in a contrary direction*
   averse means *unwilling, disinclined*

9. notorious
   notorious means *generally known in an unfavorable sense*
   noted means *celebrated*, mostly used in a *favorable sense*.

10. stimulus
    a *stimulus* as a rule refers to a *general incentive*, something that rouses the mind or spirit
    a *stimulant* is usually more concrete, like coffee or an alcoholic beverage, and produces *temporary stimulation*

11. exceptional
    exceptional means *not ordinary, superior*
    exceptionable means *liable to exception, objectionable*

12. precede
    to *precede* means to *go before*
    to *proceed* means to *go onward*, to *advance*

13. contemptuous
    contemptuous means *expressing contempt*
    contemptible means *deserving contempt, despicable*

14. indicted
    to *indict* means to *charge with a crime*
    to *indite* means to *compose and write*

15. prescribed
    to *prescribe* means to *direct the use of*
    to *proscribe* means to *outlaw, to condemn*

16. elevator
    the *elevator* is the cage that carries you up and down in a building
    the *elevated* is the railway built above the street level

17. prosecution
    a *prosecution*, as opposed to the *defense, is the carrying on of a judicial proceeding in behalf of the complaining party*
    a *persecution* is a *campaign to subjugate or to destroy the adherents of a religion or a way of life*, or *repeated acts intended to harass or annoy*

18. avocation
   a man's *avocation* is his *hobby*
   his *vocation* is his *work*
19. disinterested
   disinterested means *free from selfish motive*
   uninterested means *not interested*
20. council
   a *council* means an *assembly gathered for consultation*
   counsel means (a) *advice*, (b) *a lawyer or group of
   lawyers engaged to try a case*

B

Try to get the word that fits each of the following persons
or situations:

1. He wore a tuxedo at the party.   He dressed
                                      f_____
2. He is dotingly attentive to his   He's u_____
wife.
3. She said yes to his proposal.   She a_____
4. The danger is coming very   It's i_____
close.
5. The house is full of costly   It's lu_____
things.
6. His estate covers many acres.   It's s_____
7. Hawthorne had an outstanding   He was
reputation as a novelist.   e_____
8. The present company is not   It's e_____
included in what I say.
9. He says he is an ex-communist.   He was
                                      f_____ a
                                      communist
10. His argument sounded plausi-   It was
ble, but it was untrue.   s_____
11. He shows great cleverness in   He's i_____
devising new ideas.
12. After the applause, he went on   He p_____
with his speech.
13. Bluebeard was well known for   He was
his murders.   n_____
14. I can well believe your story.   It sounds
                                      c_____
15. A glass of sherry may arouse   It's a
you for a time.   s_____

166

16. The dawn comes before the sunrise.

It p___ the sunrise

17. His action is something to be ashamed of.

It's c___

18. He was disinclined to take the risk.

He was a___ to it

19. She believes everything people tell her.

She's c___

20. The doctor is renowned for his skill.

He's n___

21. The criticism of the book was unfavorable.

It was a___

22. Faith helps us to greater effort.

It's a s___

23. The singer's voice is extraordinary.

It's ex___

24. He treats others disdainfully.

He's c___

25. His conduct was such that they all objected to it.

It was ex___

26. He composed a poem.

He i___ it

27. His motive was entirely unselfish.

He was d___

28. The lawyers acted in his behalf.

They were his c___

29. Nero ordered the extinction of the Christians.

He was guilty of p___

30. His answers were frank and above board.

They were i___

31. He was charged at the trial with assault and battery.

He was i___

32. They are elected to help the mayor in his deliberations.

They are his c___

33. The doctor ordered sleeping pills for his patient.

He p___ the pills

34. He shows no inclination to listen to your story.

He's u___

35. He rode up to the twentieth floor.

He used the e___

36. The doctor ordered his patient to omit sugar from his diet.

He p___ it

37. He travels to work on the overhead railway.

He uses the e___

38. He works as an accountant at the bank.

Accounting is his v___

39. He tried the case for the government against the defendant.

He represented the p_____

40. He plays golf on his holidays.

It's his a_____

—Answers—

1-formally, 2-uxorious, 3-accepted, 4-imminent, 5-luxurious, 6-spacious, 7-eminent, 8-excepted, 9-formerly, 10-specious, 11-ingenious, 12-proceeded, 13-notorious, 14-credible, 15-stimulant, 16-precedes, 17-contemptible, 18-averse, 19-credulous, 20-noted, 21-adverse, 22-stimulus, 23-exceptional, 24-contemptuous, 25-exceptionable, 26-indited, 27-disinterested, 28-counsel, 29-persecution, 30-ingenuous, 31-indicted, 32-council, 33-prescribed, 34-uninterested, 35-elevator, 36-proscribed, 37-elevated, 38-vocation, 39-prosecution, 40-avocation

C

After each of the following words, write the word that is sometimes confused with it. If you do not fully understand the difference, look it up among the answers in A, the first part of this word game.

1. accept   e_____
2. adverse   a_____
3. avocation   v_____
4. credible   c_____
5. contemptible   c_____
6. council   c_____
7. disinterested   u_____
8. elevated   e_____
9. eminent   i_____
10. exceptional   e_____
11. formerly   f_____
12. indict   i_____
13. ingenuous   i_____
14. luxurious   u_____
15. noted   n_____
16. persecution   p_____
17. precede   p_____
18. prescribe   p_____
19. spacious   s_____
20. stimulant   s_____

1-except, 2-averse, 3-vocation, 4-credulous, 5-contemptuous, 6-counsel, 7-uninterested, 8-elevator, 9-imminent, 10-exceptionable, 11-formally, 12-indite, 13-ingenious, 14-uxorious, 15-notorious, 16-prosecution, 17-proceed, 18-proscribe, 19-specious, 20-stimulus

D

Several of these words are easy to pronounce. But here are the more difficult ones:

adverse: ad-VURS, or AD-vurs
credulous: KRED-you-lus
eminent: EM-in-ent
imminent: IM-in-ent
indict: in-DITE
ingenious: in-JEEN-yus
ingenuous: in-JEN-you-us
luxurious: lux-YOU-ree-us, or lug-ZHOO-ree-us
specious: SPEE-shus
uxorious: uks-OWE-ree-us, or ugz-OWE-ree-us

Don't mistake the apparently similar words in this chapter for synonyms. Synonyms are words that have like meanings, which these deceptive words certainly do not.

Incidentally, always try to think of synonyms and antonyms. It's one of the best ways to build your vocabulary.

17

THE WHEN, WHERE, AND HOW WORDS

ADVERBS ARE CONFUSING

The use of slovenly English is not confined to the uneducated man in the street. Even those who have had the advantage of a college education are guilty of many a slip of the tongue and the pen. Note, for example, the following typical error taken from a college song:

> She treats us *royal*,
> To her be loyal.

The above statement may be emotionally impressive, but it is grammatically incorrect. The author of the song failed to distinguish between the adjective *royal* and the adverb *royally*.

This confusion between the adjective and the adverb has occasionally stumped even the college teacher. In his excellent book, *We Who Speak English*, Charles Allen Lloyd tells an "almost incredible" but true story about the head of the English department in one of our leading universities. This learned gentleman, writes Mr. Lloyd, was asked to settle an argument about the usage of the word *high*. And his amazing decision was that this word could not be used as an adverb, "because the dictionary does not record it as one."

The professor was apparently relying upon his tricky memory. For, if he had taken the trouble to look this word up in any standard dictionary, he would have noticed that *high* is an adverb as well as an adjective and a noun.

When people of such high caliber can get tripped up on the adverb, it is time for the rest of us to watch our step.

HOW TO TELL ADVERBS FROM ADJECTIVES

You have already noticed the difference between the noun and the adjective. But what is the difference between the adjective and the adverb? To be specific, when is the word *high* an adjective, and when is it an adverb?

It is an adjective when it modifies, limits, qualifies, or describes a noun or a pronoun. It is an adverb when it modifies, limits, qualifies, or describes a verb.

For example:

Adjective: They climbed upon the high mountain. In this sentence, *high* modifies (limits the meaning of) the noun *mountain.*

Adverb: They climbed high upon the mountain. In this sentence, *high* modifies the verb climbed.

An adverb can also modify an adjective:

He looks supremely happy.
He was evidently sure of himself.

In the preceding sentences, *supremely* modifies the adjective *happy,* and *evidently* modifies the adjective *sure.*

An adverb can also modify another adverb:

She speaks more fluently than her brother.
The man was very greatly amused.

More modifies the adverb *fluently,* and *very* modifies the adverb *greatly,* in the two preceding sentences.

Thus an adverb is a word which qualifies a verb, an adjective, or another adverb.

TRICKY ADVERBS

Several of the adverbs in the above examples, as you may have noticed, end in *-ly: royally, supremely, evidently, fluently, barely, perceptibly.* But don't let this ending mislead you into thinking that every adverb ends in *-ly,* or that every word ending in *-ly* is an adverb. Don't, for example, commit errors such as the following:

1. The ice melted *fastly.*
2. She sang *lovely.*
3. She set her hair *curly.*

The first sentence should read: The ice melted *fast.* The old word *fastly* is not used in modern English. Nowadays the word *fast* is both an adjective and an adverb.

The second sentence should be corrected somewhat as follows: She sang in a *lovely manner.* The word *lovely* is an adjective in present-day use. Its use as an adverb, according to the best authorities, including Webster, is now obsolete.

Correct the third sentence to read: She set her hair *in curls*. The word *curly* is not an adverb but an adjective.

Some words ending in *-ly*—such as *daily, weekly, monthly, early, kindly*—may be used both as adverbs and as adjectives. When in doubt about the usage of a word ending in *-ly*, consult a good dictionary. But remember the distinction: adjectives go with nouns or pronouns; and adverbs go with verbs, adjectives, or other adverbs.

ADVERBS ARE POWERFUL WORDS

The role played by the adverb is very important. For it tells you not only *when, where,* and *how* an action takes place, but also *why, whence, whither, wherefore,* and *to what degree* or *extent.* Here is just a sample of the varied and flexible uses of the English adverb:

You can see Mr. Brown *tomorrow* (time). He will be *here* (place), at his office. You will have to talk *fast* (manner), since he is a *very* (degree) busy man. You are expected to tell him *why* (reason) you want to interest him in your new sales idea, *where* (source) you got this idea, and *how far* (extent) it will carry us in our expansion plans. Mr. Brown will want to make his decision *promptly* (manner), *so* (consequence) be ready to "shoot the works."

The adverb is as essential to the verb as the adjective is to the noun. As a rule, the adverb is easy to recognize. But it is not always easy to handle. Many of the common errors in English are due to the incorrect use of the adverb.

Let us look at some of these errors:

MOST, MOSTLY, AND ALMOST

Seven of the following eleven sentences are wrong. See if you can find and correct the mistakes:

1. The test was so hard, he most flunked it.
2. They elect mostly men to the senate.
3. The game was most over when he threw a forward pass.
4. This is the mostly beautiful woman I have seen for a long time.
5. He partly walked but mostly ran to the station to be on time for the train.
6. The bridegroom was the mostly elated man at the wedding.

7. He was almost, but not quite, successful in his venture.
8. My work is most finished; it will be all finished in fifteen minutes.
9. The pages in the book are most uncut.
10. He was most generous to give away all his money.
11. He mostly collapsed from his hard work.

—Answers—

1. Change *most* to *almost*.
   The word *most* as an adverb means *in the highest degree*. It is used with an adjective or another adverb to form the superlative, as *most interesting, most frequently*.
   The word *almost* is an adverb which means *nearly, all but*.
2. This sentence is correct.
   The adverb *mostly* means *for the greatest part, chiefly*.
3. Change *most* to *almost*.
4. Change *mostly* to *most*.
5. This sentence is correct.
6. Change *mostly* to *most*.
7. This sentence is correct.
8. Change *most* to *almost*.
9. Change *most* to *mostly*.
10. This sentence is correct.
11. Change *mostly* to *almost*.

COMPARING THE ADVERB

In several of the above sentences, you have noted the adverb *most*. This word, when used with an adjective or another adverb, indicates the superlative degree. The adverb, like the adjective, can be compared either by the addition of *-er* and *-est* to the positive degree, or by placing *more* and *most* before the positive degree.

For example:

Positive	Comparative	Superlative
soon	sooner	soonest
fast	faster	fastest
high	higher	highest
royally	more royally	most royally
awkwardly	more awkwardly	most awkwardly
graciously	more graciously	most graciously

173

A few adverbs, like a few adjectives, are compared irregularly:

Positive	Comparative	Superlative
far	farther, further	farthest, furthest
little	less	least
much	more	most
well	better	best

The use of adverbs in comparison offers little difficulty. A dwindling number of purists still make a distinction between *farther* and *farthest* on the one hand, and *further* and *furthest* on the other hand. The words *farther* and *farthest,* according to these grammarians, refer to distance in space; the words *further* and *furthest* refer to distance in time or degree. The modern tendency, however, is toward the use of *further* and *furthest* even when you want to express space.

WELL AND GOOD

Several of the common errors in English are due to the misuse of *well* and *good,* and their antonyms *badly* and *bad.* Are you sure you know how to use these words correctly? See if you can check the right word in the parentheses in each of the following sentences:

1. I dined (good, well).
2. He knows me (well, good).
3. They need it very (bad, badly).
4. Everybody thinks (good, well) of you.
5. The tree stood out (well, good) against the horizon.
6. He fought very (bad, badly) in the third round.
7. The soup tastes (good, well).
8. Johnny's chances for graduation look (well, good).
9. But Billy's chances look (bad, badly).
10. I feel (well, good).
11. Certain chemicals smell (badly, bad).
12. Johnny smells (bad, badly).

—Answers—

1. The correct word is *well.* In this sentence it is used as an adverb to qualify the verb *dined.* But, as we shall see in the comment on Sentence 10, *well* may also be used as an adjective. The word *good* is used only rarely as an adverb, and in a restricted sense. For example: He *as good as* finished his work.

2. The correct word is *well*, an adverb which qualifies the verb *knows*.

3. Use *badly*, an adverb which qualifies the verb *need*. The word *bad* is generally an adjective. It is used as an adverb in a colloquial sense only. Several of the leading authorities have not as yet admitted it into the society of good English.

4. Use *well*, in this sentence an adverb which qualifies the verb *thinks*.

5. Use the adverb *well*, to qualify the verb *stood out*.

6. Use *badly*, to qualify *fought*.

7. The correct word here is *good*. And this involves a principle which it is well for you to remember. With certain intransitive verbs that describe an action of the senses —such as *feel*, *look*, *smell*, *sound* and *taste*—you must use adjectives where you might (erroneously) expect adverbs. For the adjectives, in all such instances, modify or describe the noun which is the subject of the sentence.

A few illustrations will make this point clear:

> The *day* feels *humid*.
> The *doctor* looks *good* (that is, *efficient*).
> The *rose* smells *sweet*.
> The *music* sounds *pleasant*.
> The *milk* tastes *sour*.

How can you tell when to use an adjective with these verbs? Very easily. You do it when the verb can be translated into the word *is*:

> The day *is* humid.
> The doctor *is* good.
> The rose *is* sweet.
> The music *is* pleasant.
> The milk *is* sour.

8. Use *good*, the adjective that qualifies the noun *chances*.

9. Here the adjective *bad* qualifies the noun *chances*.

10. This is a sentence in which both adjectives are correct. *I feel well* means *I feel in good health*. *I feel good* generally means *I feel in good spirits*.

11. Use the adjective *bad*, to qualify the noun *chemicals*.

12. In this sentence you can use either the adjective *bad* or the adverb *badly*. It depends upon the meaning that you wish to convey. Thus:

Johnny smells bad means that Johnny has a bad odor. Here the adjective *bad* qualifies the noun *Johnny*.

Johnny smells badly implies that Johnny's nasal passage is obstructed. In this instance, the adverb *badly* qualifies the verb *smells*.

So be sure you don't insult Johnny by describing his condition with the wrong part of speech.

GO SLOW AND THINK FAST

As you drive through the country, you often see the warning: BAD CURVES—GO SLOW. Is this grammatically right or wrong?

It is right. The word *slow* can be an *adverb* as well as an *adjective*. Such expressions as *go slow, speak slow, do it slow* are to be found in the works of the best writers. It is a usage that dates back further than the time of Shakespeare, who wrote: "How slow the time goes!" A pedantic motorist recently tore down a road sign, GO SLOW, and replaced it with another sign, GO SLOWLY IF YOU WANT TO BE CORRECT. The traffic commissioner restored the original words, with an additional warning: GO SLOW IF YOU WANT TO BE SAFE.

But the other form of the adverb—*slowly*—can also be used. For example:

> He picked his way *slowly* through the traffic.
> *Slowly* he gave out his instructions, one by one.

In the above sentences, *slowly sounds* better because it is the form established by long usage in such sentences. Educated people would not use the shorter form here.

So here is the rule:

Use *slow* as an informal adverb with such verbs as *go, walk, speak*, when it is more important than the verb, as in a command, or is required by idiom; use *slowly* as a more formal adverb with the less common verbs.

The same principle applies to a number of similar adverbs —*close, deep, fair, hard, high, low, quick, right, straight*. Each of these adverbs has another form ending in *-ly*. Use the longer form when the sound and the usage require it.

For example:

> Stand *close*.
> Breathe *deep*.
> Play *fair*.
> Study *hard*.
> Aim *high*.
> Sing *low*.

176

Strike *quick*.
Step *right*.
Shoot *straight*.

But, on the other hand:

They feel *deeply* hurt.
He treated me *fairly*.
She *hardly* knew him. (The adverb *hardly* is generally used in the sense of *scarcely*.)
I think *highly* of him.
Rightly handled, he will make a good fighter.

MISPLACED ADVERBS

Adverbs, like adjectives, are frequently misplaced—sometimes with ridiculous results. Consider the following sentence:

The candidates for the Senate filed their intentions to run rapidly.

Which of the words does *rapidly* modify—*filed*, or *run*?
To avoid this confusion in the meaning of the sentence, place the adverb as near as possible to the word or words that it modifies:

The candidates for the Senate rapidly filed their intentions to run.

The position of the adverb *only* may have caused you some trouble in the past. There are times when a change in the position of this word may change the meaning of the sentence. For example:

1. *Only John* invited us to take the trip. (John, and nobody else, invited us.)
2. John *only* invited us to take the trip. (John invited us, but didn't urge us.)
3. John invited *only us* to take the trip. (John invited us, and nobody else.)
4. John invited us *only to take* the trip. (John invited us to take, but not to pay for, the trip.)
5. John invited us to take *only the trip*. (John invited us to take the trip, but to take nothing else.)

The orthodox rule, therefore, is to place this word in the precise part of the sentence which it qualifies. Yet in modern usage it is sometimes idiomatic and quite correct to depart from the orthodox usage of *only*. It is good English, for example, to say: *He only passed away a month ago.*

The principle to follow, therefore, is to stick to the established position of *only* when any other position would confuse the meaning. But when there is no possibility for such confusion, you are safe in adopting the colloquial and idiomatic position.

OTHER ADVERBIAL ERRORS

Have you ever made any of the following common errors?

> I *haven't only* one dollar.
> They *don't hardly* expect it.
> We *didn't meet scarcely* anybody.
> He *hasn't barely* begun.

The above adverbs—*only, hardly, scarcely, barely*—have a negative meaning. You must therefore use them with positive verbs. Otherwise you will have double negatives. "I haven't only one dollar" is just as incorrect as "I don't have no more than one dollar." Correct the wrong sentences to read:

> I *have only* one dollar.
> They *hardly expect* it.
> We *met scarcely* anybody.
> He *has barely* begun.

Another common error is to use the expression *equally as.* This is an unnecessary repetition of words that have the same meaning. Use either *equally* or *as* by itself:

1. I enjoyed yesterday's dinner, but today's is *equally* good.
2. His wife is *as* pretty as a movie star.

Along with *equally as,* try to avoid such repetitious expressions as *return back* for *return, repeat again* for *repeat, collaborate together* for *collaborate, descend down* for *descend.* In each of these examples, the verb is adequate by itself. Adding the adverb is a mistake.

QUIZ TIME

Do you think you can now use the adverb with sufficient accuracy and skill? Try this quiz, and see how good a score you can make. If you have done this chapter carefully, you should be able to give the correct answer to every one of the questions:

A

In each of the following sentences, check the correct word enclosed in parentheses:

1. He pronounces his words too (indistinct, indistinctly).
2. She didn't do so (well, good) in the last test.
3. Don't take my words too (serious, seriously).
4. The carpet feels (softly, soft) under our feet.
5. Don't shout; I can hear you (plainly, plain) enough.
6. There's nothing that smells so (sweet, sweetly) as a rose.
7. Leave your work not when it is (most, almost) finished but all finished.
8. It's such a surprise, I (can, can't) hardly believe it.
9. This food tastes (sour, sourly).
10. Turn (rightly, right) when you come to the next traffic light.
11. He hit the ball (hardly, hard) for a home run.
12. She speaks (beautiful, beautifully).
13. Don't treat him so (cruelly, cruel).
14. The cold air feels (good, well).
15. He has now recovered from his infection and looks (good, well) again.
16. He likes both friends (equally as, equally) well.
17. He kicked the ball (highly, high) and right over the goal line.
18. You'll have to do this (differently, different) if you want to do it right.
19. "I am (mostly, most) delighted with your singing," he said enthusiastically.
20. This candy tastes rather (sweetly, sweet).
21. He (returned, returned back) from the hospital in (as well as, as good as) perfect health.

B

The following sentences contain twenty-two adverbs. See how many of them you can point out:

1. He served his master faithfully and wisely.
2. We mutually pledge to each other our lives, our fortunes, and our sacred honor.
3. He is a friendly gentleman who treats all people well.
4. Live dangerously if you want to live happily.

5. She worked so hard, she hardly had any time for relaxation.

6. Speak fast, but let your diction be good.

7. She was a homely person, yet everybody felt strangely attracted to her.

8. He struck the blow swiftly and with deadly aim.

9. She was madly in love with her unreasonably jealous husband.

10. Everybody loves a person who finds contentment nearly everywhere.

11. He ran furiously and fast and straight to the goal.

12. Buy the paper anywhere and come right to the office.

13. The cook behaves badly because the soup tastes bad.

14. "I hope you will soon be well," he said to his convalescent friend.

—Answers—

A: 1-indistinctly, 2-well, 3-seriously, 4-soft, 5-plainly, 6-sweet, 7-almost, 8-can, 9-sour, 10-right, 11-hard, 12-beautifully, 13-cruelly, 14-good, 15-well, 16-equally, 17-high, 18-differently, 19-most, 20-sweet, 21-returned, as good as

B:
1. faithfully, wisely
2. mutually
3. well
4. dangerously, happily
5. hard, hardly
6. fast
7. strangely
8. swiftly
9. madly, unreasonably
10. nearly, everywhere
11. furiously, fast, straight
12. anywhere, right
13. badly
14. soon

While checking your adverbs in the foregoing quiz, you may have found a little trouble with some of the other words. How, for example, would you classify such words as *and, if, in, to, with?* Chapter 18 will give you the answer to this question.

But first—an intermission for another word game.

Time out for the Fifteenth Word Game
WORDS ABOUT VARIOUS PERSONS,
THINGS AND IDEAS

Do you know the meanings of all of the more difficult words you hear in lectures and in cultured conversation, or read in magazines and in books? Take a number of these words, for example, and see how many of them you can define. Try to check the statement which most nearly applies to each of the following italicized words:

A

1. John Smith is an *amicable* person.
    a. He likes to quarrel.
    b. He runs amuck.
    c. He has a friendly disposition.

2. Some people are *gregarious*.
    a. They like to live alone.
    b. They like to flock together.
    c. They tell you what they think.

3. He suffers from *schizophrenia*.
    a. His business is in bad shape.
    b. He is mentally ill.
    c. He has a jaundiced liver.

4. He lives a *sequestered* life.
    a. His home is in a solitary place.
    b. His home is in the heart of the city.
    c. His home is full of guests.

5. He believes in *reciprocity*.
    a. He is very ambitious.
    b. He likes to provoke a quarrel.
    c. He adheres to the Golden Rule.

6. The lawyer used *chicanery*.
    a. He bullied the witness.
    b. He resorted to tricky practice.
    c. He flattered the judge.

7. He is an *egocentric* person.
    a. He goes to the center of an argument.

    b. His actions are peculiar.

    c. He rarely thinks of the other fellow.

8. They talked *acrimoniously* to each other.

    a. Their talk was friendly.

    b. Their talk was about money matters.

    c. Their talk was bitter.

9. He gave *irrelevant* testimony.

    a. His testimony was irreligious.

    b. His testimony had nothing to do with the case.

    c. His testimony had to do with a cocktail party.

10. He is an *ebullient* type of person.

    a. He is subject to enthusiasm.

    b. He is inclined to be a bully.

    c. He suffers from excessive boils.

11. He spoke in a *dispassionate* voice.

    a. His voice was calm.

    b. His voice was hot-tempered.

    c. His voice was sympathetic.

12. They looked through his *dossier*.

    a. They examined the secret drawers of his desk.

    b. They examined his love letters.

    c. They examined his record.

13. He has a *raucous* laugh.

    a. His laughter is hearty.

    b. His laughter is sarcastic.

    c. His laughter is harsh.

14. He delivered a *panegyric*.

    a. It was a valuable package.

    b. It was a panicky command.

    c. It was a speech of praise.

15. He offered a *parsimonious* dinner to his guests.

    a. It had Persian dishes.

    b. It was very stingy.

    c. It came to a lot of money.

16. The doctor prescribed an *anodyne* for the patient.

    a. It was some form of iodine.

    b. It was a reducing diet.

    c. It was a soothing medicine.

17. Wolves and tigers are *carnivorous*.

    a. They like carnivals.

    b. They like to eat meat.

    c. They are inclined to worry.

18. He has a *bovine* temperament.
  a. He likes alcoholic drinks.
  b. He is sluggish like an ox.
  c. He is a regular Beau Brummell.

19. They indulged in *badinage*.
  a. Their talk was light and frivolous.
  b. Their talk was obscene.
  c. Their talk was about the evils of old age.

20. He acts *surreptitiously*.
  a. He gives up without a fight.
  b. He does things by stealth.
  c. He believes in the supernatural.

—Answers—

1-c, 2-b, 3-b, 4-a, 5-c, 6-b, 7-c, 8-c, 9-b, 10-a, 11-a, 12-c, 13-c, 14-c, 15-b, 16-c, 17-b, 18-b, 19-a, 20-b

B

In this section, try to play the game the other way around. Check the word that best fits each of the following statements:

1. His life is solitary—away from society.
  a. It is vicarious.
  b. It is sequestered.
  c. It is schizophrenic.

2. He thinks only of himself.
  a. He is egocentric.
  b. He is lethargic.
  c. He is gregarious.

3. He likes to make friends.
  a. He is ebullient.
  b. He is dispassionate.
  c. He is amicable.

4. His words were bitter and stinging.
  a. He spoke irrelevantly.
  b. He spoke surreptitiously.
  c. He spoke acrimoniously.

5. Tigers live on the flesh of other animals.
  a. They are gregarious.
  b. They are carnivorous.
  c. They are schizophrenic.

6. His behavior is slow and oxlike.

a. He is raucous.
b. He is acrimonious.
c. He is bovine.

7. Birds of a feather flock together.
a. They are surreptitious.
b. They are gregarious.
c. They are ebullient.

8. He suffers from a disintegrated personality—a serious mental disorder.
a. He's amicable.
b. He's dispassionate.
c. He's schizophrenic.

9. He is fond of playful "small talk."
- a. He likes a sequestered life.
b. He likes badinage.
c. He likes acrimony.

10. Confucius believed in mutual dependence and coöperation.
a. He advocated irrelevance.
b. He advocated reciprocity.
c. He advocated acrimony.

11. He cheated them out of their rights.
a. He employed irrelevance.
b. He employed an anodyne.
c. He employed chicanery.

12. His enthusiasm is effervescent.
a. He's egocentric.
b. He's ebullient.
c. He's bovine.

13. The judge considered the evidence impartially.
a. He was reciprocal.
b. He was parsimonious.
c. He was dispassionate.

14. What he said was beside the point.
a. It was irrelevant.
b. It was reciprocal.
c. It was lethargic.

15. His words soothed her pain.
a. They served as a panegyric.
b. They served as an anodyne.
c. They served as a dossier.

16. He gave the committee his records on the case.

          a. He presented his dossier.
          b. He presented his chicanery.
          c. He presented his panegyric.

17. His stinginess was notorious.
          a. He was acrimonious.
          b. He was parsimonious.
          c. He was surreptitious.

18. He delivered a speech in praise of the dead man.
          a. It was an anodyne.
          b. It was an irrelevance.
          c. It was a panegyric.

19. He removed the evidence by stealth.
          a. His action was parsimonious.
          b. His action was surreptitious.
          c. His action was acrimonious.

20. His voice sounded like a buzz saw.
          a. It was raucous.
          b. It was bovine.
          c. It was surreptitious.

—Answers—

1-b, 2-a, 3-c, 4-c, 5-b, 6-c, 7-b, 8-c, 9-b, 10-b, 11-c, 12-b, 13-c, 14-a, 15-b, 16-a, 17-b, 18-c, 19-b, 20-a

C

Using the key words of this game, try to get the correct synonym for each of the following terms:

1. secluded, isolated   s_____
2. banter   b_____
3. stingy, niggardly   p_____
4. unrelated, not applicable   i_____
5. judicial, calm, unruffled   d_____
6. peaceable, friendly   a_____
7. living in flocks or herds   g_____
8. caustic, stinging, bitter   a_____
9. a split personality   s_____
10. mutuality   r_____
11. boiling up or over, effervescent   e_____
12. sharp practice, trickery   c_____
13. interested only in one's self   e_____
14. a written detailed record   d_____

185

15. oxlike, sluggish and patient   b_____
16. disagreeably harsh in sound   r_____
17. a medicine that soothes pain   a_____
18. a formal speech of praise   p_____
19. stealthily, secretly   s_____
20. eating flesh   c_____

—*Answers*—

1-sequestered, 2-badinage, 3-parsimonious, 4-irrelevant, 5-dispassionate, 6-amicable, 7-gregarious, 8-acrimonious, 9-schizophrenia, 10-reciprocity, 11-ebullient, 12-chicanery, 13-egocentric, 14-dossier, 15-bovine, 16-raucous, 17-anodyne, 18-panegyric, 19-surreptitiously, 20-carnivorous

D

Several of the words in this game are frequently mispronounced. Here is their correct pronunciation:

acrimony, noun: AK-ri-moe-nee
acrimonious, adjective: ak-ri-MOE-nee-us
amicability, noun: am-ik-a-BIL-i-tee
amicable, adjective: AM-ik-a-bl
anodyne: AN-o-dine
badinage: bad-i-NAZH, or BAD-i-nazh, or BAD-i-nij
bovine: BOE-vine, or BOE-vin
carnivore, noun: CAR-ni-vor
carnivorous, adjective: car-NIV-o-rus
chicanery, noun: she-KANE-er-ee
to chicane, verb: she-KANE
dossier: DOSS-ee-ay as in *may*, or DOSS-ee-er
ebullient: e-BUL (to rhyme with *dull*)-i-ent, or e-BUL-yent
egocentricity, noun: ee-go-sen-TRISS-i-tee
egocentric, adjective: ee-go-SENT-rik
gregarious: gre-GARE (to rhyme with *care*)-ee-us
irrelevant: ir-REL-e-vant (don't confuse this word with *irreverent*.)
panegyric: pan-e-JIR-ik
parsimony, noun: PAR-si-moe-nee, or, especially British, PAR-si-mun-i
parsimonious, adjective: par-si-MOE-nee-us
reciprocity, noun: ress-i-PROSS-i-tee
reciprocal, adjective: re-SIP-ro-kal

to reciprocate, verb: re-SIP-ro-kate
schizophrenia, noun: ski-zo-FREE-nee-a
schizophrenic, noun and adjective: ski-zo-FREN-ik
surreptitious: sir-ep-TISH-us

18

LINKS AND LOOSE ENDS

DON'T ABUSE THEM

We now come to a group of words whose abuse, to quote H. W. Fowler, represents "almost the worst element in modern English."

The words that Fowler has in mind are the conjunctions and the prepositions—the so-called common links in our language.

Let us look at some of the frequent errors in their use.

THE DIFFERENCE BETWEEN CONJUNCTIONS AND PREPOSITIONS

In one respect, conjunctions and prepositions are alike. They both serve as *connective* words. They help to *tighten* a sentence into a unit that holds together. For example:

1. *Conjunction:* To do a good job, act *as* she does.
2. *Preposition:* To do a good job, act *like* her.

But notice the difference between *as* and *like:*

The conjunction *as* merely connects words or word groups.

The preposition *like* does not merely *connect* words—it *shows the relation of a pronoun (or a noun)* to another part of the sentence.

Note the word *her* in Sentence 2. After *like* or other prepositions, we say *me, him her, us,* or *them;* not *I, he, she, we,* or *they.* Or, to put it in grammatical terms, we use the objective case of the pronoun after a preposition.

A conjunction is not followed by the objective case. Observe the difference in the following sentences:

Conjunctions

He *and* I took the journey together.
I shall come *if* you promise to be there.
He told her *that* he was afraid.
The book was found *where* he had put it.

He is as strong *as* I.
He is taller *than* I.

In the last two sentences, many grammarians would hold that the verb *am* is understood after the pronoun *I*. According to these authors it is not the best formal usage to say: "He is as strong as me. He is taller than me." The word *me* is in the objective case, they tell us, and therefore cannot be used after a conjunction. More liberal grammarians would permit *me* and describe *as* as a preposition in this instance. Here we shall recommend the more formal usage as less likely to provoke criticism.

Prepositions

He took the journey together *with* me.
He lives not far *from* us.
I am sending a present *to* them.
Without her he is lost.
I hold a position *under* him.
Between her and me there will always be an understanding.

It is wrong to say: "Between her and I there will always be an understanding." *Between* is the controlling word here, and it is a preposition, requiring the objective case in the second pronoun as well as in the first.

Some of the conjunctions most frequently used are *and, although, as, because, if, since, so, than, that, unless, when, where, while.*

Some of the prepositions most frequently used are *above, at, by, except, for, from, in, into, like, of, on, to, upon, with, without.*

WORDS THAT ARE CONJUNCTIONS OR PREPOSITIONS

There are some words which can be used either as conjunctions or as prepositions—depending upon the structure of the sentence.

Conjunctions	Prepositions
Don't leave *before* I come.	Don't leave *before* me.
Everybody left, *but* we remained.	Everybody left *but* (meaning *except*) us.
They like him, *for* he is a good man.	They like him *for* himself.

189

He has lived with us *since*   He has lived with us *since* he sold the house.   last year.

Wait *till* (or *until*) I come.   Wait *till* (or *until*) my arrival.

He came *after* I did.   He came *after* me.

The preposition *till* plays an interesting part in a rather amusing anecdote. A beggar once accosted Will Rogers and asked him for a dime. Reaching into his pocket, Rogers found he had nothing less than a quarter.

"Here's a quarter," he said. "But don't forget you owe me fifteen cents."

"Thank you, sir," said the beggar. "And may you live *till* the day I pay you!"

TEST YOUR SKILL

Do you now see the difference between the conjunction and the preposition? If you do, you can easily check the correct word in the parentheses in each of the following sentences:

1. I shall not be there (without, unless) you also come.
2. You don't look as if you are older than (me, I).
3. You are just as good as (they, them), but you are more modest.
4. No one but (her, she) could ever get away with it.
5. Let there be an understanding between you and (I, me).
6. Everyone was invited except (him, he).
7. Is this ticket for you and (I, me)?
8. He came after you and (me, I) had left.
9. He came after you and (me, I).
10. (Like, As) you may know, he made a very good profit on the deal.

—Answers—

1-unless, 2-I, 3-they, 4-her, 5-me, 6-him, 7-me, 8-I, 9-me, 10-As

TWO TROUBLESOME WORDS—*LIKE* AND *AS*

We frequently hear the expression "Like I said." Is this correct?

The answer to this question has given rise to a great deal of controversy. Generally speaking, *like* is a preposition and not a conjunction. The correct form, therefore, would be "As

190

I said." For *as* is a conjunction and can therefore be followed by a clause.

Thus, it is correct to say:

> Work hard *as* I do.
> Work hard *like* me.

But it is incorrect to say:

> Work hard *like* I do.

Yet there are some professional speakers and writers—especially radio announcers and journalists—who use *like* instead of *as*. Shakespeare and other noted writers occasionally did the same. This usage, however, has not as yet received the sanction of some of the best authorities. According to Fowler, the use of *like* as a conjunction is "vulgar and slovenly." And according to Webster, this sort of construction "is freely used only in illiterate speech."

So the safest thing for you to do is to avoid this usage in your speaking and writing of better English. Say, "*As* I told you," and not, "*Like* I told you."

But there are other pitfalls in the usage of these two parts of speech. Let us look at some of the more common ways in which they may trip you up.

DOUBLE CONJUNCTIONS

There is one sort of conjunction that requires a little extra care on your part. This is the *double conjunction*, such as *either . . . or, neither . . . nor, not only . . . but also, both . . . and*. This sort of double conjunction connects *parallel ideas*. The two parts of the conjunction, therefore, should be followed by *parallel constructions* in careful writing. Don't place one of the parts before a verb and the other before a noun or an adjective or an adverb.

Don't, for example, say:

> You *either* have to accept our terms *or* none at all.
> He *neither* likes mustard *nor* pickles.
> DiMaggio *not only* found profit *but also* pleasure in baseball.
> She *both* helped him mentally *and* financially.

Most of these are fairly acceptable in informal speech, but all are considered rather careless in more formal speaking and writing. Say, instead:

191

You have to accept *either* our terms *or* none at all.

He likes *neither* mustard *nor* pickles.

DiMaggio found *not only* profit *but also* pleasure in baseball.

She helped him *both* mentally *and* financially.

Warning: In using your double conjunctions, don't couple a positive with a negative, such as *neither . . . or, either . . . nor.*

Wrong form: He wanted *neither* sympathy *or* advice.
Correct form: He wanted *neither* sympathy *nor* advice.

NOT SO AND NOT AS

You've often heard such expressions as the following:

She is *not so* good *as* her brother.
She is *not as* good *as* her brother.

Which of the two statements is grammatically correct? The more tradition-bound teachers still insist that after a negative verb the proper word is *so* instead of *as*. But, as most educated speakers and writers will tell you, this is not true and has never been true. It is simply an arbitrary convention.

So *it's not as bad as you think*—in fact, it's perfectly correct—to use the more colloquial-sounding expression. There is no grammatical rule that requires the use of *so* after a negative. It's merely an old-fashioned custom, like stiff collars and long skirts. "The use of *as* in this construction," according to Professor S. A. Leonard, in *Current English Usage*, "is established in cultivated English."

PREPOSITIONS AT THE END OF A SENTENCE

Another point that teachers traditionally insist upon is that a preposition is a bad word to end a sentence with. When I went to school, I was taught that there were "two unforgivable crimes: to end a man's life with a bullet, and to end a sentence with a preposition."

This taboo against final prepositions is just another of those old-fashioned conventions that have no basis in traditional usage. It was borrowed from Latin, whose grammar once dominated the thinking of English writers. A preposition at the end of a sentence is not only permissible but at times necessary in our language.

Take the following statement, for example:

It all depends on what the money is meant *for*.

Now try to transfer the preposition from the end to another part of the statement, and see how clumsy it becomes:

It all depends on *for* what the money is meant.

When you end a sentence with a preposition, you find yourself in the company of some of the greatest writers—all the way from Shakespeare ("We are such stuff as dreams are made *on*") down to Kipling ("Too horrible to be trifled *with*"). The 1953 Nobel Prize winner for literature, Sir Winston Churchill, was once taken to task for his use of "that is something I shall not put up with." In reply to this criticism, Sir Winston observed, "That is something up with which I shall not put."

There are times when a preposition is a very convenient word to end a sentence with. But, on the other hand, don't overdo the idea. Here's a sentence quoted from *The Reader's Digest*, with no less than five prepositions at the end:

Little Tommy, ill upstairs, complained to his mother as she sat down to read to him: "What did you bring that book I didn't want to be read *to out of up for?*"

The best rule to follow in this matter is to follow no artificial rule. End your sentences with those words that will give them the greatest vigor and naturalness and ease.

PREPOSITIONAL BOOBY TRAPS

There are many traps that lie in wait for the unwary in their daily use of the preposition. Take care to obey the following rules:

1. Don't use *of* after *off*.

Wrong form: He fell *off of* the bridge.
Correct form: He fell *off* the bridge.

2. Don't use *of* as a substitute for *have*.

Wrong form: You ought to *of* known better.
Correct form: You ought to *have* known better.

3. Don't misuse *to* and *for*.

Wrong form: She brought little Johnny *for* dinner.
Correct form: She brought little Johnny *to* dinner.
Correct form: She brought a steak *for* dinner.

4. Don't use *without* for *unless*.

Wrong form: I shall not do this *without* you consent to it.
Correct form: I shall not do this *without* your consent.
Correct form: I shall not do this *unless* you consent to it.

Without is a preposition; *unless* is a conjunction.

5. Don't use *by* for *with*.

Wrong form: I am staying *by* my daughter.
Correct form: I am staying *with* my daughter.

6. Don't muddle your thought through the omission of necessary prepositions. For example:

> John thought more of money than his wife.
> John thought more of money than of his wife.

Both sentences are correct, but their meanings are different. The first means that John liked money more than his wife liked it. The second means that John liked money more than he liked his wife. Be sure that your prepositions help you to say exactly what you *want* to say.

7. Don't misplace your prepositional phrases.

Wrong form: Toscanini will return to the city where he was born in two months.
Wrong form: He testified that the bus had run into him and thrown him down in the court house.
Correct form: In two months Toscanini will return to the city where he was born.
Correct form: He testified in the court house that the bus had run into him and thrown him down.

8. Don't omit a preposition when it is required in a compound phrase.

Wrong form: He had a fear and a respect for his father.
Wrong form: He had a profound interest and a wide knowledge of books.
Correct form: He had a fear *of* and a respect *for* his father.
Correct form: He had a profound interest *in* and a wide knowledge *of* books.

9. There are more than a thousand idiomatic phrases in which the preposition is often used incorrectly. Here are

some of the more familiar among them, together with their correct usage:

Acquiesce in (not *to*): He acquiesced *in* the decision of the majority.

Angry with (a person): Don't be angry *with* him.

Angry at (a thing): Don't be angry *at* his silence.

Apply to (a person): He applied *to* Mr. Peters.

Apply for (a thing): He applied *for* a job.

Concur with (a person): He concurs *with* the other members.

Concur in (an idea): He concurs *in* their plans.

Conducive to (not *of*): Prayer is conducive *to* peace of mind.

Connive with (a person): They connived *with* each other.

Connive at (an act or thought): They connived *at* his treachery.

Contemporary (adjective) *with:* Shakespeare was contemporary *with* Queen Elizabeth I.

A contemporary (noun) *of:* Walt Whitman was a contemporary *of* Lincoln.

Disagree with (not *from*): She disagrees *with* him.

Enraged against (a person): They are enraged *against* the spy.

Enraged at (a thing): They are enraged *at* his betrayal.

Familiar with (not *to*): He is familiar *with* Homer.

Identical with (not *to*): Jimmy is identical *with* his twin brother.

Inferior to (not *than*): Today's steak is inferior *to* yesterday's.

In search of (not *for*): The sailor was in search *of* adventure.

Involved in (not *by*): Five persons were involved *in* the plot.

Of his own accord (not *on*): He did it *of* his own accord.

On his own account (not *of*): He did it *on* his own account.

Originate with (a person): The idea originated *with* Edison.

Originate in (a thing or place): The idea originated *in* Edison's laboratory.

Preferable to (not *than*): Peace is preferable *to* war.

195

Protest against (not *at*): They protested against the verdict.

Similar to (not *with*): My job is similar to yours.

Suffer from (not *with*): He suffered from the heat.

Superior to (not *than*): She considers herself superior to her friends.

Tendency to (not *for*): He has a tendency to forgiveness.

QUIZ TIME

Here is a quiz that will show you how carefully you have done this chapter:

A

The italicized words in the following sentences are either conjunctions or prepositions. Check the correct or preferred form of the pronouns that come after them:

1. I am sure you can live as comfortably *as* (me, I).
2. She has a little girl who looks just *like* (she, her).
3. Our friends have gone, *but* (we, us) have stayed behind.
4. Everybody has gone *but* (we, us).
5. *Between* you and (me, I), there's nothing to this story.
6. Nobody *but* (him, he) would take such a risk.
7. She deserves more *than* (him, he), but she gets less.
8. She is not as tall *as* (he, him).
9. He feels lost *without* (she, her).
10. There's nothing left *for* you and (I, me) to do here.

B

In the following sentences, tell whether the positions of the double conjunctions are right or wrong:

1. He *neither* likes tomatoes *nor* his wife. Right Wrong
2. You can *either* exchange this for another tie *or* get your money back. Right Wrong
3. He likes *not only* his job, *but* he *also* gets good pay. Right Wrong
4. He *neither* praised her singing *nor* her acting. Right Wrong
5. I admire *both* your courage *and* your ability. Right Wrong

196

C

Point out the correct word in the parentheses in each of the following sentences:

1. Some people maintain that seeing a prize fight on TV is preferable (to, than) having a seat at the ringside.
2. The hero of one of Tennyson's poems is in search (for, of) the Holy Grail.
3. This is neither here (or, nor) there.
4. I hope you have consented to come (on, of) your own accord.
5. Caesar was a contemporary (of, with) Brutus.
6. Her story on the whole was similar (to, with) that of her husband.
7. This custom originated (in, with) the early history of the United States.
8. Don't be angry (at, with) each other.
9. The dissenting juror at last concurred (with, in) the decision of the others.
10. He acquiesced (in, to) a verdict which he didn't altogether approve.
11. Don't act (like, as if) you had never seen him.
12. He may be richer than (I, me), but he doesn't enjoy life (like, as) I do.

—*Answers*—

A:1-I, 2-her, 3-we, 4-us, 5-me, 6-him, 7-he, 8-he, 9-her, 10-me

B:1-wrong, 2-right, 3-wrong, 4-wrong, 5-right

C:1-to, 2-of, 3-nor, 4-of, 5-of, 6-to, 7-in, 8-with, 9-in, 10-in, 11-as if, 12-I, as

A NOTE ABOUT INTERJECTIONS

We have now considered the uses and the abuses of seven parts of speech—verbs, nouns, adjectives, pronouns, adverbs, conjunctions, and prepositions.

In addition to these, there are a number of words that cannot be classified under any of the seven parts of speech. They bear no grammatical relationship to the rest of the sentence. They are "thrown in," so to speak, in order to express great emotion. These words, classified as the eighth part of speech, are the exclamatory *interjections*.

The most common interjections are *ah! alas! damn! dear me! fie! gosh! heck! hello! indeed! nonsense! pshaw! really!*

rot! rubbish! well! wow! But any word or phrase may be used as an interjection: *go! for heaven's sake! get out! leave the room at once! so this is it!* And sometimes you can express an interjection by a mere gesture or look. A professor at Harvard has a good interjectional recipe for closing an interview. He rises from his desk, holds out his hand to his visitor, and glances at the door.

And, without a single word, the visitor knows that the conference is over. The unspoken interjection has done the trick.

The interjection, whether expressed or implied, is an important part of your daily intercourse. Don't neglect it. But don't overuse it, or your style may become too emotional and therefore less capable of convincing your friends.

Time out for the Sixteenth Word Game
FRENCH AND LATIN PHRASES

The tendency nowadays, according to most authorities, is to avoid foreign expressions in English speech and writing. The frequent use of such expressions makes it look as though we were showing off our knowledge too much. Our own language is rich enough in picturesque words and idioms to express our everyday thoughts.

Yet any reader will encounter a fair number of foreign words and phrases in books, newspapers, and magazines. A few are even common in speech—so common, in fact, that they are part of our language, or are rapidly becoming so. This game contains twenty-four of the most widely used foreign expressions—twelve French and twelve Latin. Those considered to be completely "naturalized" in our language are printed in roman type; it is standard practice to print the others in *italics*.

A

French

Check the phrase which best completes each of the following statements:

1. The merciful blow that puts a suffering creature to ath is a

    a. *faux pas*
    b. *de trop*
    c. *coup de grâce*

2. When a person is alive to all that is going on, he is the

    a. potpourri
    b. *qui vive*
    c. *esprit de corps*

3. When a person pays a fixed rate for board or lodging, is charged .

    a. *de trop*
    b. *en rapport*
    c. *en pension*

4. Shakespeare, preëminent in his plays, was a dramatist

    a. *savoir-faire*
    b. *de trop*
    c. par excellence

5. An assorted mixture of great variety is a

    a. par excellence
    b. potpourri
    c. *coup de grâce*

6. A person with perfect poise rarely commits a

    a. *faux pas*
    b. *double-entendre*
    c. *savoir-faire*

7. An act that is already done and cannot be recalled is

    a. *coup de grâce*
    b. *fait accompli*
    c. *de trop*

8. Sophisticated people who "know their way around" e generally endowed with

    a. *esprit de corps*
    b. *savoir-faire*
    c. *fait accompli*

9. When Johnny insisted on staying in the living room ith his sister and her boy friend, they considered him

    a. *faux pas*
    b. *savoir-faire*
    c. *de trop*

10. A remark which has two meanings, one of them possibly slightly off color, is a

      a. *fait accompli*
      b. *double-entendre*
      c. *coup de grâce*

11. Two minds that have a perfect understanding may be said to be

      a. *double-entendre*
      b. par excellence
      c. *en rapport*

12. A player who prefers his own glory to the good of the team has no

      a. *esprit de corps*
      b. *coup de grâce*
      c. *fait accompli*

—Answers—

1-c, 2-b, 3-c, 4-c, 5-b, 6-a, 7-b, 8-b, 9-c, 10-b, 11-c, 12-a

B

Latin

Check the correct reference to each of the following phrases:

1. *Deo volente* refers to

      a. a flight in an airship
      b. the will of God
      c. the difference in people's tastes

2. *cui bono* refers to

      a. a game of dice
      b. a well-baked bun
      c. a question as to who benefits by a certain action

3. *in medias res* refers to

      a. the rays of the midday sun
      b. plunging into the midst of things
      c. a midday siesta

4. *de mortuis nil nisi bonum* refers to

      a. respect for the dead
      b. the bones of a skeleton
      c. people's tastes

5. *de gustibus non est disputandum* refers to
  - a. people's tastes
  - b. disgust with one's condition
  - c. a lover's quarrel
6. *per aspera ad astra* refers to
  - a. the value of aspirin in certain diseases
  - b. astronomical figures
  - c. attainment through hardship
7. *persona grata* refers to
  - a. an aggressive person
  - b. a thankful person
  - c. an acceptable person
8. a *non sequitur* refers to
  - a. a thing that cannot be dissected
  - b. a region that is not sequestered
  - c. a fallacy in an argument
9. a *rara avis* refers to
  - a. a bird-house
  - b. an unusually excellent person
  - c. an occasional air attack
10. *ne plus ultra* refers to
  - a. the summit of achievement
  - b. a business statement in the red
  - c. an example in addition and subtraction
11. *multum in parvo* refers to
  - a. a multitude on parade
  - b. a tumultuous parley
  - c. saying much in a few words
12. *e pluribus unum* refers to
  - a. the United States
  - b. the pointer on a sundial
  - c. the pluralization of nouns

—*Answers*—

1-b, 2-c, 3-b, 4-a, 5-a, 6-c, 7-c, 8-c, 9-b, 10-a, 11-c, 12-a

C

True or False?

State whether each of the following statements is true or false—that is, whether it does or does not make sense:

1. The Russian Revolution in 1917 was a *multum in parvo.* True False

2. He found himself out of place and *de trop* at the party. True False

3. A runner who could do 100 yards in 9 seconds would be a *rara avis.* True False

4. The restaurant specializes in roast duckling *en rapport.* True False

5. *"Cui bono?"* asked Senator Smith, referring to a new advance in prices. True False

6. Mrs. Jones ran a boarding house for students *en pension.* True False

7. Having wounded the fox, he administered a *double-entendre* to put it out of its pain. True False

8. Some authors believe that a good way to start a story is to plunge *in medias res.* True False

9. The U. S. Marines are noted for their *esprit de corps.* True False

10. *De mortuis nil nisi bonum* is a good motto to remember when people disagree about a book. True False

11. He prepared a *savoir-faire* dish of many appetizing ingredients. True False

12. *Deo volente,* new cures may be discovered for many diseases. True False

13. He was so stupid he often blundered into a *fait accompli.* True False

14. Now that he is dead, let us not attack his character; *de gustibus non est disputandum.* True False

15. President Eisenhower rose through sheer ability *per aspera ad astra.* True False

16. Watch your step, or you may make a *faux pas.* True False

17. He was so clever, he always made a *coup de grâce* when he spoke. True False

18. The soldiers were ordered to be on the *qui vive.* True False

19. Many regard the "Mona Lisa" as the *ne plus ultra* in portrait painting. True False

20. Caesar was a military leader par excellence. True False

21. Lincoln was a sociable and therefore a *non sequitur* type of statesman. True False

22. An ill-dressed man is *persona grata* at a formal banquet.   True   False

23. The phrase *e pluribus unum* describes our country—one unit consisting of many states.   True   False

24. He was ashamed of the potpourri he had committed against social convention.   True   False

—*Answers*—

1-False, 2-True, 3-True, 4-False, 5-True, 6-True, 7-False, 8-True, 9-True, 10-False, 11-False, 12-True, 13-False, 14-False, 15-True, 16-True, 17-False, 18-True, 19-True, 20-True, 21-False, 22-False, 23-True, 24-False

D

Matching

From the general meaning of the foreign expressions in the foregoing rounds, see if you can match the phrases in the first column with the literal translations in the second column. In the parentheses that follow the phrases, F stands for French and L for Latin:

1. *coup de grâce* (F)
2. *cui bono* (L)
3. *de gustibus non est disputandum* (L)
4. *de mortuis nil nisi bonum* (L)
5. *Deo volente* (L)
6. *de trop* (F)
7. *double-entendre* (F)
8. *en pension* (F)
9. *en rapport* (F)
10. *e pluribus unum* (L)
11. *esprit de corps* (F)
12. *fait accompli* (F)
13. *faux pas* (F)

a. (to plunge) into the midst of things
b. a thing accomplished and presumably irrevocable
c. the common enthusiasm of individuals toward their group
d. the summit of achievement; literally, nothing more beyond
e. an acceptable person
f. a rare bird
g. of the dead (say) nothing but good
h. knowing how to do, tact
i. a merciful blow
j. one out of many
k. a double meaning
l. with God's will
m. after the custom of a boarding house

14. *in medias res* (L)	n. much in little
15. *multum in parvo* (L)	o. there is no disputing about tastes
16. *ne plus ultra* (L)	p. for whose benefit
17. *non sequitur* (L)	q. it doesn't follow, referring to an illogical statement
18. par excellence (F)	r. too much or too many, superfluous
19. *per aspera ad astra* (L)	s. a medley or mixture
20. *persona grata* (L)	t. who goes there? (literally, who lives?)
21. potpourri (F)	u. by hard ways to the stars
22. *qui vive* (F)	v. pre-eminently
23. *rara avis* (L)	w. a false step
24. savoir-faire (F)	x. in a harmonious relationship

—Answers—

1-i, 2-p, 3-o, 4-g, 5-l, 6-r, 7-k, 8-m, 9-x, 10-j, 11-c, 12-b, 13-w, 14-a, 15-n, 16-d, 17-q, 18-v, 19-u, 20-e, 21-s, 22-t, 23-f, 24-h

E

As you learn the pronunciation of these phrases, be sure that you understand their literal meaning as well as their idiomatic usage.

Note: The pronunciations are in accordance with Webster:

coup de grâce: koo-de-GRAHSS
cui bono: KIGH BONE-oh, or KWEE BONE-oh
de gustibus non est disputandum: de GUS-ti-bus non est dis-pu-TAN-dum
de mortuis nil nisi bonum: de MOR-tu-iss nil NIS-si BONE-um
Deo volente: DEE-owe vo-LEN-te
de trop: de TROE, to rhyme with *foe*
double-entendre: DOO-bl ahn-TAHN-dr
en pension: ahn pahn-si-ONG (slur the g)
en rapport: ahn ra-POR
e pluribus unum: ee-PLOO-ri-bus YOU-num
esprit de corps: ess-PREE de KOR
fait accompli: fet a-kong(slur the g)-PLEA
faux pas: foe PA
in medias res: in MEE-dee-as REEZ

204

multum in parvo: MUL-tum in PAR-vo
ne plus ultra: knee plus UL-tra
non sequitur: non SEK-wit-er
par excellence: par ek-se-LAHNS
per aspera ad astra: per ASS-per-a ad ASS-tra
persona grata: per-SO-na GRAY-ta
potpourri: poh-poo-REE
qui vive: kee-VEEV
rara avis: RAY-ra AY (to rhyme with day)-vis
savoir-faire: sav-WAHR FAIR

19

THE EASY WAY TO CORRECT SPELLING

A teacher asked three little boys to write on the blackboard a sentence containing the word *beans*.

The first boy wrote: "My mother cooks beans."
The second boy wrote: "My father eats beans."
The third boy wrote: "All of us are human beans."
This boy spelled *beings* the way he pronounced it.

POOR PRONUNCIATION

One of the commonest reasons for bad spelling is bad pronunciation. The very word *pronunciation* is often mispronounced and misspelled as *pronounciation*.

There are many other words that are misspelled because they are mispronounced. Watch out for the most familiar among them (the correct spelling appears in the right-hand column):

Wrong Pronunciation	Right Pronunciation
ac-ci-dent-ly	ac-ci-dent-al-ly
ath-e-let-ic	ath-let-ic
ar-tic	arc-tic
bar-brous	bar-ba-rous
cram-berry	cran-berry
dis-as-ter-ous	dis-as-trous
gov-er-ment	gov-ern-ment
i-den-ity	i-den-tity
ir-rev-e-lent	ir-rel-e-vant
lab-ra-tory	lab-o-ra-tory
lin-a-ment	lin-e-a-ment
min-er-ol-ogy	min-er-al-ogy
min-a-ture	min-i-a-ture
Ni-ag-ra	Ni-ag-a-ra
pro-gi-dy	pro-di-gy
rec-o-nize	rec-og-nize

Wrong Pronunciation	Right Pronunciation
su-prise	sur-prise
tre-men-jous	tre-men-dous
twelth	twelfth
val-u-ble	val-u-a-ble

A pupil in one of my classes wrote a composition about his father's house. Among the articles in the dining room, he mentioned a *sum-of-art*. I was puzzled about this expression, and I asked him to describe the object. It turned out to be a *samovar*.

SILENT PARTNERS

Another common reason for poor spelling is the frequency of silent partners in the business of word construction. The presence of silent letters in many of our words is one of the most troublesome hurdles on the road to better English. So let us look at some of them.

Words with silent *b*: climb, crumb, dumb, lamb, plumber, tomb

Silent *g*: gnarl, gnash, gnat, gnome

Silent *h*: ghastly, ghetto, ghost, ghoul (pronounced *gool*)

Silent *k*: knack, knave, knead, knife, know

Silent *l*: almond, alms, balk, balm, talk

Silent *p*: pneumonia, psalm, pseudo, psychic

Silent *s*: aisle, island, lisle

Silent *t*: apostle, bristle, castle, thistle, whistle

Silent *w*: wrap, wretch, wrist, wrong, wry

Other silent letters:

align
besought
brougham (pronounced *broom* or BROO-um
dahlia
diaphragm
extraordinary
guerrilla
handkerchief
handsome
indict
luncheon
parliament

business
campaign
catarrh
cocoa
redoubt
rhythm
solemn
toward (pronounced *tord*)
victuals (pronounced *vittles*)
yacht

Handicapped as we are in the matter of silent letters, it seems we are more fortunate than the British. An American who visited England was talking to an Oxford professor. "Let me congratulate you," he said, "on your many famous people and places. Take Lord Cholmondeley, for instance."

"Pardon me, sir," said the Oxford professor, "but the name is pronounced *Chumly*."

"And the other day," continued the American, "I read an article by that brilliant essayist, Howard Saint John."

"Again I must ask you to pardon me, sir. The name is *SIN-jun*."

"And only yesterday," went on the American, "I visited Saint Magdalene College."

"Please don't feel offended, sir, but we call it Saint *Maudlin* College."

And then the Englishman, to put the American at ease, said: "You, too, have famous people and places. When I visited your country several years ago, I met President Roosevelt."

"The name, sir," said the American with a twinkle in his eye, "is President *Rivet*."

"And," continued the Englishman, "I never beheld a more imposing spectacle than Niagara Falls."

"Pardon me, sir," said the American, "but the right way to say it is *Niffles*."

British English may be harder to spell than American English. But we, too, must be on our guard. So watch out for the words with the silent letters.

The *second* aid to good spelling, then, is to *keep your eyes open*.

TEN SIMPLE RULES FOR BETTER SPELLING

English is perhaps the most difficult language to spell. For it contains too many words in which the spelling is divorced from the sound. "No wonder," said Mark Twain, "that so many good English writers are such poor *spelers*."

Yet the majority of our troublesome words can be classified under a few easy-to-remember rules. Learn these rules, and you will be able to eliminate many of your spelling difficulties.

1. Take your words apart, and see what makes them tick. Note, for example, the synonym for *rivalry*. How would you spell that word—*compitition* or *competition*?

Well, let's see. A *competition* is a *petition* of two or more people for the same thing. And thus you get the spelling by dividing the word into its two parts—*com* + *petition*.

In like manner, the synonym for *witty* is *humorous* (allied with *humor*), and not *humerous*. And the synonym for *great joy* is *exhilaration* (allied with *hilarious*), and not *exhiliration*.

2. When a word has a prefix (a letter or group of letters at the beginning), imagine that there is a hyphen between the word and the prefix and you will generally see the correct spelling.

Thus: *dissolve* consists of *dis-solve*, but *disappear* consists of *dis-appear*. Hence a word that is combined with the prefix *dis* is spelled with a *double s* if it originally begins with the letter *s*, but with a *single s* if it begins with any other letter.

Other examples: *dissatisfy, disservice, dissension, dissimilar;* but *disappoint, disbelieve, dislocate, disregard.*

Words compounded with the prefix *mis* are subject to the same rule: *misstep, missent, misstatement;* but *misapplied, mishap, misunderstand.* It also applies in the case of some of the other prefixes. Thus:

> *overrated, overripe, overrun;* but *overextend, overindulge, overexpose*
> *unnatural, unnecessary, unnoticed;* but *unavoidable, uninteresting, unimpressed*
> *underrate, underrun;* but *underestimate, underexpose*

3. When a word has a suffix (a letter or group of letters at the end, like *ly, ness,* or *ed*), you can generally apply a similar test. Imagine a hyphen between the word and the suffix; double the letter if the word ends and the suffix begins with the same sound; but do not double when the two letters are different.

> Examples: *actually, drunkenness, soulless;* but *sincerely, cleverness, heartless*

4. When a monosyllable (a word of one syllable) ends in a *single consonant* preceded by a *single vowel*, you *double* the consonant before *ing, ed, er, est.*

> Examples: *star, starring, tap, tapped, wrap, wrapper, big, biggest*

5. When a word of more than one syllable ends in a *single consonant* preceded by a *single vowel*, and when the accent is on the last *syllable*, you *double* the consonant before *ing, ed, er, est* (the same as in Rule 4).

209

Examples: *concur, concurring, commit, committed, forbid, forbidden, compel, compelling*

If you remember Rules 4 and 5, you will see why the following words are spelled with a *single* instead of a *double* consonant: *beating* (from *beat*), *heater* (from *heat*), *conquering* (from *conquer*), *softest* (from *soft*). *Beat* and *heat* end in a single consonant, but the consonant follows a diphthong (two vowels) instead of a single vowel; *conquer* does not have the accent on the last syllable; *soft* ends in two consonants. Just ask yourself these questions:

Is the word a monosyllable?

If not, is the accent on the last syllable?

Does it end in a single consonant?

Is there a single vowel before this consonant?

If the answer to all the questions is *yes*, you double the consonant when you add the suffix.

But not otherwise. For then you might repeat the error made by the prospective bridegroom who wrote to his prospective bride: "I am treading on air and *hopping* for the day of our approaching bliss."

6. When a word ends in a consonant followed by a silent *e*, drop the *e* before you add *ing: bribe, bribing; drive, driving; save, saving; urge, urging.*

7. When a word ends in *y* preceded by a consonant, keep the *y* before you add *ing*, but change the *y* to *i* before you add *es* or *ed: cry, crying, cries, cried; reply, replying, replies, replied.*

8. Rule for *ei* or *ie*, when pronounced like *ee* in *seem*. Use *ei* after *c*, and *ie* after the other consonants: *receive, perceive; field, believe, niece, siege.*

But there are a number of exceptions to this rule: *financier, neither, seize, weird.*

Other apparent exceptions are such words as *eight, freight, reign, sleigh*. But in these words, as you will note, the letters *ei* are pronounced like *a* in *late*.

9. Rule for words ending in *sede, ceed, cede:*

Only one word ends in *sede: supersede.*

Only three words end in *ceed: exceed, proceed, succeed.*

All the other words in this group end in *cede: concede, precede, recede, secede*, etc.

10. This is not a rule, but rather a helpful guide to the spelling of such words as *dispensable* and *digestible*. If the word is allied to another word ending in *ation*, you generally

spell it with an *a—able*. Otherwise you generally spell it with an *i—ible*.

Thus:

dispensable is allied to *dispensation*
estimable is allied to *estimation*
irritable is allied to *irritation*

But:

digestible has no allied word like *digestation*
irresistible has no allied word like *irresistation*
reprehensible has no allied word like *reprehensation*

The above rules will not cover *all* the words you may have occasion to spell. But they will take care of *a good many* of them. As a general aid to better spelling, check the words that have given you trouble in the past. Try to learn them not only with your ears, by pronouncing them, but also with your eyes, by observing them carefully and photographing them upon your consciousness.

This procedure applies especially to the tricky words that you will find in the next word game.

Time out for the Seventeenth Word Game
LET US RELAX FOR A SPELL

In this game you will play with a hundred words that are frequently misspelled. These words are arranged in the order of their difficulty—from the least troublesome in the first round to the most troublesome in the last.

Yet even the easiest words in the first round may have confused you in the past. See what you can do with them.

A

Words That Are Fairly Easy to Spell

Check the one word that is spelled *wrong* in each of the following groups:

1. (a) tyranny, (b) malign, (c) efervescent, (d) abscess, (e) separate

2. (a) assassinate, (b) priviledge, (c) accommodate, (d) resistant, (e) insistent

3. (a) hippocrisy, (b) penitentiary, (c) chrysanthemum, (d) picnicking, (e) anoint

4. (a) analyze, (b) noticable, (c) drunkenness, (d) permissible, (e) dissipate

5. (a) assassinate, (b) penitentiary, (c) separate, (d) permissible, (e) resistent

6. (a) annalyze, (b) anoint, (c) effervescent, (d) privilege, (e) tyranny

7. (a) picknicking, (b) noticeable, (c) malign, (d) insistent, (e) abscess

8. (a) drunkenness, (b) chrisanthemum, (c) accommodate, (d) dissipate, (e) hypocrisy

9. (a) separate, (b) tyrrany, (c) insistent, (d) hypocrisy, (e) dissipate

10. (a) resistant, (b) picnicking, (c) permissable, (d) drunkenness, (e) chrysanthemum

11. (a) malign, (b) analyze, (c) annoint, (d) abscess, (e) accommodate

12. (a) privilege, (b) effervescent, (c) noticeable, (d) penitentiary, (e) assasinate

13. (a) resistant, (b) tyranny, (c) abcess, (d) insistent, (e) analyze

14. (a) anoint, (b) drunkeness, (c) malign, (d) picnicking, (e) separate

15. (a) acommodate, (b) assassinate, (c) chrysanthemum, (d) dissipate, (e) effervescent

16. (a) privilege, (b) picnicking, (c) permissible, (d) noticeable, (e) pennitentiary

17. (a) analyze, (b) tyranny, (c) seperate, (d) anoint, (e) abscess

18. (a) accommodate, (b) chrysanthemum, (c) mallign, (d) noticeable, (e) penitentiary

19. (a) insistant, (b) resistant, (c) privilege, (d) hypocrisy, (e) effervescent

20. (a) assassinate, (b) dissippate, (c) drunkenness, (d) permissible, (e) picnicking

—*Answers*—

1-c (effervescent), 2-b (privilege), 3-a (hypocrisy), 4-b (noticeable), 5-e (resistant), 6-a (analyze), 7-a (picnicking), 8-b (chrysanthemum), 9-b (tyranny), 10-c (permissible), 11-c (anoint), 12-e (assassinate), 13-c (abscess), 14-b (drunkenness), 15-a (accommodate), 16-e (penitentiary), 17-c (separate), 18-c (malign), 19-a (insistent), 20-b (dissipate)

B

Words That Are a Little Harder to Spell

Did you do pretty well on the first round? Fifteen out of twenty would be a good score. Your score on the second round will probably be a little lower. But see for yourself. Check the one word that is spelled *right* in each of the following groups:

1. (a) batallion, (b) anihilate, (c) alright, (d) questionnaire, (e) geneology
2. (a) beneficent, (b) innoculate, (c) proffessor, (d) irresistable, (e) parralel
3. (a) conscienscious, (b) discrimanate, (c) ecstasy, (d) ocurrence, (e) exhilirate
4. (a) embarrassment, (b) sacreligious, (c) superintendant, (d) tarriff, (e) supercede
5. (a) benificent, (b) genealogy, (c) inocculate, (d) ecstacy, (e) battallion
6. (a) annihilate, (b) descriminate, (c) alright, (d) consientious, (e) occurence
7. (a) proffesor, (b) embarassment, (c) paralell, (d) questionare, (e) irresistible
8. (a) sacrelegious, (b) tariff, (c) superseed, (d) superrintendant, (e) exhillirate
9. (a) all right, (b) annihillate, (c) questionaire, (d) conscienshus, (e) descriminate
10. (a) benefissent, (b) battalion, (c) extassy, (d) tarrif, (e) exillirate
11. (a) geneallogy, (b) inocullate, (c) iresistable, (d) occurrence, (e) paralel
12. (a) embarressment, (b) superceed, (c) superinttendant, (d) proffesor, (e) sacrilegious
13. (a) conscientious, (b) discrimminate, (c) annihalate, (d) allrite, (e) beneficcent
14. (a) batalion, (b) ecstassy, (c) embarassment, (d) exhilarate, (e) genialogy
15. (a) taraff, (b) supersede, (c) sacrillegious, (d) innoculate, (e) iresistable

16. (a) occurrance, (b) parallel, (c) proffesser,
(d) questionnair, (e) superintendant
17. (a) alrite, (b) battalyon, (c) discriminate, (d) extacy,
(e) sacrelligious
18. (a) superintendent, (b) supercede, (c) questionaire,
(d) parrallel, (e) innocculate
19. (a) beneficcent, (b) tarriff, (c) professor,
(d) ocurence, (e) irresistible
20. (a) anihalate, (b) conscienceous, (c) embarassment,
(d) exilharate, (e) inoculate

—*Answers*—

1-d (questionnaire), 2-a (beneficent), 3-c (ecstasy), 4-a
(embarrassment), 5-b (genealogy), 6-a (annihilate), 7-e
(irresistible), 8-b (tariff), 9-a (all right), 10-b (battalion),
11-d (occurrence), 12-e (sacrilegious), 13-a (conscientious),
14-d (exhilarate), 15-b (supersede), 16-b (parallel), 17-c
(discriminate), 18-a (superintendent), 19-c (professor), 20-e
(inoculate)

C

Words That Stump Teachers

This round is somewhat harder than the second round.
Several of the words in the following list have occasionally
stumped even high school and college teachers. How many
of them have stumped *you* in the past? One of the spellings
for each of the words in this list is correct, and the other is
incorrect. Check *a* or *b*, whichever spelling you think is
correct:

	a	b
1.	innocuous	inocuous
2.	dissappear	disappear
3.	vacillate	vaccillate
4.	dilettante	dilletante
5.	pharoah	pharaoh
6.	consensus	concensus
7.	innuendo	inuendo
8.	dissention	dissension
9.	abstention	abstension
10.	erisypelas	erysipelas
11.	desiccate	dessicate
12.	liquify	liquefy

13. iridescent	irridescent
14. apellation	appellation
15. guttural	gutteral
16. colonnade	collonade
17. phlem	phlegm
18. villainy	villany
19. suppoena	subpoena
20. hidrangea	hydrangea
21. moccasin	mocassin
22. altogether	alltogether
23. Brittanic	Britannic
24. catarrh	cattarh
25. delapidated	dilapidated
26. fuselage	fusillage
27. fuselade	fusillade
28. gaseous	gasseous
29. incidently	incidentally
30. secreterial	secretarial

—*Answers*—

1-a, 2-b, 3-a, 4-a, 5-b, 6-a, 7-a, 8-b, 9-a, 10-b, 11-a, 12-b, 13-a, 14-b, 15-a, 16-a, 17-b, 18-a, 19-b, 20-b, 21-a, 22-a, 23-b, 24-a, 25-b, 26-a, 27-b, 28-a, 29-b, 30-b

Did you get twenty out of the thirty? Then you are a pretty good speller. Did you get twenty-five or more? In that case you are almost an expert. But watch out for the next round, where you will meet some real demons.

D

Try to Get the Spelling

I will give the pronunciation and the definition of each of the words in this round, and you try to get the spelling:

1. sit-a-KOE-sis, a parrot disease communicable to humans

2. NICE, a granite-like kind of rock

3. her-BAY-shus, having the characteristics of a herb or a leaf

4. NOS-tik, pertaining to knowledge

5. TAR-mi-gan, a species of grouse (a bird)

6. pres-ti-DIJ-i-tay (as in *pray*)-ter, a juggler

7. SIL-ee-um, a plant whose seeds are used as a laxative

215

8. sap-o-NAY-shus, resembling soap, soapy, slippery
9. nem-ON-ik, assisting the memory
10. DES-we-tude, state of being no longer in use
11. i-dee-o-SIN-kra-see, a peculiarity of temperament, ec centricity
12. im-BROE (to rhyme with *foe*)-lee-owe, a serious mis understanding or an intricate situation
13. AN-si-ler-ee, subordinate or auxiliary
14. KOO-chook, or koo-CHOOK, India rubber, pure rub ber
15. JOUR (to rhyme with *hour*), an infidel (a Turkish word referring to anyone who is not a Mohammedan)

—Answers—

1-psittacosis, 2-gneiss, 3-herbaceous, 4-gnostic, 5-ptarmi gan, 6-prestidigitator, 7-psyllium, 8-saponaceous, 9-mnemonic 10-desuetude, 11-idiosyncrasy, 12-imbroglio, 13-ancillary 14-caoutchouc, 15-giaour

How many of these did you get? Five? Less? Never mind you know them all now. And you can have lots of fun trying them on your friends.

But here comes perhaps the stiffest list of them all.

E

More of the Same

Just as in the fourth round, I will give you the pronunci ations and the definitions, and you spell the words:

1. TIZ-ik, consumption, tuberculosis
2. DELL-ee-um, or DELL-yum, a gum resin
3. si-ROWE-sis, a disease of the liver
4. HAR-ik-owe, a stew of lamb or mutton with vegetable
5. rash-ee-o-si-NAY-shun, a piece of reasoning, a train o thought
6. AP-o-them (the *th* is pronounced as in *think*), a short pithy and instructive saying, a maxim
7. ser-Al-yoe (to rhyme with *foe*), a harem
8. or-DUV-r (pronounce the *u* as in *urge*), a kind o appetizer
9. GUR-kin, a small cucumber
10. GUR-dun, a reward
11. SIZ-i-jee, a joining together—a term used in astron omy, grammar, mathematics and zoölogy

12. SAWL-ter-ee, a musical instrument mentioned in the Bible

13. HEM-o-rij, a flow of blood from the blood vessels

14. fi-LOJ-i-nus, fond of women

15. fa-ri-NAY-shus, referring to a diet that consists of meal or flour

—Answers—

1-phthisic, 2-bdellium, 3-cirrhosis, 4-haricot, 5-ratiocination, 6-apophthegm, or apothegm, 7-seraglio, 8-hors d'oeuvre; plural, hors d'oeuvres, pronounced the same as the singular, 9-gherkin, 10-guerdon, 11-syzygy, 12-psaltery, 13-hemorrhage, or haemorrhage, 14-philogynous, 15-farinaceous

Before we leave this game, let's have a look at the longest English word listed in *Webster's Unabridged Dictionary*. This word, *antidisestablishmentarianism*, has 28 letters. Actually, there are a few medical terms which contain a greater number of letters, but these terms are Greek or Latin compounds of the names of chemicals used in certain drugs.

So remember *an-ti-dis-es-tab-lish-men-TAY-ri-an-ism* as a handy word to spring on your friends. It denotes opposition to the doctrine of withdrawing state patronage from an established church.

And by the way, do you remember the old joke of your school days? It goes something like this:

"What is the longest word in the English language?"

"The longest word is *smiles*."

"Why?"

"Because there is a *mile* between the first letter and the last."

20

WORDS THAT TRIP THE TONGUE

YOUR TELLTALE SPEECH

The way you talk may reveal a good deal about you. At the very least, it indicates where you come from. For example, when I was in high school at Boston, a new boy came into the class just after New Year's Day. We had a geometry lesson. The teacher called upon the boy to define *circle* and *point*. The boy gave excellent definitions, but he referred to these terms as *soicle* and *pernt*. We knew at once that our new classmate had moved to Boston from a certain district in Brooklyn.

Contrariwise, if you ask an educated New Yorker the way to *Central Pahk*, he'll know that you are a native of Boston. But if you ask him the way to *Central Pawrk*, he'll guess correctly that you probably come from the Midwest or the West.

How do you pronounce the word *vase?* If you're a New Englander, you call it *vace;* a Philadelphian, *vahz;* a Southerner, *vawz.*

Have you ever run into a person who pronounces *j* or soft g like *y—Do you like yinyer-ale, by yiminy?* He doesn't have to explain that he is a Scandinavian; and if *'e hasks a policeman to 'elp 'im because 'e 'as been 'eld hup*, the intelligent listener will recognize him as a Cockney visitor from London.

Suppose someone tells you he wants to take his *"vite voolen sveater out of de vardrobe."* You may be fairly certain he's an immigrant from Germany, or nearby parts. What, however, is the nationality of the person who says *chaise lounge* for *chaise longue, togedder* for *together*, and *dincha* for *didn't you?* He may well be a native American—but we would not judge him to have had much education.

By the way you speak, you may create an impression that is good, bad, or indifferent. Naturally, what you say is more important than how you say it, but clear, correct speech will immediately win you the respect of your listeners, whether or not they agree with what you say.

MUTED AND MUTILATED SOUNDS

When we come across new words in our reading, we cannot always be sure how we should pronounce them. As we noted in Chapter 19, the spelling is often different from the sound.

There are too many silent letters in our written vocabulary. For example, if *r-o-u-g-h* is pronounced *ruff*, why isn't *p-l-o-u-g-h* pronounced *pluff?* It is the silent *gh* (plus the varying vowel sound) in many words—like *brougham, drought, thorough, slaughter, fraught*—that makes them so difficult for some people to pronounce as well as to spell.

DID SHAKESPEARE SPEAK IRISH?

One reason why unfamiliar English words are so hard to pronounce or spell—and therefore hard to learn—is that our language is closely linked to its past. The spelling of many words was fixed long ago. It may accurately record the pronunciation of three or five hundred years back—the pronunciation of a different time and place, not of here and now. Pronunciation keeps changing from time to time. For example, spoken English in Shakespeare's day was quite different from spoken English today. In the opinion of many scholars, the Englishmen of the Elizabethan era—men like Bacon and Shakespeare—pronounced their words with an "Irish" brogue. And Chaucer, a major literary figure of the fourteenth century in England, was, as Bernard Shaw remarked, a great poet, but "he spoke English with a foreign accent."

Here are just a few specimens of English words that were spoken with a "foreign accent" in the past:

Folk was formerly spoken with an audible *l.*

England was formerly pronounced with a short *e* sound at the start.

Name was formerly pronounced NAHM-uh.

House was once pronounced HOOS.

Comb formerly had a different vowel sound, and the *b* was sounded; the word was pronounced KAWMB.

In words like *simple* and *angle*, the final *e* was sounded; so, too, was the *gh* in a word like *plough*, where it was pronounced like the *ch* in the German word *ach.*

English is a living language, and living things are always subject to development and change. It is only the dead languages whose pronunciation has been mummified into a rigid system of inflexible sounds. The living languages, on the other hand, keep varying with the variety of the human tongues that utter them. Pronunciation is not a science, but an art. "In matters of pronunciation," declared Professor Thomas R. Lounsbury, "one thoroughly educated man is as good an authority as another."

The thing to do, then, is to adopt the pronunciation approved by the *greatest* number of the *best* authorities. This is what we are trying to do in the present book.

SIMPLE GUIDES TO CORRECT PRONUNCIATION

First of all, here are a few simple rules on which all the authorities agree:

1. Many words are differently accented when they are used as different parts of speech. In general, they have the accent on the *first* syllable when used as nouns: on the *second* syllable when used as verbs. Thus:

Noun	*Verb*
CONduct	conDUCT
CONscript	conSCRIPT
CONtest	conTEST
CONverse	conVERSE
CONvict	conVICT
CONvoy	conVOY
DEsert	deSERT
OBject	obJECT
PREview	preVIEW
PROject	proJECT
PROtest	proTEST
SUBject	subJECT

2. There are three ways to pronounce the consonant combination, *ng*:

ng as in *bring*, in which the *g* is somewhat slurred
ng as in *clangor*, in which the *g* is distinctly pronounced
ng as in *fringe*, in which the *g* is sounded like *j*

A. Use the slurred *ng* sound as in *bring* when you find these two letters—*ng*—at the *end* of a word:

among	making
fling	ping-pong
gripping	sing

hang	swing
king	thong

B. Retain the slurred *ng* sound as in *bring* when you add a suffix to words such as those included in List A above:

flinging (*not* fling-ging)
hanging (*not* hang-ging)
singing (*not* sing-ging)

To this rule there are a few exceptions:

long-ger (*not* longer)
strong-ger (*not* stronger)
young-ger (*not* younger)

C. Pronounce *ng* as in *fringe* in words that end in *nge*:

binge	hinge	plunge
change	lounge	revenge
cringe	orange	twinge

3. The pronunciation of *a* and *the*. The article *a* is pronounced like *u* in *hut*, and it is used only before words that begin with a consonant sound: a (u) book, a (u) dollar, a (u) union (pronounced as though the first letter were *y*).

The article *the* is pronounced like *thee* when it is used before a word that begins with a *vowel* sound: the (thee) apple, the (thee) egg, the (thee) opera.

The is pronounced like *thuh* when it is used before a word that begins with a *consonant* sound: the (thuh) pencil, the (thuh) table, the (thuh) water.

4. Don't "swallow" any letters or syllables in such words as the following:

Right	*Wrong*
correct	c'rect
federal	fed'ral
liability	li'bility
perhaps	p'raps
poem	pome
recognize	reco'nize
restaurant	rest'rant
strength	stren'th
superstition	sup'stition
suppose	s'pose
temperature	temper'ture

221

5. Don't put any extra letters or syllables into words where they don't belong:

Right	Wrong
across	acrosst
athletic	atheletic
burglar	burgalar
chimney	chimeney
column	colyumn
drowned	drownded
elm	ellum
fiend	feeund
hindrance	hinderance
mayoralty	mayorality
translate	transalate
umbrella	umberella

6. Don't use "illiterate" pronunciations in your everyday talk:

Right	Wrong
Atlantic	Alannic
audience	aujence
butter	budda
buying	buyin'
could you	couldja
don't you	doncha
drawing	drawring
going to	gonna
got to	godda
journey	choiney
let him	led'm
let me	lemme
let's go	less go
ought to	odda
something	sumpin
spoil	sperl
third	toid
want to	wanna
what do you mean	wadjameen
will you	willyer
would you	wouldja

7. Here are the correct pronunciations of 50 place names that are frequently mispronounced:

Ankara, capital of Turkey: AHN-ka-ra
Ajaccio, the Corsican birthplace of Napoleon: a-YAT-cho
Boston: BOSS-ton, *not* BAWS-ton
Butte: BEWT
Calaveras, a river in California: kal-a-VAY-ras
Canaan, the promised land of the Israelites: KAY-nan
Canberra, a city in Australia: KAN-ber-a
Cannes, a French winter resort: KAN
Chalcidice, a Greek peninsula: kal-SID-i-see
Champlain, a lake between New York and Vermont: sham-PLAIN
Chickamauga, a battlefield in the Civil War: chik-a-MAW-ga
Delhi, India: DELL-ee, to rhyme with *Nellie*
Des Moines, Iowa: de MOIN
Derwent, name of several rivers in England: DUR-went
Edinburgh: ED-in-buh-ruh
Eiffel: EYE-fel
Eire, another name for Erin or Ireland: AIR-a
Eolus, a mountain in Colorado: EE-o-lus
Genoa: JEN-oh-a
Gloucester: GLOS-ter
Gobi Desert: GO-bee
Gravesend, a district in the borough of Brooklyn: GRAVE-zend
Greenwich, Connecticut: GREN-itch, GRIN-witch, GREEN-witch; Greenwich, England: GREN-ij
Houston: HEW-stun
Hyderabad, a state in India: high-der-a-BAD
La Jolla, California: lah HAW-ya
La Junta, Colorado: lah HOON-ta
Mojave: mo-HAH-vay
Nez Perce, Idaho: NAY per-SAY
Niger River, in West Africa: NIGH-jer
Peiping: pay-PING
Rio de Janeiro: REE-oh-day-zha-NAY-ro (*zh* like *s* in *pleasure*)
Rio Grande, boundary river between Texas and Mexico: REE-o-GRAN-day
Salisbury, Massachusetts: SAWLZ-bree
Sandringham, British royal residence: SAND-ring-am
San Joaquin, California: san Wah-KEEN
San Juan: san HWAN

Sault Sainte Marie, Michigan: soo-saint-ma-REE
Spokane, Washington: spo-KAN
Thailand, another name for Siam: TIE-lahnd
Tucson: too-SUN
Vladivostok: vla-di-vos-TOK
Worcester: WOOS-ter
Yosemite: yoh-SEM-i-tee

And here, as an extreme example of our rather illogical pronunciation, are the names of two American towns—associate the sounds with the spelling if you can:

Siasconset, New York: SKON-sit
Shawangunk, New York: SHON-gum

Time out for the Eighteenth Word Game
HOW IS YOUR PRONUNCIATION?

It is amazing how many people who ought to know better are careless about their pronunciation. And this carelessness applies even to some of our leading radio and television announcers. Within a single week I have heard the following words mispronounced in various broadcasts and telecasts:

ephemeral	grimace
lingerie	finis
impotency	cerebral
bestial	Uranus

What about yourself? Do you know how to pronounce the above words, and the dozens of other words that are all too frequently mispronounced?

Let's see. In this game you are going to play with a hundred words, arranged according to the difficulty of their pronunciation. The words in the first round are fairly easy to pronounce; those in the second round are a little harder; and those in the third round are the most likely to trip you up.

Yet even the first round contains a number of "tricky" words. So watch out!

(*Note:* You will find brief definitions after the less familiar words in this game.)

A

Check the correct pronunciation of the following words:

1. museum: (a) MYOO-zee-um, (b) myoo-ZEE-um
2. library: (a) LYE-bre-ree, (b) LYE-be-ree
3. February: (a) FEB-roo-er-ee, (b) FEB-you-er-ee
4. visage: (a) VISS-ij, (b) VIZ-ij
5. mischievous: (a) miss-CHEE-vee-us, (b) MISS-chi-vuss
6. athletic: (a) ath-e-LET-ik, (b) ath-LET-ik
7. film: (a) FILL-um, (b) FILM
8. length: (a) LENGTH, (b) LENTH
9. genuine: (a) JEN-you-in, (b) JEN-you-wine
10. aviator: (a) AY (as in *day*)-vee-ay-ter, (b) AVV-ee-ay-ter
11. elm: (a) ELL-um, (b) ELM
12. grievous: (a) GREE-vus, (b) GREE-vee-us
13. percolator: (a) PER-ko-lay-ter, (b) PER-kyo-lay-ter
14. preferable: (a) PREF-er-a-bl, (b) pre-FER-a-bl
15. accessory: (a) a-SESS-o-ree, (b) ak-SESS-o-ree, (c) AK-sess-o-ree
16. combatant: (a) KOM-bat-ant, (b) kom-BAT-ant
17. dirigible: (a) di-RIJ-i-bl, (b) DIR-i-ji-bl
18. coupon: (a) KOO-pon, (b) KEW-pon, (c) koo-PONG
19. human: (a) HEW-man, (b) YOU-man
20. eczema: (a) ek-ZEE-ma, (b) EK-ze-ma, (c) EK-se-ma
21. inclement: (a) in-KLEM-ent, (b) IN-klem-ent
22. adversary: (a) AD-ver-se-ree, (b) ad-VERSE-e-ree
23. incorrigible: (a) in-kor-RIJ-i-bl, (b) in-KOR-ij-i-bl
24. infamous: (a) IN-fam-us, (b) in-FAME-us
25. oblique: (a) ob-LEEK, (b) ob-LIKE
26. intricacy: (a) in-TRICK-a-see, (b) IN-tri-ka-see
27. lamentable: (a) la-MEN-ta-bl, (b) LAM-en-ta-bl
28. pecan: (a) pe-KAN, (b) PEA-kan
29. radiator: (a) RAY-dee-ay-ter, (b) RAD-ee-ay-ter
30. relapse: (a) REE-laps, (b) re-LAPS
31. sedentary: (a) SED-en-ter-ee, (b) se-DEN-ter-ee
32. tumult: (a) TOO-mult, (b) TEW-mult
33. villain: (a) VIL-yun, (b) VIL-in
34. status: (a) STAY-tus, (b) STAT-us

—Answers—

1-b, 2-a, 3-a, 4-b, 5-b, 6-b, 7-b, 8-a, 9-a, 10-a, 11-b, 12-a, 13-a, 14-a, 15-b, 16-a, 17-b, 18-a or b, 19-a, 20-b or c, 21-a,

22-a, 23-b, 24-a, 25-a (b in military use), 26-b, 27-b, 28-a, 29-a, 30-b, 31-a, 32-b, 33-b, 34-a

Did you pronounce 25 or more out of the 34 words correctly? Then you are a better orthoepist (OR-tho-ep-ist, or or-THO-ep-ist) than the average high school graduate. (The word *orthoepist* means a person skilled in pronunciation.)

But now comes the second round, consisting of words that are not quite so easy.

B

See if you can get at least 25 of the following 36 words. As in Round A, check the pronunciations which you think are correct:

    1. vice versa: (a) VEE-che VUR-sa, (b) VICE VUR-sa, (c) VIE-se VUR-sa

    2. bestial: (a) BES-chal, (b) BEAST-yal, (c) BEST-yal

    3. thyme (one of the mint plants): (a) TIME, (b) THIME

    4. efficacy (power to produce effects): (a) ef-FIK-a-see, (b) EF-fi-ka-see

    5. impotent: (a) IM-po-tent, (b) im-POE-tent

    6. impotency: (a) im-POE-ten-see, (b) IM-po-ten-see

    7. valorous: (a) val-OWE-rus, (b) VAL-er-us

    8. ephemeral (existing only for a day): (a) ef-e-MER-al, (b) ef-EM-er-al, (c) ef-EEM-er-al

    9. dolorous (grievous, causing pain): (a) DOL-er-us, (b) do-LOR-us, (c) DOE-ler-us

    10. Belial (Satan): (a) Be-LIE-al, (b) BEE-lee-al, (c) BEEL-yal

    11. machination (an artful plot): (a) mash-in-AY-shun, (b) mak-in-AY-shun, (c) MATCH-in-AY-shun

    12. irrevocable (past recall): (a) ir-REV-o-ka-bl, (b) ir-re-VOKE-able

    13. lingerie: (a) lon-zhe-RAY, (b) lan-zhe-RAY, (c) lan-zhe-REE

    14. inebriate (intoxicated): (a) in-EE-bri-ate, (b) in-EB-ri-ate

    15. adjudicate (to adjudge, to act as judge): (a) ad-JUD-i-kate, (b) ad-JOOD-i-kate

    16. acumen (keenness of mind): (a) a-KEW-men, (b) AK-you-men

    17. verbatim: (a) ver-BAY-tim, (b) ver-BAT-im

18. sachem (a chief): (a) SATCH-em, (b) SACK-em, (c) SAY-tchem

19. clandestine (kept secret by craft): (a) KLAN-des-tine, (b) klan-DES-tin

20. culinary: (a) KULL-in-er-ee, (b) KEW-lin-er-ee

21. heinous (hateful): (a) HE-in-us, (b) HANE-us

22. gratis: (a) GRAY-tiss, (b) GRAT-iss

23. chiropodist (a foot doctor): (a) kigh-ROP-o-dist, (b) CHIR-op-o-dist

24. somnolent (sleepy): (a) som-NO-lent, (b) SOM-no-lent

25. impious: (a) IM-pee-us, (b) im-PIE-us

26. indefatigable (not yielding to fatigue): (a) in-de-FAT-i-ga-bl, (b) in-de-fa-TIG-a-bl

27. longevity (length of life): (a) long-EV-i-ti, (b) lon-JEV-i-ti

28. robust: (a) ro-BUST, (b) ROE-bust

29. disheveled: (a) dis-HEV-eld, (b) di-SHEV-eld

30. dishabille (a loose negligee): (a) dis-a-BEEL, (b) dish-a-BEEL

31. grimace: (a) GRIM-iss, (b) grim-ACE

32. secretive: (a) se-KREE-tiv, (b) SEE-kre-tiv

33. Uranus (one of the major planets): (a) YOU-ra-nus, (b) you-RAY-nus

34. cerebral: (a) SER-e-bral, (b) se-REE-bral

35. comparable: (a) COM-par-a-bl, (b) com-PAR-a-bl

36. respite (interval of rest): (a) re-SPITE, (b) RES-pit

—*Answers*—

1-c, 2-a and c, 3-a, 4-b, 5-a, 6-b, 7-b, 8-b, 9-a and c, 10-b and c, 11-b, 12-a, 13-c, 14-a, 15-b, 16-a, 17-a, 18-c, 19-b, 20-b, 21-b, 22-a or b, 23-a, 24-b, 25-a, 26-a, 27-b, 28-a, 29-b, 30-a, 31-b, 32-a, 33-a, 34-a, 35-a, 36-b

Have you made a score of 25 out of 36, or better? In that event, you have good reason to be proud of your speech. You may be prouder still if you can handle most of the words in the next round. The *average* college graduate will get about 15 out of the 30 words in Round C.

C

Check the correct pronunciation for each of the following words:

1. gondola: (a) gon-DOLE-a, (b) GON-do-la
2. flaccid (flabby), (a) FLAS-sid, (b) FLAK-sid
3. vagary (a caprice): (a) VAG-a-ree, (b) va-GAY-ree
4. precedent, noun: (a) pre-SEE-dent, (b) PRESS-i-dent
5. precedent, adjective: (a) PRESS-i-dent,
(b) pre-SEE-dent
6. dour (hard, severe): (a) rhymes with *hour,* (b)
rhymes with *poor*
7. congeries (a heap): (a) KON-gur-eez,
(b) kon-JEER-ee-eez
8. antipodes (the exact opposite): (a) AN-ti-podes,
(b) an-TIP-owe-deez
9. lascivious (lewd, lustful): (a) la-SHIV-ee-us,
(b) las-SIV-ee-us
10. finis: (a) FIN-is, (b) FIGH-nis
11. eighth: (a) AYTH, (b) ATE-th
12. succinct (concise, compressed): (a) sus-SINKT,
(b) suk-SINKT
13. ignominy (disgrace): (a) ig-NOM-in-ee,
(b) IG-no-min-ee
14. anathema (a ban or curse): (a) an-a-THEEM-a,
(b) an-ATH-e-ma
15. diphtheria: (a) dip-THEE-ree-a, (b) dif-THEE-ree-a
16. splenetic (depressed, melancholy): (a) sple-NET-ik,
(b) SPLEN-et-ik
17. palanquin: (a) pal-an-KEEN, (b) pal-AN-kwin
18. vinous: (a) VIGH-nus, (b) VIN-us
19. satiety (excessive gratification): (a) sa-TIGH-e-tee,
(b) SAY-she-a-tee
20. piquant (tart, pungent): (a) PEA-kant, (b) pe-KANT
21. adjunct (an appendage or a colleague): (a) AJ-unkt,
(b) a-JUNKT
22. appositeness (appropriateness): (a) AP-po-zit-ness,
(b) ap-POZ-it-ness
23. acclimatize: (a) a-KLIME-at-ize, (b) AK-lim-at-ize
24. credence: (a) KREE-dens, (b) KRED-ens
25. dotage: (a) DOE-tij, (b) DOT-ij
26. lichen: (a) LIKE-en, (b) LITCH-en
27. remediable: (a) re-MEE-dee-a-bl, (b) REM-e-dee-a-bl
28. inchoate (to begin): (a) in-KOE-it, (b) in-CHOE-ate
29. sepulchral: (a) se-PUL (to rhyme with *dull*)-kral,
(b) SEP-ul-kral
30. viscount: (a) VIGH-count, (b) VIS-count

The words numbered 1 to 15 are pronounced in accordance with *b*; those numbered 16 to 30, in accordance with *a*.

Don't be perturbed if you have not done too well in this game. As suggested, it really is a hard one. We rarely hear many of these words spoken, so it is easy to go wrong on them. When in doubt about any pronunciation or definition or point of grammatical usage, be sure to consult a good dictionary. *Webster's Unabridged Dictionary* has been our final authority in this game.

21

HOW TO BUILD YOUR WORDS INTO THOUGHTS

PHRASES, CLAUSES, AND SENTENCES

Are the two following sentences correct or incorrect?

1. Everybody went to the party but him.
2. His sister was older than he.

These two sentences, as you probably remember from your study of Chapter 18, are correct. Can you tell the reason why? This, too, you should be able to answer from what you learned in Chapter 18.

In the first sentence, *but* is a preposition which forms a *phrase* with the objective pronoun *him*.

In the second sentence, *than* is usually interpreted as a conjunction which joins two *clauses—His sister was older than he (was)*.

But what are *phrases* and *clauses?*

They are groups of words combined into parts of sentences.

A *phrase* is a related group of words which does not contain a subject and a verb. The following, for example, are phrases:

a group of words
the taming of the shrew
sweets to the sweet
parting of the ways
a thing of beauty
but him

A *clause* is a group of words which does contain a subject and a verb. For example:

and he came later
or it will never be done
but (*conjunction*) he will not consent

when Eisenhower was elected President
which he sent to his mother

Phrases and clauses are *parts* of sentences. A *whole* sentence is a group of words that contains a *completed thought*.

So far, this is easy enough. But the structure of the sentence, with its combination of phrases and clauses, is not always so easy. So let us consider the different kinds of sentences, the common errors in their formation, and the general principles that govern their correct usage.

FOUR KINDS OF SENTENCES

Every sentence contains two basic elements—the subject and the predicate. Some sentences contain a single subject and a single predicate; others contain two or more subjects and two or more predicates. The subject of a sentence, you will recall, is the person, thing, or idea you are talking about. The predicate is what you are saying about the subject.

1. A sentence that contains a single subject and predicate is a *simple sentence*.

Example:

Eisenhower was elected President of the United States in 1952.

The above sentence has several phrases; but it has only one subject, *Eisenhower*, and only one predicate, *was elected President of the United States in 1952*. You will find little difficulty with this type of sentence. So let us go on to the other types.

2. A sentence that contains more than one subject and predicate—that is, more than one clause—joined by the conjunction *and, or, but, for*, or *nor*, is a *compound sentence*.

Example:

In 1952 Eisenhower was elected President, and Nixon was elected Vice-President; but Stevenson and Sparkman were defeated.

This sentence contains three *co-ordinate* clauses—that is, clauses of equal grammatical order or importance—each of which could be a simple sentence:

In 1952 Eisenhower was elected President.
Nixon was elected Vice-President.
Stevenson and Sparkman were defeated.

When you use a compound sentence of co-ordinate clauses be sure that your co-ordination is grammatically logical. The following sentence, for example, is wrong:

A good man *respects* his neighbors and never *seeking* a quarrel with them.

Change the sentence to read:

A good man *respects* his neighbors and never *seeks* a quarrel with them.

In the following anecdote, there is one incorrect sentence. See if you can spot it and make the correction:

A corpulent and exhausted shopper at Macy's found herself pushed to the rear of a crowded elevator. Glancing back, she was delighted to see a small brown seat in the corner. She sank down upon it thankfully, but it bursting into a loud yell. The seat turned out to be a little boy in a brown beret.

The incorrect sentence is: She sank down upon it thankfully, but it bursting into a loud yell.

Correct it to read: She sank down upon it thankfully, but it burst into a loud yell.

Errors in the compound sentence are not too frequent. Much more common are those committed in the next two types.

3. A sentence whose clauses are connected by conjunctions other than *and, but, or, for,* or *nor* is usually a *complex sentence*.

Example:

Eisenhower was elected by an overwhelming majority when he ran for the Presidency in 1952.

This complex sentence contains one principal clause, *Eisenhower was elected by an overwhelming majority*, and one subordinate clause, *when he ran for the Presidency in 1952*.

4. The most complicated type of sentence is a combination of co-ordinate clauses which are connected by the co-ordinating conjunctions *and, but, or, for,* or *nor,* and of subordinate clauses which are connected by the subordinating conjunctions, *that, if, when, although, where, why, since, because, unless,* and the like.

Example:

Eisenhower was elected by an overwhelming majority and most of the Republican candidates were swept into office when many of the voters decided that it was time for a change.

This sentence has four clauses:

Eisenhower was elected by an overwhelming majority
and most of the Republican candidates were swept into office
when many of the voters decided
that it was time for a change

The second clause, introduced by the co-ordinating conjunction *and,* makes the sentence *compound.*

The third and the fourth clauses, introduced by the subordinating conjunctions *when* and *that,* make the sentence *complex.*

Please note that the words *by, into, of,* and *between* are not conjunctions introducing clauses, but prepositions used in phrases.

AVOID SLOVENLY SENTENCES

Here are some of the pitfalls that you must avoid in the usage of the complex and the compound-complex sentences.

1. Don't confuse clauses with phrases. Don't say, for example:

Referring to Mrs. Jones, Mrs. Smith said, "I wish I were rich like she."

The word *like* is a preposition which takes the objective case in the phrase *like her.* Correct the sentence to read:

Referring to Mrs. Jones, Mrs. Smith said, "I wish I were rich like her."

2. Don't use an incorrect complex sentence where a simple sentence is required. Don't say:

A tornado is where a whirlwind blows under a funnel-shaped cloud.

Or:

A tie in a game is when the scores are equal.

The above errors are due to the substitution of subordinating conjunctions (where and when) for nouns. Correct the sentences to read:

A tornado is a whirlwind under a funnel-shaped cloud.
A tie in a game is an equal score.

3. Don't mix up your constructions in compound-complex sentences. The following sentence, for example, is wrong:

I should like to know how he came so quickly and did he take a taxi.

The two parallel things you would like to know should have parallel constructions. Correct the sentence as follows:

I should like to know *how* he came so quickly and *whether* he took a taxi.

4. Don't lose track of your construction in a compound-complex sentence. Can you tell, for example, why the following sentence is wrong?

She invited my brother and my sister to the party, and she invited even the girl who had taken her fiancé away from her, but never I, who had done her so many favors.

The pronoun *I* should be changed to *me*, the object of the verb *invited*. Don't let the distance between the subject and the object mislead you into the wrong case.

5. Don't use the expression *no sooner . . . when* in sentences such as the following:

I had no sooner arrived when he asked me for a loan.

The error in the above sentence is the result of confusing two ways of expressing the same idea. Either of the following two constructions will enable you to correct the sentence:

I had *hardly* (or *scarcely*) arrived *when* he asked me for a loan.
I had *no sooner* arrived *than* he asked me for a loan.

But the combination of *no sooner* with *when* is incorrect.

6. Don't make a subordinate clause look (incorrectly) like a co-ordinate clause through the insertion of the wrong conjunction. The following anecdote, for example, has one incorrect clause. See if you can spot it:

A famous biologist, who had unsuccessfully tried to teach a monkey to play ball, and who decided as a last resort to leave the little animal alone in a room with a bat and a ball. He closed the door, waited a moment, and then, very quietly, stooped and peered through the keyhole.

He found himself staring into an intent brown eye. The monkey was no less curious than he.

To correct the grammatical error in this anecdote, omit the words *and who* before the word *decided* in the first sentence.

7. Don't omit the connectives that introduce subordinate clauses. The following sentence is wrong:

The worst thing about history every time it repeats itself the price goes up.

The corrected sentence should read:

The worst thing about history *is that* every time it repeats itself the price goes up.

A comma might be substituted for *that*, and the sentence would be equally correct.

8. Don't mix up your subjects in the clauses of a complex sentence. One of the sentences in the following anecdote contains such a mix-up. Can you spot it?

A candidate for county sheriff was canvassing for votes in a small town in Oklahoma. After he had delivered an impassioned campaign speech to a prospective voter, the man was asked for his vote.

"Well, sir," said the voter, "you are my second choice."

The candidate, concluding that he could easily eliminate the voter's first choice by maligning the man, asked patronizingly, "And who is your first choice?"

"Well, sir, just anybody."

The second sentence in the first paragraph is wrong. Change the clause *the man was asked for his vote* to *he asked the man for his vote*. Both clauses in this sentence should have the same subject—the pronoun *he*, referring to the candidate.

9. Don't place your subordinate clauses in an awkward position. Note how ridiculous the following sentences sound because of misplaced clauses:

The teacher worked out a number of instructions for the students in his class which he had copyrighted.

I want a check book to present to my boy friend that folds in the middle.

Wanted—a boy to deliver telegrams that can ride on a bicycle.

These sentences, with the clauses properly rearranged, should read:

The teacher worked out for the students in his class a number of instructions which he had copyrighted.

I want a check book that folds in the middle to present to my boy friend.

Wanted—a boy that (or who) can ride on a bicycle to deliver telegrams.

The subordinate connectives, together with their clauses, should be placed near the words they modify: *instructions which, check book that, boy that.*

10. Don't put into a subordinate clause the principal idea of a sentence. The following sentence, while not incorrect, is rather feeble:

They dare not speak for the fallen and the weak, a fear which makes them slaves.

See how much more powerfully this idea has been expressed, in the words of James Russell Lowell:

They are slaves who dare not speak for the fallen and the weak.

Here the principal idea—*They are slaves*—becomes grammatically, as well as logically, the principal clause of the sentence.

In Chapter 22, we shall have more to say about the structure of the sentence—how to build it into a clear and logical and powerful unit. But, for the present, suppose you put to the test what you have thus far learned about the various types of sentences.

QUIZ TIME

Check and correct those of the following sentences that are wrong:

1. A wise statesman builds upon the past, but not overturning it.

2. He was examined by the draft board and found fit for service.

3. The superior man, said Confucius, is kind to his friends and just to his enemies.

4. The trouble with many of us we just slide along in life.

5. The difference between the right word and the almost right word, said Mark Twain, is the difference between the lightning and the lightning bug.

6. To insure a long life, observed Dr. Adolf Lorenz, be moderate in all things, but not missing anything.

7. They had a quarrel, whereupon he left the house, and his wife slamming the door after him.

8. She really believes that nobody is wiser than she.

9. Most men can stand up to their opponents, but a few men can stand up to their friends.

10. "When I first saw my face on the screen in a close-up, I jumped up and yelled, 'It's a lie!'" (*Joe E. Brown*)

11. A picnic is when people eat ham and egg and mosquito sandwiches.

12. The girl who thinks no man is good enough for her may be right—and she also may be left.

13. No sooner had he got into bed when the telephone rang.

14. Many of us, said Alexander Woollcott, spend half our time wishing for things we could have if we didn't spend half our time wishing.

15. It's one thing to itch for something and quite another thing scratching for it.

16. Wanted—a man to work on a Pennsylvania Dutch farm, to take care of chickens, cows and pigs who can speak German.

17. He was a boy scout, said Bob Hawk, until he was 16, and then becoming a girl scout.

18. Said the flea to the elephant as they crossed the little bridge, "Nobody can shake this bridge harder than you and me."

19. She wore a dress that the stripes made her look like a stick of Christmas candy.

20. She asked her brother could she borrow his car.

CORRECTIONS

1. A wise statesman builds upon the past, but does not overturn it.

2. This sentence is correct.

3. Correct.

4. The trouble with many of us is that we just slide along in life.

5. Correct.

6. To insure a long life, observed Dr. Adolf Lorenz, be moderate in all things, but don't miss anything.

7. Change the word *slamming* to *slammed*.

8. Correct.

9. Correct.

10. Correct.

11. A picnic is an occasion when people eat, etc.

12. Correct.

13. Change *when* to *than*.

14. Correct.

15. Change *scratching* to *to scratch*.

16. Wanted—a man who can speak German to work on a Pennsylvania Dutch farm, to take care of chickens, cows and pigs.

17. He was a boy scout, said Bob Hawk, until he was 16, and then he became a girl scout.

18. Change *me* to *I*.

19. Change *that the stripes* to *whose stripes*.

20. She asked her brother whether she could borrow his car.

Time out for the Nineteenth Word Game
FAMOUS NAMES IN HISTORY

Suppose you have been invited to a gathering where the conversation turns to historical matters. Would you be able to identify the great names that are mentioned, and would you know whether or not these names are correctly pronounced?

Let's put it to the test.

A

Check the correct calling, or profession, for each of the following names:

1. Amundsen, Roald
   (a) physician, (b) poet, (c) explorer, (d) soldier
2. Aquinas, Thomas
   (a) philosopher, (b) scientist, (c) painter,
   (d) crusader
3. Archimedes
   (a) dramatist, (b) statesman, (c) sculptor,
   (d) mathematician
4. Bartholdi, Frédéric Auguste
   (a) basketball star, (b) sculptor, (c) banker, (d) actor
5. Bolivar, Simon
   (a) composer, (b) capitalist, (c) liberator, (d) dancer
6. Cézanne, Paul
   (a) economist, (b) statesman, (c) motion picture
   producer, (d) painter
7. Damien, Joseph
   (a) missionary, (b) inventor, (c) general in Napoleon's
   army, (d) violinist
8. Demosthenes
   (a) philosopher, (b) orator, (c) dramatist,
   (d) marathon runner
9. De Soto, Hernando
   (a) automobile manufacturer, (b) inventor,
   (c) archbishop, (d) explorer
10. Ehrlich, Paul
    (a) short-story writer, (b) theatrical producer,
    (c) physician, (d) educator
11. Empedocles
    (a) philosopher, (b) general, (c) dramatist,
    (d) sculptor
12. Euripides
    (a) dramatist, (b) philosopher, (c) mathematician,
    (d) sculptor
13. Faraday, Michael
    (a) poet, (b) capitalist, (c) clergyman, (d) scientist
14. Fitzgerald, Edward
    (a) statesman, (b) poet, (c) manufacturer,
    (d) college president
15. Fox, George
    (a) judge, (b) motion picture producer,
    (c) religious leader, (d) revolutionary soldier
16. Garibaldi, Giuseppe
    (a) wrestler, (b) actor, (c) patriot, (d) composer

17. Genghis Khan (also spelled Jenghiz Khan)
    (a) crusader, (b) wrestler, (c) conqueror,
    (d) capitalist
18. Grenfell, Wilfred Thomason
    (a) medical missionary, (b) admiral, (c) playwright,
    (d) football coach
19. Herodotus
    (a) statesman, (b) philosopher, (c) physician,
    (d) historian
20. Homer, Winslow
    (a) poet, (b) inventor, (c) painter, (d) historian
21. Howe, Elias
    (a) chain-store owner, (b) astronomer,
    (c) college president, (d) inventor
22. Kepler, Johannes
    (a) astronomer, (b) admiral, (c) poet, (d) statesman
23. Lavoisier, Antoine Laurent
    (a) revolutionist, (b) opera singer, (c) statesman,
    (d) chemist
24. Livingstone, David
    (a) explorer, (b) inventor, (c) educator,
    (d) statesman
25. Lucretius
    (a) emperor, (b) soldier, (c) poet, (d) conspirator
26. Montezuma
    (a) capitalist, (b) emperor, (c) dancer,
    (d) swordsman
27. Phidias
    (a) general, (b) philosopher, (c) playwright,
    (d) sculptor
28. Reinhardt, Max
    (a) theater director, (b) dancer, (c) composer,
    (d) philanthropist
29. Rembrandt van Rijn
    (a) clergyman, (b) statesman, (c) educator,
    (d) painter
30. Rimski-Korsakov
    (a) composer, (b) dancer, (c) emperor,
    (d) revolutionist
31. Robespierre
    (a) pianist, (b) orchestra conductor, (c) revolutionist,
    (d) sculptor
32. Rodin, Auguste

240

(a) sculptor, (b) tennis champion, (c) singer, (d) educator

33. Savonarola, Girolamo
    (a) religious reformer, (b) sculptor, (c) statesman, (d) composer

34. Sienkiewicz, Henryk
    (a) pianist, (b) wrestler, (c) writer, (d) emperor

35. Synge, John Millington
    (a) poet, (b) football star, (c) labor leader, (d) capitalist

36. Tagore, Rabindranath
    (a) magician, (b) poet, (c) prince, (d) biologist

37. Toussaint L'Ouverture
    (a) poet, (b) composer, (c) liberator, (d) opera singer

38. Thucydides
    (a) historian, (b) general, (c) dramatist, (d) orator

39. Undset, Sigrid
    (a) delegate to the U.N., (b) tennis star, (c) novelist, (d) swimming star

40. Vespucci, Amerigo
    (a) soldier, (b) navigator, (c) painter, (d) scientist

—*Answers*—

1-c, Swiss explorer who discovered the South Pole (1911)

2-a, famous Catholic philosopher (1225?–1274?)

3-d, Greek mathematician, famous for the "displacement principle" in physics, a law he discovered while taking a bath (3d century B.C.)

4-b, French sculptor of the Statue of Liberty (1834–1904)

5-c, South American liberator (1783–1830)

6-d, French painter (1839–1906)

7-a, Belgian missionary to the lepers in Molokai (1840–1889)

8-b, Athenian orator (4th century B.C.)

9-d, Spanish explorer who was the first European to cross the Mississippi (in 1541)

10-c, German physician (1854–1915) who discovered the famous "606 drug" for syphilis

11-a, Greek philosopher (5th century B.C.)

12-a, Greek dramatist (5th century B.C.)

13-d, English chemist and physicist (1791–1867)

14-b, English poet (1809–1883), translator of the *Rubaiyat* by Omar Khayyam

15-c, English founder of the Society of Friends, or Quakers (1624–1691)

16-c, Italian patriot (1807–1882)

17-c, Asiatic conqueror (1162?–1227)

18-a, English medical missionary to Labrador (1865–1940)

19-d, Greek historian (5th century B.C.), known as the "Father of History"

20-c, American painter (1836–1910)

21-d, American inventor of the sewing machine (1819–1867)

22-a, German astronomer (1571–1630)

23-d, French chemist (1743–1794), who died on the guillotine in the Reign of Terror

24-a, Scottish explorer in Africa (1813–1873)

25-c, Roman poet (1st century B.C.)

26-b, last Aztec emperor of Mexico (1480?–1520)

27-d, Greek sculptor (5th century B.C.)

28-a, German dramatist and theater director (1873–1943)

29-d, Dutch painter (1609–1669)

30-a, Russian composer (1844–1908)

31-c, one of the leaders of the French Revolution (1758–1794)

32-a, French sculptor (1840–1917)

33-a, Italian religious reformer, excommunicated, tortured and hanged (1452–1498)

34-c, Polish novelist, author of *Quo Vadis* (1846–1916)

35-a, Irish poet and playwright (1871–1909)

36-b, Hindu poet (1861–1941)

37-c, Haitian general and liberator (1743–1803)

38-a, Greek historian (5th century B.C.)

39-c, Norwegian novelist, author of *Kristin Lavransdatter* (1882–   )

40-b, Italian navigator (1451–1512), after whom America is named

B

Check whether each of the following statements is right or wrong:

1. Thomas Aquinas lived before Phidias. Right Wrong
2. Amundsen discovered the South Pole. Right Wrong
3. Demosthenes wrote a history of Greece. Right Wrong
4. Faraday was the author of *Robinson*

242

Crusoe. Right Wrong

5. George Fox was a famous Quaker. Right Wrong

6. Garibaldi was one of Mussolini's generals. Right Wrong

7. Edward Fitzgerald wrote *Tales of the Jazz Age* (1922). Right Wrong

8. Winslow Homer is most famous for the *Iliad* and the *Odyssey*. Right Wrong

9. Herodotus is known as the "Father of History." Right Wrong

10. Elias Howe was the inventor of the sewing machine. Right Wrong

11. Montezuma was a South American financier. Right Wrong

12. Bartholdi designed the Empire State Building. Right Wrong

13. Archimedes lived before Christ. Right Wrong

14. Bolivar was a Mexican explorer. Right Wrong

15. Cézanne was a painter. Right Wrong

16. Euripides was a great dramatist. Right Wrong

17. Damien was a medical missionary in Labrador. Right Wrong

18. Lavoisier lived before Stalin. Right Wrong

19. Livingstone discovered the "606 drug." Right Wrong

20. Lucretius was a Latin poet. Right Wrong

21. De Soto organized the De Soto Automobile Company. Right Wrong

22. Empedocles was a great Athenian orator. Right Wrong

23. Ehrlich was a psychoanalyst. Right Wrong

24. Kepler was an astronomer. Right Wrong

25. Genghis Khan was the grandfather of Ali Khan. Right Wrong

26. Grenfell was a British admiral. Right Wrong

27. Toussaint L'Ouverture fought for the liberation of Haiti. Right Wrong

28. Phidias was a famous general. Right Wrong

29. Tagore lived before Christ. Right Wrong

30. Reinhardt did his important work in the 20th century. Right Wrong

31. Synge was a great Irish playwright. Right Wrong

32. Rembrandt was a Dutch painter. Right Wrong

33. Sienkiewicz wrote *Quo Vadis*.   Right   Wrong

34. Rimski-Korsakov was a Russian
general in World War II.   Right   Wrong

35. Savonarola was a religious martyr.   Right   Wrong

36. Vespucci was a composer of grand
operas.   Right   Wrong

37. Robespierre was a French
revolutionist.   Right   Wrong

38. Rodin lived in the 18th century.   Right   Wrong

39. Sigrid Undset was a famous opera
singer.   Right   Wrong

40. Thucydides and Herodotus are famous
in the same field.   Right   Wrong

—Answers—

1-wrong, 2-right, 3-wrong, 4-wrong, 5-right, 6-wrong, 7-wrong (the author of that book was F. Scott Fitzgerald), 8-wrong, 9-right, 10-right, 11-wrong, 12-wrong, 13-right, 14-wrong, 15-right, 16-right, 17-wrong, 18-right, 19-wrong, 20-right, 21-wrong, 22-wrong, 23-wrong, 24-right, 25-wrong, 26-wrong, 27-right, 28-wrong, 29-wrong, 30-right, 31-right, 32-right, 33-right, 34-wrong, 35-right, 36-wrong, 37-right, 38-wrong, 39-wrong, 40-right

C

As you get the pronunciation of the names of the great characters of history, make sure that you can identify their occupations and recall their approximate dates:

Amundsen: AM-und-sen
Aquinas: a-KWIGH-nas
Archimedes: ar-ki-MEE-deez
Bolivar: BOL-i-ver, or bo-LEE-var
Cézanne: say-ZAHN
Damien: dahm-YAN
Demosthenes: de-MOS-the-neez
Ehrlich: AIR-lik
Empedocles: em-PED-o-kleez
Euripides: you-RIP-i-deez
Genghis Khan: JEN-gis KAHN
Herodotus: her-OD-o-tus
Lavoisier: lav-woz-YAY, to rhyme with pay
Lucretius: loo-KREE-shus, or loo-KREE-shi-us
Montezuma: mon-te-ZOO-ma

Phidias: FID-ee-as
Reinhardt: RINE-hart
Rembrandt van Rijn: REM-brant van RINE
Rimski-Korsakov: RIMS-ki-KOR-sa-koff
Robespierre: robe-es-PYAIR
Rodin: roe-DAN
Savonarola: sav-o-na-ROE-la
Sienkiewicz: shenk-YAY (to rhyme with *may*)-vich
Synge: SING
Tagore: ta-GORE
Toussaint L'Ouverture: too-SAN loo-ver-TURE
Thucydides: thew-SID-i-deez
Undset: OON-set
Vespucci: ves-POOT-chee

22

HOW TO HANDLE YOUR SENTENCES

SIMPLE SENTENCES AND COMMON SENSE

The sentence is the basic unit in the expression of your thoughts. To make yourself clearly understood, you must learn to use clear-cut sentences. As a general rule, the *simple* sentence is the best conveyer of facts and ideas.

In other words, plain talk is the surest way to a better understanding between yourself and the rest of the world.

This truth was recognized three hundred years ago, when Samuel Butler objected to the use of complicated sentences. "Some writers," he declared, "have the unhappiness . . . to affect an obscurity in their styles, endeavoring by all means not to be understood, but rather to cast a mist before the eyes of their readers . . . To write not to be understood is no less vain than to speak not to be heard . . . [such writers] are like citizens that choose the darkest streets [for selling their goods], or make false lights that the spots and stains of their stuffs may not be perceived . . . [These obscure writers aim at] the admiration of the weak and ignorant, who are apt to contemn whatsoever they can understand, and admire anything they cannot."

This advice is as sound today as it was in the day of Samuel Butler. The *best* writing, from the Bible to Hemingway, is the *simplest* writing. And this holds equally true of the best speaking. The ultimate goal of effective English is plain talk, conveyed in sentences that are easy to understand.

Before we come to the formula for plain and easy-to-understand sentences, let us look at a few samples—some of them clear, and others obscure:

1. "Let every man honor and love the land of his birth and the race from which he springs. It is a pious and honorable duty. But let us have done with British-Americans and Irish-Americans and German-Americans, and so

on. If a man is going to be an American at all, let him be so without any qualifying adjectives. And if he is going to be something else, let him drop the word American from his personal description."

—*Henry Cabot Lodge, Senior*

2. In a lecture on the simplicity of Lincoln's style, a college professor made the following erudite observation: "May I call your attention to the monosyllabic lucidity of Abraham Lincoln, who generally—nay, almost always—expressed his thoughts in uninvolved phraseology, devoid of any abstractions and allegorical allusions that might have mystified the minds of his none too intellectual constituents."

3. "I saw a tanager flying through the foliage as if it would set the leaves on fire."   —*Henry David Thoreau*

4. "Saddle your dream before you ride it if you want to avoid a painful jolt."

5. And Jesus said unto a certain lawyer:
"A certain man went down from Jerusalem to Jericho, and fell among thieves, who stripped him and wounded him and left him half dead. And by chance there came down a certain priest that way; and when he saw him, he passed by on the other side. And, likewise, a Levite came and looked on him, and passed by on the other side.

"But a certain Samaritan, as he journeyed, came where he was; and when he saw him, he had compassion on him, and went to him, and bound up his wounds, pouring in oil and wine, and set him on his own beast, and brought him to an inn, and took care of him.

"And on the morrow, when he departed, he took out two pence, and gave them to the host, and said unto him, 'Take care of him; and whatsoever thou spendest more, I will repay thee.'

"Which now of these three, thinkest thou, was neighbour unto him that fell among the thieves?"
And the lawyer said, "He that showed mercy to him."
Then said Jesus, "Go, and do thou likewise."

In these selections, it is easy to distinguish between the clear and the obscure sentences. Now if you will glance at them again, you will find that the clearest among them possess one or more features in common.

The clear sentences are generally short. They consist largely of simple words. They are built around verbs of action. They move in a straight line, containing either a single idea or a group of associated ideas. They are free from expressions that would clutter up the thought. And they talk, as a rule, about people; in other words, they have human interest.

Suppose we look a little more closely at these common features of the more effective sentences.

1. GOOD SENTENCES ARE SHORT

A number of tests have been made to determine the standard length of a sentence that is neither too elementary nor too advanced for the average person. It has been found that the best sentences of this type contain about 17 words. This does not mean that all your sentences should be cut to this exact measure. But it does mean that your speech or your writing is too "low-brow" if it averages much *less* than 17 words to a sentence, and too "high-brow" if it averages much *more* than 17 words.

The 17-word average, you will find, comes pretty close to the standard of such popular magazines as the *Reader's Digest* and the *Saturday Evening Post*. No doubt this is one of the reasons for the wide circulation of these magazines. The less popular (or more intellectual) magazines, like *Harper's* and the *Atlantic Monthly*, generally contain longer and more involved sentences.

If, therefore, you want an *immediate and popular* response to your own speaking or writing, try to adapt your sentences to the standard size. You will find an excellent example of this sort of style in Lincoln's First Inaugural Address. Here are a few sentences taken from the ending of this address:

"... I am loath to close. We are not enemies, but friends. We must not be enemies. Though passion may have strained, it must not break, our bonds of affection. The mystic chords of memory, stretching from every battlefield and over this broad land, will yet swell the chorus of the Union when again touched, as surely they will be, by the better angels of our nature."

Note the combination of shorter and longer sentences that average into a balance of plain and beautiful and effective speech. Though the average is somewhat less than 17 words, it is close enough to fit the required standard.

And note also, in the last and longest sentence, the un-broken continuity of the thought, which conveys the single idea of a reunited nation from beginning to end.

And so the first requisite for a clear, comprehensible style is to write sentences that, on the whole, are not very long, although they may vary in length.

2. GOOD SENTENCES CONSIST OF SIMPLE WORDS

The second requisite for a good style is to use simple instead of difficult words in the building of your sentences. As a general rule, it is best to avoid such words as *transcend*, *annihilate*, *redress*, *presuppose*, *quiescence*, *circumlocution*, *conducive*, and the like. All these words, you will note, have either a *prefix*, like *trans-*, or a *suffix*, like *-cence*, tacked on to the beginning or to the end. These additional syllables tend to complicate the meanings of your words and to stifle your sentences.

Here are some simple translations for the above *prefix* or *suffix* words:

transcend, to rise above (in excellence or degree)
annihilate, to wipe out
redress, to right (a wrong) by payment or punishment.
presuppose, to take for granted
quiescence, silent, still, quiet
circumlocution, roundabout talk
conducive, helpful toward a result

Try, for the most part, to use words that are short, familiar, clear, and direct—such as *renew* instead of *renovate*, *ease* instead of *facility*, *goal* instead of *objective*, *a red sunset* instead of *a crimson reflection of the declining sun*, *he wrote the story out of his own head* instead of *he conceived and executed the story solely and entirely by himself*.

It is the simple words, combined into simple sentences, that produce the most powerful results. Note, for example, the following passage from the *Sermon on the Mount*—the greatest of all speeches ever delivered on earth:

"You are the salt of the earth; but if the salt have lost its savor, wherewith shall it be salted? It is thenceforth good for nothing but to be cast out, and to be trodden underfoot.

"You are the light of the world. A city that is set on a hill cannot be hid. Neither do men light a candle, and put it under a bushel, but on a candlestick . . . Let your light so shine before men, that they may see your good works, and glorify your Father in Heaven."

And this brings us to the third requisite for a good English sentence.

3. GOOD SENTENCES HAVE COLORFUL VERBS

As we noted in an earlier part of this book, it is the verb that gives the go and the glow to a sentence. Look again at the vivid picture of the tanager painted against the background of the trees: "I saw a tanager flying through the foliage as if it would set the leaves on fire." Can you ever forget this picture as it darts into living color before your eyes? And all this color comes to life and catches fire through the skillful handling of the verb. See how much of the vitality you would lose if you omitted the verb phrase *set on fire*. The sentence, with this omission, would fade into some such inferior picture as the following: "I saw a tanager flying through the foliage with wings suggesting a kindling flame."

And now recall the story of the Good Samaritan. You get the vigorous effect of this story through the actions of several verbs—*fell* among thieves, *stripped* him, *wounded* him, *passed* by on the other side, *had compassion* on him, *bound up* his wounds, *set* him on his own beast, *brought* him to an inn, and so on.

Note also how the story moves into its climax with the two simple verbs of action—*go*, and *do* thou likewise.

4. GOOD SENTENCES ARE DIRECT

The fourth requisite for a good sentence is to keep it free from cumbersome constructions. Don't crisscross your phrases and clauses into a tangle that might confuse your listener or reader. This sort of tangled confusion has been called "tapeworm English." Try to avoid it if you want to be clearly understood. Make your sentences move in a straight line from beginning to end.

Here is an example of "tapeworm English"—a good idea that has become snarled into a mass of crisscross phrases and clauses:

In the journey of life, whatever paths it may be our choice or fortune to pursue, and whatever vehicles—however slow or fast their motion—we may decide or be compelled to use, we shall all arrive at one and the same destination. Consequently, even though some of us may crawl on our knees, while others may ride on horseback or in motor-cars, while still others, for the purpose of earlier arrival, outspeed the carrier-pigeon in airplanes, we shall find that there has been no necessity for undue haste, since it is certain that all of us shall duly arrive at the journey's end.

See how much better this idea sounds if you break it up into shorter sentences, untangle the constructions, and omit or simplify the words that tend to obscure the thought:

"In the journey of life, all roads lead to the same destination. And all vehicles, however slow or fast, will bring us to the goal at the appointed time. Some of us crawl on our knees, some ride on horseback or in motor-cars, others fly past the carrier-pigeon in airplanes. There is no need for hurry; we are all sure to reach the journey's end."
—*Axel Munthe*

One of the chief improvements in the above passage, as you may have noted, is the omission of unnecessary words or digressions. And this brings us to the fifth requisite for a good sentence.

5. GOOD SENTENCES HAVE FEW EMPTY WORDS

Unnecessary or "empty" words—words that add nothing to the force, color, clarity, or meaning of your sentence—ought to be avoided. Such words make your writing weak or fuzzy. Here is a partial list of them:

along the lines of	instead of	*like*
consequently	" "	*and so,* or *so*
dead rather than alive	" "	*dead*
red in color	" "	*red*
for the purpose of	" "	*to*
for the reason that	" "	*since*
furthermore	" "	*then*
in the event that	" "	*if*
in the nature of	" "	*like*
likewise	" "	*and*
during the time that	" "	*while*
come in contact with	" "	*meet*
one and the same	" "	*the same*

251

panacea for all ills	"	"	panacea
seems evident	"	"	seems
five in number	"	"	five
different in character	"	"	different
with the result that	"	"	so that

These are but a few samples of the verbal deadwood that may clutter up the current of your thought. Avoid these, as well as any other expressions that are obscure, superfluous, cumbersome, or abstract. Keep your sentences free of any words or phrases that fail to carry your thought straight ahead.

6. GOOD SENTENCES HAVE HUMAN INTEREST

In addition to making your sentences short, simple, colorful, connected, and straight to the point, try to make them alive. One of the best ways to do this is to talk about living people. No matter what your subject, you can give it the human touch if you relate it to the human interests of your audience.

Suppose, for example, you want to show how cheerfulness is superior to sadness. See how vivid the idea becomes when you apply it to the actual experience of your reader, and note particularly the use of the pronouns:

> "Laugh, and the world laughs with you; weep, and you weep alone."

Or suppose you want to consider a question that is purely philosophical: Is there any divine pattern in the universe? This question, you will agree, is quite abstract and remote. And yet see how concrete and immediate it becomes when you describe it in terms of everyday experience. Note the following, for example:

> "Some say that to the gods we are like the flies that the boys kill on a summer day; and some say, on the contrary, that the very sparrows do not lose a feather that has not been brushed by the finger of God." —*Thornton Wilder*

People are the most interesting subject in the world. "I am a man," wrote the Latin poet, Plautus, "and everything that is human is close to my heart." Bear this in mind whenever you speak or write. If you want your sentences to strike home, address them to the personal interests of your listeners or readers. People are most concerned either about themselves or about other people. So talk about people. If you want to discuss a battle, tell about an eye-witness *to the* battle or, still better, about a participant *in* the battle. If you want to report a Congressional hearing, don't talk abstractly about the various views represented at the hearing; talk about them rather in terms of the various people who represent these views. If you tell about a tornado, the best way to describe its fury is to describe the plight of those who are caught in its path. The same principle applies to any subject you may discuss—all the way from an atom to a star. Any idea becomes alive when you exhibit it in the light of human experience. In all your speaking and writing, try to picture *persons* as well as *things* and *ideas*.

TEST YOUR SKILL

Rewrite the following quotation in accordance with the principles outlined in this chapter. That is, make the sentences shorter, simpler, more colorful, more direct, less clumsy, and more alive. Delete superfluous words. Where you find an abstract word or phrase, make it concrete. Use short words. Use plenty of personal pronouns to connect the reader with your text.

The following is, in substance, an excerpt from the philosophy of Jesus:

"The principal considerations in this life, as many would assume, are food and drink and clothing—a philosophy with which I thoroughly disagree. Consequently I declare that the core of existence is concerned with other issues besides mere subsistence and raiment. Let me emphasize this idea by means of a number of comparisons between human beings on the one hand, and the much lower, ephemeral forms of living things on the other hand. Just as the birds and the flowers and the grasses are fed and sheltered and gorgeously tinted and supplied with feathers and foliage, even though they are without labor or care or even awareness of their needs, so too must you, in spite of the inadequacy of your faith, assume the providential goodness of God to supply the necessities of your life without any vexation on your part."

Now compare your version with the words of Jesus as translated in the King James version of the Bible:

"Therefore I say unto you, take no thought for your life, what ye shall eat, or what ye shall drink; nor yet for your body, what ye shall put on. Is not the life more than meat, and the body than raiment? Behold the fowls of the air.

For they sow not, neither do they reap, nor gather into barns; yet your heavenly Father feedeth them. Are ye not much better than they? Why take ye thought for raiment? Consider the lilies of the field, how they grow. They toil not, neither do they spin; and yet I say unto you that even Solomon in all his glory was not arrayed like one of these. Wherefore, if God so clothe the grass of the field, which today is, and tomorrow is cast into the oven, shall He not much more clothe you, O ye of little faith?"

And now, having observed how some of the greatest writers have turned their sentences into instruments of beauty and understanding and persuasion and power, "Go, and do thou likewise."

Time out for the Twentieth Word Game
MANIAS AND PHOBIAS

One of the most important sciences of our day is psychiatry, which is the treatment of mental illness. Although it is a relatively new field, many of its discoveries have been made widely known by books and motion pictures. We frequently come across the words used by psychiatrists, especially those that describe the various abnormalities known as *manias* and *phobias*.

The Greek word *mania* means *madness*, and the Greek word *phobia* means *fear*. Every English word that ends in *mania* denotes a strong or irrational craving for something, or an infatuation with it. Words that end in *phobia* mean just the opposite; they describe a deep fear or hatred of something.

In this game we shall play with the words that denote some of the more common manias and phobias. See how many of them apply to your own or to your friends' pet addictions or aversions:

A

1. *Agromania* means a morbid desire to live in the open country, especially in solitude.
2. *Bibliomania* means an intense passion for collecting books.

3. *Dipsomania* means an abnormal craving for drink.

4. *Egomania means* an excessive and morbid love of oneself.

5. *Kleptomania* means an uncontrollable urge to steal.

6. *Megalomania* means an exaggerated worship of one's own greatness. There is, for example, an interesting story told about Teddy Roosevelt, who, according to some of his contemporaries, was addicted to megalomania. When Roosevelt came to heaven, so the story goes, he set about reorganizing the celestial choir. "What you need," he said to Saint Peter, "is a hundred thousand sopranos, a hundred thousand tenors, and a hundred thousand baritones."

"What about the bassos?" asked Saint Peter.

"I," replied Teddy Roosevelt, "sing basso."

7. *Monomania* means an obsession with one particular object or idea. On everything else except his own pet delusion the monomaniac may be absolutely sane.

8. *Nymphomania* means ungovernable sexual desire on the part of a woman.

9. *Plutomania* means a madness for money.

10. *Pyromania* means a morbid urge to set things on fire.

And now, for the other side of the picture—the mental disorders known as *phobias:*

1. *Ailurophobia* means a strong fear of cats.

2. *Androphobia* means an irrational fear of men.

3. *Claustrophobia* means an excessive dread of enclosed places, a deep fear of being locked in.

4. *Cynophobia* means a morbid fear of dogs.

5. *Hydrophobia* means an overpowering dread of water; this is also the medical term for the disease resulting from the bite of a mad dog.

6. *Hypsophobia* (also called *Acrophobia*) means an uncontrollable fear of high places.

7. *Nyctophobia* means an excessive fear of night or of darkness.

8. *Thanatophobia* means an irrational fear of death.

9. *Triskaidekaphobia* means fear of the number 13.

10. *Xenophobia* means an aversion to strangers or foreigners.

B

Have you learned the meanings of the above *manias* and *phobias?* See if you can check them for yourself. State the disease which would apply to each of the following statements:

Statement	*Disease*

1. She gets frightened at the sight of a dog.   c_____

2. She is an inveterate shoplifter.   k_____

3. Poor fellow, he can't help his craving for drink.   d_____

4. He is obsessed with a single passion, an overpowering desire for revenge.   m_____

5. She gets frightened when she looks down over a precipice.   h_____

6. He exaggerates his own greatness.   m_____

7. He is afraid of the number 13.   t_____

8. She gets frightened when she is left alone in a small room.   c_____

9. She fears men.   a_____

10. He has a morbid hunger for the wide open spaces.   a_____

11. She loves herself to distraction.   e_____

12. The little boy has been bitten by a mad dog.   h_____

13. He has an excessive fear of death.   t_____

14. She spends all her time collecting books.   b_____

15. He loves riches above everything else.   p_____

16. He is suspicious of all strangers.   x_____

17. She is terribly afraid of the dark.   n_____

18. The sound of a cat's meow makes her flee.   a_____

19. She has an insatiable passion for sex.   n_____

20. He can't help setting fires.   p_____

—Answers—

1-cynophobia, 2-kleptomania, 3-dipsomania, 4-monomania, 5-hypsophobia or acrophobia, 6-megalomania, 7-triskaidekaphobia, 8-claustrophobia, 9-androphobia, 10-agromania, 11-egomania, 12-hydrophobia, 13-thanatophobia, 14-bibliomania, 15-plutomania, 16-xenophobia, 17-nyctophobia, 18-ailurophobia, 19-nymphomania, 20-pyromania

C

And now, check the words on the right with the definitions on the left:

1. agromania	a. an irrational aversion to men
2. kleptomania	b. an irrational love for riches
3. androphobia	c. a fear of heights
4. monomania	d. a fear of cats
5. xenophobia	e. a morbid self-love
6. nyctophobia	f. a passion for collecting books
7. dipsomania	g. a morbid fear of night
8. bibliomania	h. a fear of number 13
9. triskaidekaphobia	i. an uncontrollable urge to steal
10. ailurophobia	j. a passion for open spaces
11. egomania	k. a morbid fear of enclosed places
12. cynophobia	l. delusions of grandeur
13. megalomania	m. a fear of dogs
14. nymphomania	n. a morbid fear of death
15. hydrophobia	o. an abnormal obsession with a single object or idea
16. plutomania	p. a morbid fear of water
17. claustrophobia	q. a compulsion to set fires
18. pyromania	r. a woman's excessive desire for sex
19. thanatophobia	s. an uncontrollable thirst for alcoholic drink
20. hypsophobia	t. an aversion to strangers

—*Answers*—

1-j, 2-i, 3-a, 4-o, 5-t, 6-g, 7-s, 8-f, 9-h, 10-d, 11-e, 12-m, 13-l, 14-r, 15-p, 16-b, 17-k, 18-q, 19-n, 20-c

D

Some of the words we have used in this game are fairly common; others, I grant, are on the learned side, and do not crop up in conversation much. However, you should know their pronunciation. Here are the harder-to-pronounce words:

egomania: ee-go-MAY-nee-a, or egg-o-MAY-nee-a
megalomania: meg-a-lo-MAY-nee-a
pyromania: pigh-ro-MAY-nee-a
ailurophobia: ay (as in *may*)-lew-ro-FOE-bee-a
claustrophobia: closs-tro-FOE-bee-a
cynophobia: sin-o-FOE-bee-a
hypsophobia: hip-so-FOE-bee-a
nyctophobia: nik-to-FOE-bee-a

thanatophobia: than-a-to-FOE-bee-a (pronounce the *th* as in *thank*)

triskaidekaphobia: triss-kigh-dek-a-FOE-bee-a

xenophobia: zen-o-FOE-bee-a

23

THE TRAFFIC LIGHTS OF MEANING—PUNCTUATION

SENSE AND NONSENSE

A young man, having quarreled with his fiancée, sent her the following note:

"Woman without her man is a savage."

In reply, the young lady returned the note with some additional "explanatory" punctuation:

"Woman! without her, man is a savage."

Punctuation is often of the utmost importance in bringing out the meaning of a sentence. Change the punctuation, and you may change the meaning. There is a classic story about the manner in which the philosopher Voltaire "outpunctuated" his friend, King Frederick the Great. Once, when the king was offended with Voltaire, he issued a public message: "Frederick the Great declares Voltaire is an ass." But the philosopher turned the tables against the king by the insertion of two commas: "Frederick the Great, declares Voltaire, is an ass."

Here are two bits of doggerel that sound nonsensical without the proper punctuation:

1. Every lady in this land
   Hath twenty nails upon each hand
   Five and twenty on hands and feet
   This is true without deceit

2. A funny little man told this to me
   I fell in a snowdrift in June said he
   I went to a ball game out in the sea
   I saw a jellyfish float up in a tree
   I fed the birds with a big brass key

I opened my door on my bended knee
I beg your pardon for this said he
But 'tis true when told as it ought to be

Punctuate these poems properly, and you get complete sentences and a semblance of sense:

1. Every lady in this land
   Hath twenty nails; upon each hand,
   Five, and twenty on hands and feet;
   This is true without deceit.

2. A funny little man told this to me:
   "I fell in a snowdrift; in June," said he,
   "I went to a ball game; out in the sea
   I saw a jellyfish float; up in a tree
   I fed the birds; with a big brass key
   I opened my door; on my bended knee
   I beg your pardon for this," said he,
   "But 'tis true when told as it ought to be."

AN IMPORTANT RULE

In the matter of punctuation (and word spacing) we are luckier than the ancients. The Greek and the Latin manuscripts that have come down to our own day are written in solid lines without any breaks whatsoever. It is a physical and mental torture to read them, as you can see for yourself when you try to read the following English passage arranged in the non-punctuated style of the classical manuscripts:

Tellusnotinmournfulnumberslifeisbutanemptydreamand-
thesoulisdeadthatslumbersandthingsarenotwhattheyseem

It was not until the fifteenth century that punctuation was invented. Today it serves as a convenient system of "stop" and "go" signals in reading a manuscript. It enables you to reach the writer's mind as quickly as possible without getting snarled up in the traffic of the sentences.

One of the purposes of punctuation is to represent the modulations of the voice. When you speak, you raise or lower your voice, you make shorter or longer pauses, and you emphasize some words or phrases at the expense of others. You use all these pauses and inflections to convey the subtle coloring of your thoughts. But when you put your thoughts in writing, you substitute symbols for sounds. Punctuation does for the eye what inflection does for the ear.

Bear this in mind, and you will find punctuation rather easy to handle most of the time. As a general rule, you can rely upon your common sense in selecting the correct and emphatic punctuation marks. Use a comma to mark a slight pause, a semicolon to denote a somewhat longer pause, and a period to indicate a full stop.

But this isn't the whole story. You can't always rely upon your own judgment. Writers, printers, and publishers have set up a conventional system of punctuation. If you don't follow this system, you are likely to disturb or confuse your reader sometimes.

This conventional punctuation, however, should cause you little trouble if you remember a few simple rules.

Here they are:

COMMA—SLOW DOWN

1. Use commas to separate the equal parts of a series. For example:

He was determined to advance, to persevere, and to reach the goal.

The following inscription marked the grave of an army mule in France:

"In memory of Maggie who in her time kicked two colonels, four majors, ten captains, a hundred privates, and one stick of dynamite."

The present tendency is to *omit* the comma before the last item of a series: "a hundred privates and one stick of dynamite." But if you prefer to use a comma in such a construction, you have plenty of good authority for your preference.

2. Use a comma at the end of a series when the omission would confuse the meaning. For example:

The Communists allowed nothing to be published except books, pamphlets, and papers, which had secured the approval of the dictator.

The omission of the comma after *papers* would seem to imply that the papers alone needed the approval of the dictator. The inclusion of the comma makes it clear that the books and the pamphlets are included with the papers in the Communist order against the publication of material without the permission of the dictator.

3. Use a comma to introduce a short quotation. Example:

Explaining his forced retirement from West Point on his failure in a chemistry examination, Whistler remarked, "If silicon had been a gas, I would have been a major general."

4. Use commas to set off addresses and dates. Example:

Here is the epitaph on a tombstone set up at Medway, Massachusetts, to Peter Daniels, who was born August 7, 1688, and died May 20, 1746:

> Beneath this stone, a lump of clay,
> Lies Uncle Peter Daniels
> Who too early in the month of May
> Took off his winter flannels.

5. Use commas to separate a parenthetical expression (a word or phrase inserted by way of comment, and not strictly required) from the rest of the sentence:

This sentence, for example, is an illustration of the above rule.

6. Use a comma to separate a dependent clause from the principal clause, when the principal clause *follows* the dependent clause:

When they arrived at the theater, the curtain had already gone up.

But you may omit the comma when the principal clause *precedes* the dependent clause:

The curtain had already gone up when they arrived at the theater.

7. Use a comma to separate the contrasted elements in a sentence. For example:

Many are called, but few are chosen.

The true spirit of conversation consists in building upon another man's observation, not in arguing against it.

8. Use commas to set off the name of a person who is addressed, as in the second of the following sentences:

One day an annoying bore accosted Mark Twain on the street.

"Well, Mr. Clemens, what's going on?"

"I am," replied Mark Twain as he hurried away.

9. Use commas to set off an absolute expression—that is, an expression which is grammatically independent of the rest of the sentence:

"I'm a smash hit," boasted a conceited actor to Bernard Shaw. "Yesterday, the closing scene having been practically finished, I had the audience glued in their seats to the very last word."

"Wonderful!" exclaimed Shaw. "How clever of you to think of the glue!"

10. Use a comma between any two parts of a sentence which, without the comma, would be improperly connected and therefore misunderstood by the reader of the sentence.

Example:

He decided to go home, as I was coming to relieve him.

The word *as*, in the above sentence, means *since*, or *because*. Omit the comma, and the same word might mean *when*.

The above rules will not cover every use of the comma. But, together with the general formula that a comma represents a slight pause in the reading, they should help you to decide when this mark of punctuation is needed.

SEMICOLON—WATCH YOUR STEP

1. Use a semicolon between co-ordinate clauses when there is no co-ordinating conjunction:

An optimist is a man who sees the world in a rosy light; a pessimist is one who sees it in its true light.

2. Use a semicolon between two co-ordinate clauses, even when a co-ordinating conjunction is present, if the clauses are long or emphatic, or if they contain commas within themselves.

Example:

One night a tourist stopped at a Russian inn; and the

next morning, when the landlady asked him how he had slept, the tourist replied:

"I was awake all night; for the bed, I am sorry to report, was infested with vermin."

"But that, my dear sir, is impossible!" cried the indignant landlady. "We have not a single bug in the house!"

"No, madam," retorted the tourist, "not single. They are all married; and, from what I have observed, they have enormous families."

3. Use semicolons to show the balance between the co-ordinate parts of a sentence:

If a man runs after money, he's greedy; if he keeps it, he's stingy; if he spends it, he's extravagant; if he doesn't get it, he's shiftless; and if he gets it after a lifetime of hard labor, he's a fool who has never stopped to enjoy the good things of the world.

4. Never use a semicolon to join the subordinate parts of a sentence. Don't ever write a sentence such as the following:

I hardly think, the field being so soggy after the rain; that the football team will roll up a big score.

Place a comma, instead of a semicolon, after the word *rain* in the preceding sentence. The semicolon joins only the *co-ordinate* parts of a sentence.

PERIOD—FULL STOP

1. Use a period to indicate the full stop at the end of a sentence.

This rule is too obvious to need further amplification. But remember *not* to use a period unless you have a *full sentence*, with a *subject* and a *predicate*.

2. Use periods to mark abbreviations:

pp.—*pages*
A.M.—*Master of Arts*
A.M.—*ante meridiem*, the Latin for *before noon*

3. Use three periods to indicate the omission of words from a quoted passage:

For by thy words . . . thou shalt be condemned. (*Matthew XII:37*)

4. Use a period, instead of a question mark, after an indirect question:

He asked the traffic officer whether he was on the right road to Washington.

The direct question was, "Am I on the right road to Washington?"

COLON

1. Use a colon, instead of a comma, before a long or a formal quotation—especially when the introduction is formal and no verb meaning *to say* introduces the speech.
Example:

At a public dinner in Boston, Chief Justice Joseph Story made the following toast to the guest of honor, Edward Everett:
"Fame follows merit where Everett goes."
Whereupon Everett returned the compliment in the following words:
"To whatever heights judicial learning may attain in this country, it will never rise above one Story."

2. Use colons to introduce explanations or illustrations:

These are his reasons for dissolving the partnership: he wants to set up an independent business; he finds it hard to get along with Mr. Smith; and he is anxious to work without the feeling that he is being watched.

3. Use the colon after the salutation in a formal letter:

A tenant, when asked by his landlord to vacate his apartment, sent him the following reply:

"Dear Sir:
    I remain,
            Yours truly,
                John Doe."

4. Use the colon to separate the hours from the minutes when they are written in numerals:

Meet me at the restaurant at 6:15.

QUESTION MARK

1. Use a question mark after a direct, but not after an indirect, question.

2. Use a question mark after a date to indicate a doubt as to its correctness:

Rabelais, 1490?–1553, was a physician, philosopher, satirist, and humorist.

EXCLAMATION POINT

Use an exclamation point to indicate a strong emotion. But don't overuse it, or your style may sound hysterical.

DASH

1. Use a dash to indicate an abrupt or unexpected change in thought:

"Do you believe in clubs for women?"
"Yes—if every other form of persuasion fails."

2. Use dashes to enclose a parenthetical word, or group of words, to show a break in the thought, or to summarize or explain what has just been said:

My best friend—John—is coming to visit me.
The last big snowstorm—the one just before Christmas —was the severest I have ever seen.

Don't overuse the dash, as it produces a choppy style.

QUOTATION MARKS

1. Use quotation marks to enclose direct quotations, or words used in a special sense.

The following anecdote shows both these uses of quotation marks:

A "soak-the-rich" socialist once expounded his views to Rockefeller. "It isn't fair," he said, "for one man to have millions, while his neighbor has nothing at all."

"What would you do about it?" asked Rockefeller.

"Redistribute the wealth, so that everybody will have his equal share."

"Very well," said Rockefeller to the "social-minded" dreamer, "my total wealth is 260 million dollars. The total population of the world is 2 billion. Here is your exact share of my wealth—13 cents."

2. When a quotation extends over several paragraphs, put quotation marks at the beginning of each paragraph, but at the end of the last paragraph only.

3. Use single quotation marks to indicate a quotation within a quotation.

Examples:

"Of all sad words of tongue and pen," wrote Whittier, "the saddest are these: 'It might have been.'"

"I believe," said a friend to Oscar Wilde, "that 'sugar' and 'sumac' are the only two English words that begin with 's-u' and are pronounced *shoo*."
"Are you sure?" was the instant retort.

4. Use quotation marks or italics to indicate the titles of books, magazine articles, lectures, sermons, and words used in a special sense.

Under this rule the words *sugar* and *sumac*, in the above anecdote, can be italicized. (Words to be printed in italics are underlined when handwritten or typewritten.)

5. If an exclamation mark or a question mark is part of a quotation, it belongs inside the closing quotation marks:

"More light!" cried the dying Goethe.
"What do you know?" he asked.

6. If the exclamation mark or question mark is not part of the quotation, place it outside the closing quotation marks:

Who dares to say, "I am not a coward"?

7. Always place commas and periods inside the closing quotation marks, even when they are not part of the quotation:

"A stitch in time saves nine," he said sagely.
The word "truth," as you know, means different things to different people.
Buddha has been called the "Light of Asia."

PARENTHESES—DETOUR SIGNS

Use parentheses (or commas or dashes) to indicate explanations or illustrations of preceding thoughts and words:

The problem (it dealt with the Einstein theory) was very difficult.

Ben Hogan, the best golfer of his day, won three championships within a single year.

You must pass these four subjects—mathematics, history, English, and French—before next September.

A final word: Note the punctuation of the news items, articles, and books you read. See how the proper marks, like good traffic signals, help to clarify the writer's ideas and to carry them most effectively into your consciousness. You will observe that writers who lived a generation or more ago used a much larger number of punctuation marks than we do today. The modern tendency to use less punctuation gives one's style the quality of speed. However, to omit marks of punctuation where they are needed will only serve to confuse the reader. Experience and observation will teach you where to use punctuation marks and where you may safely omit them. After you have finished a piece of writing, always check it over to make sure it has been punctuated adequately. For a good style of writing, clarity is as important as any other feature.

Time out for the Twenty-First Word Game
A MISCELLANEOUS GROUP OF WORDS

The words in this game are difficult, and yet they form a part of the educated person's vocabulary. In the first round of this game, you may make quite a number of errors. Don't be discouraged—you will find yourself in good company, for most people are unable to use all these words correctly. When you get through with this game, you will find yourself in still better company.

A

Check the statement which, in your opinion, applies most closely to each of the following words in *italics:*

1. He is a man of great *perspicacity*.
     a. He loves comfort
     b. He perspires freely
     c. He has a keen mind

2. His sister is a *flamboyant* woman.
   a. She is flighty
   b. She is easily deceived
   c. She is showy

3. The story is *scintillating*.
   a. It sparkles
   b. It deals with sex
   c. It deals with a ticklish situation

4. According to the law the child was a result of *miscegenation*.
   a. It was born in sin
   b. It was the offspring of a white person and a member of another race
   c. It was a premature birth

5. He was a man of *intrepidity*.
   a. He had great courage
   b. He was quick to act
   c. He liked to interfere with other people

6. He made a *gratuitous* statement.
   a. It was uncalled for
   b. It was full of gratitude
   c. It was very clever

7. The book was published *posthumously*.
   a. It was published in haste
   b. It was published expensively
   c. It was issued after the author's death

8. His argument was *tenuous*.
   a. It was long-winded
   b. It was flimsy
   c. It was intense

9. His conduct was *ignominious*.
   a. It was dishonorable
   b. It was stupid
   c. It was abusive

10. He made a *scurrilous* attack on his rival.
    a. The attack was very stupid
    b. It was very offensive
    c. It was a hit-and-run affair

11. They were a *homogeneous* group.
    a. They were like one another
    b. They were brilliant
    c. They were very kind

12. His face was *cadaverous.*
   a. He looked like an average person
   b. He looked like a corpse
   c. He looked like a cad

13. He advocated *genocide.*
   a. He wanted to kill germs
   b. He believed in destroying whole groups or races
   c. He urged people to read the Bible

14. His talk was *euphemistic.*
   a. He substituted pleasant for disagreeable words
   b. He spoke in an effeminate voice
   c. He talked in riddles

15. His joy was *evanescent.*
   a. It kept increasing all the time
   b. It disappeared soon
   c. It kept him on an even keel

—*Answers*—

1-c, 2-c, 3-a, 4-b, 5-a, 6-a, 7-c, 8-b, 9-a, 10-b, 11-a, 12-b, 13-b, 14-a, 15-b

B

Match the words on the right with the definitions on the left:

1. cadaverous   a. passing away before long
2. euphemistic   b. given freely, uncalled for
3. evanescent   c. intermarriage between different races
4. flamboyant   d. despicable, dishonorable
5. genocide   e. absence of fear, great courage
6. gratuitous   f. thin, flimsy
7. homogeneous   g. pale, like a corpse
8. ignominious   h. occurring after a person's death
9. intrepidity   i. sparkling
10. miscegenation   j. using a pleasant word for a disagreeable idea
11. perspicacity   k. grossly offensive
12. posthumously   l. extermination of a racial or a national group
13. scintillating   m. showy, like a flame
14. scurrilous   n. mental keenness
15. tenuous   o. of the same kind (with another)

1-g, 2-j, 3-a, 4-m, 5-l, 6-b, 7-o, 8-d, 9-e, 10-c, 11-n, 12-h, 13-i, 14-k, 15-f

C

Answer each of the following questions:

1. Would a glutton be likely to look *cadaverous?*   Yes   No
2. Is a flimsy argument *tenuous?*   Yes   No
3. Is it *euphemistic* to say that a dead person has "passed on?"   Yes   No
4. Would you call a gentle rebuke *scurrilous?*   Yes   No
5. Would you call water and oil a *homogeneous* mixture?   Yes   No
6. Is it a sign of *intrepidity* to be afraid of the dark?   Yes   No
7. Is it *miscegenation* for two white people to marry each other?   Yes   No
8. Are rainbows *evanescent?*   Yes   No
9. Is dull conversation *scintillating?*   Yes   No
10. Is a child ever born *posthumously* when both parents are alive?   Yes   No
11. Would you call a display of too many jewels *flamboyant?*   Yes   No
12. When you get information by asking for it, is it *gratuitous?*   Yes   No
13. Was Socrates a man of unusual *perspicacity?*   Yes   No
14. Is DDT regarded as a *genocide?*   Yes   No
15. Is the conduct of a traitor *ignominious?*   Yes   No

1-no, 2-yes, 3-yes, 4-no, 5-no, 6-no, 7-no, 8-yes, 9-no, 10-no, 11-yes, 12-no, 13-yes, 14-no, 15-yes

D

Give the correct word for each of the following definitions:
1. fearlessness   i_____
2. mental keenness   p_____
3. thin, flimsy (in an abstract sense)   t_____
4. pale, ghastly like a corpse   c_____
5. grossly abusive   s_____

6. expressing something disagree-
   able in an agreeable way   e_____
7. sparkling   s_____
8. born after father's death, or
   published after author's death
   (adverb)   p_____
9. marriage between different
   races   m_____
10. despicable, disgraceful   i_____
11. given freely without claim, or
    offered without cause   g_____
12. fleeting or transient   e_____
13. of the same kind   h_____
14. extermination of a racial group   g_____
15. showy, bombastic   f_____

—*Answers*—

1-intrepidity, 2-perspicacity, 3-tenuous, 4-cadaverous,
5-scurrilous, 6-euphemistic, 7-scintillating, 8-posthumously,
9-miscegenation, 10-ignominious, 11-gratuitous, 12-evanes-
cent, 13-homogeneous, 14-genocide, 15-flamboyant

E

Here are the pronunciations of the words you have just
added to your vocabulary:

cadaverous: ka-DAV-er-us
euphemistic, adjective: you-fe-MIS-tik
euphemism, noun: YOU-fe-mizm
evanescent: ev-an-ESS-ent
flamboyant: flam-BOY-ant
genocide: JEN-o-side
gratuitous: grat-YOU-it-us
homogeneous, adjective: ho-mo-JEE-nee-us
homogeneousness, noun: ho-mo-JEE-ni-us-ness; or
homogeneity, noun: ho-mo-je-NEE-i-tee
ignominious, adjective: ig-no-MIN-ee-us
ignominiousness, noun: ig-no-MIN-ee-us-ness; or
ignominy, noun: IG-no-min-ee
intrepidity, noun: in-tre-PID-i-tee
intrepid, adjective: in-TREP-id
miscegenation: mis-se-je-NAY-shun
perspicacity, noun: per-spi-KASS-i-tee
perspicacious, adjective: per-spi-KAY-shus

272

posthumously: POS-choo (or tyoo)-mus-lee
scintillating: SIN-til-late-ing
scurrilous: SCUR-ril-us
tenuous: TEN-you-us

24

THE FUN OF GOOD CONVERSATION

YOUR VOICE AND HOW TO USE IT

Good conversation is an art that everyone should cultivate. It pays dividends in enjoyment and greater effectiveness. The ability to speak well helps you to communicate your ideas to others, and to put them across. Most leaders of men are persuasive, interesting speakers.

It isn't hard to master the art of conversation, if you really want to. All you need, to begin with, is a voice. Everyone should try to cultivate a good speaking voice. Even the most interesting of stories can be spoiled if delivered in raucous tones.

Learn to modulate your voice. You can do it even if you are not an Ezio Pinza or a Risë Stevens. If your vocal cords emit an unpleasant sound, lower your tones and you will eliminate much of their harshness. If, on the other hand, your voice is weak, raise it sufficiently to give it greater fullness and strength.

Practice at home. Learn the exact volume necessary to make your voice clear and pleasant. Reading aloud will help. Try to get variety into your voice as you read; let it rise and fall, let the words come swiftly or slowly, in keeping with the nature of the passage you are reading. It's no fun to listen to a monotonous reader or speaker.

Listen with a critical ear not only to your voice, but to your enunciation as well. If a listener says to you, "What did you say?" or "I beg your pardon?" the chances are that your words have not been well enunciated.

Don't commit the error of talking with a pipe or a cigarette or a piece of chewing gum in your mouth. It makes for slovenly speech, and it destroys whatever charm your words may contain in themselves.

Another thing to remember, especially when you speak to several people, is to show that you are speaking to the entire group. Instead of fixing your gaze upon *any one person*, look at the various people present, now at one and now at another, to show them that you are equally interested in every one of them. This is a good way to get them to be interested in you.

Finally, try to avoid mannerisms in your conversation. Don't bite your lips, or click your tongue, or suck your teeth, or roll your eyes, or use your hands excessively as you speak. Don't be like the Frenchman who said, "How can I talk if you hold my hands?"

SUBJECTS TO TALK ABOUT

As a general rule, any subject of universal interest will make good conversation. Here are just a few of them:

1. *Leading topics of the day.* These topics are selected by newspaper editors as the principal news items because of their human-interest value. Take, for example, a milk strike, or a rise in the cost of living, or the discovery of a new explosive. All topics of this nature have a threefold impact upon our interest: How do they affect *me?* How do they affect *you?* How do they affect *the rest of the world?* Any general topic with a personal implication makes a good subject for conversation.

2. *Morals.* This, if kept above the level of casting stones at our neighbors, can be one of the most intriguing subjects for conversation. In discussing the morality of a person's action, try not only to point out the action itself but the thought behind the action. Suppose a movie star has been recently divorced. A simple item of this nature can stir everybody's interest, for it strikes at the very heart of our human relationships. What were the factors that led to the divorce? What are the factors that lead to divorces in general? Is a happy marriage compatible with an artistic career? Do you personally know of any actual experience that would support either side of the question? Is there a possible remedy for divorce? Is there any formula for a happy marriage?

These are just a few of the many avenues of thought you can open up with the simple discussion of a current divorce case. Almost every other human relationship can be discussed from a similar ethical point of view.

3. *Music.* Almost everybody loves music in some form or other—from boogy-woogy to Beethoven. You can always start a stimulating conversation with one of the following questions: Is it vulgar to enjoy jazz? Are juke boxes a public

275

nuisance? Are Rodgers and Hammerstein the equal of Gilbert and Sullivan? Was George Gershwin a great composer? Has the radio advanced or retarded our musical appreciation? Are our children taught the right kind of music? Do you prefer grand opera in English or in a foreign tongue? Can you give reasons for your preference?

Conversations on music—take it from a layman who has tried them—can be among the most fascinating pastimes in the world.

4. *The stage.* The recently revived interest in the drama has made the stage a lively topic for conversation. What do you consider the greatest play of the year? Of the decade? How do TV plays compare with stage plays? With screen plays? What, in your opinion, is the best medium for drama —the stage, radio, television, the motion picture? Are playwrights underpaid as compared—let us say—to stage directors or actors? As compared to salesmen? Do we give enough recognition to our artists in general? Does the entertainment world suffer from too much commercialism? These and similar questions can provide an entire evening of zestful conversation.

5. *Sports.* It is hardly necessary to dwell upon this as one of the most interesting subjects for conversation. Practically all of us are Friday prophets and Monday quarterbacks. But let me mention one phase of this subject that a number of my friends have found unusually enjoyable. They have "conversational (but not actual) betting pools" on important games, fights and races. They get together just before an important athletic event, discuss the merits of the various contestants, and place their "bets" on their favorites. And then, when the event is over, they adjust their bets and compare the actual results with their former guesses. Nobody, of course, wins any money; but, on the other hand, nobody loses any, and everybody has had an exciting time. Try it for yourself and you will see what I mean.

6. *Hobbies.* This is a good subject for conversation provided you talk about the other fellow's rather than your own hobby. Theodore Roosevelt was aware of this fact. Whenever he was about to meet anyone he was anxious to please, he found out all he could about that person's pet hobby. When he met the person, he spoke with sympathy and enthusiasm about the thing that lay closest to his visitor's heart. This, declared Roosevelt, was the secret of his popularity.

Talk to your friends about the hobbies that interest *them*, and you will get a reputation for good fellowship, charming wit, and a brilliant mind. There is nothing that pleases people so much as *your* interest in *their* interests.

7. *Gossip.* This is perhaps the most fascinating of all subjects for conversation. For "the best of women and the wisest of men enjoy their gossip now and again."

And who of us doesn't? But let us take care to be *thoughtful* gossipers. Whenever we talk about our neighbors, let us remember the words of James Whitcomb Riley: "Let something *good* be said."

The very meaning of the word *gossip* denotes something good. Derived from the two words, *God sibb*, a *gossip* was originally a *God-relation*, a person spiritually akin to another person—a sponsor at a baptism, for example. Later on, a *gossip* came to mean a *friend*. But a friend is likely to be a frequent visitor; and a frequent visitor is a possible bringer of news. And thus, little by little, the word *gossip* acquired the unsavory meaning of a *carrier of tales*, an *idle tattler*, a *scandalmonger*.

There is nothing so vicious as evil gossip. Its effects are vividly portrayed in Sheridan's *School for Scandal*, where a character is assassinated at almost every word. But, on the other hand, there is nothing so delightful as good gossip. If you gossip about your friends in a friendly way, you make them feel important. The best novels, the best newspaper columns, and the best conversations are those that indulge in good-natured gossip about everything under the sun.

SUBJECTS TO AVOID IN CONVERSATION

It is just as important to know what subjects to avoid as what subjects to select for good conversation. If you don't want to be set down as a wet blanket or a bore, be careful to remember the following conversational taboos:

1. Avoid talking about yourself, unless you are asked to do so. People are interested in their own problems, not in yours.

2. Avoid talking about the clever sayings of your children. Your friends' children are also clever at times; and nothing perhaps is so boring to parents as to see the genius of *your* little ones paraded before *their* eyes.

3. Avoid talking about sickness or death. The only one who willingly listens to such talk is the doctor, but he gets paid for it.

4. Avoid slander. Remember the ditty:

> There is so much good in the worst of us,
>   And so much bad in the best of us,
> That it hardly behooves any of us
>   To talk about the rest of us.

If you slander your friends behind their back, your auditor may show you a certain amount of interest. But he will distrust you as a dangerous person whose very next victim for slander may be himself.

5. Avoid describing the scenery you saw on your vacation. Long descriptions, even in books written by masters, are likely to be tedious.

6. Avoid telling the story of the book you have just read. The author has probably done the job much more effectively than you can do it. If your listeners are interested in the story, they will want to go to the book and get it at first hand.

7. Avoid shoptalk, unless you are talking to people engaged in the same business or profession. Very few persons in a mixed group will be interested in the details of your particular job. Good conversation, as we have noted, must deal with subjects of *general* interest.

LANGUAGE AND SLANGUAGE

In addition to certain subjects, there are certain expressions that you should avoid in good conversation.

First and most important, avoid slang expressions in polite conversation. Slang is generally taboo in cultivated company. Such expressions as *like I said, are you kiddin', what's cookin', the lady was a knockout, the cat's whiskers, he got canned, the's some babe, hot stuff, drop dead* may lend a humorous effect in familiar speech, but they are not suitable for formal use. As H. W. Fowler points out, "many slang words and phrases perish, a few establish themselves; in either case, during probation they are counted unfit for literary use."

Here is a partial list of slangy and of other vulgar and illiterate expressions to avoid in good conversation:

> *and what have you*
> *y'understand what I mean?*
> *hadn't ought to*
> *had ought to*
> *had I of known*

so what?
I feel nauseous for I feel nauseated
equally as for equally or as
leave us go for let us go
irregardless for regardless
hisself, theirself, theirselves for himself, themselves
he learned me grammar for he taught me grammar
I got an invite for I got an invitation
he owned me five dollars for he owed, etc.
like nobody's business
the car is broke for the car is broken
atta boy, atta girl
I can't find him nowhere for I can't find him anywhere
he can't hardly stand on his feet for he can hardly stand on his feet
this here city for this city
jeepers creepers
he don't do it good for he doesn't do it well
it don't do her no good for it doesn't do her any good
I ain't talking for I'm not talking
whoopee
the Giants is dead
she's a hot tamale
was you there? for were you there?
I'm tellin' yuh!
I seen it
I done it
I ain't seen it
I ain't done it
me and you are friends for you and I are friends
believe you me!
he spoke of me being there for he spoke of my being there
sez you
nertz to you
oh, yeah?

SAY IT RIGHT

Get into the habit of avoiding vulgarisms and using better English in your conversation. By way of practice, try to give a good English equivalent for each of the following bits of slang:

1. They're in cahoots.
2. Quit kiddin' me.
3. You slay me.
4. They gave her the raspberry.
5. Lay off him.
6. He gave him the low-down.
7. I'm falling for you, babe.
8. He was a punk with a lousy puss.
9. He's my side-kick.
10. Stop dishing out the applesauce.
11. That's a lot of baloney.
12. He's nuts about her.
13. I'll have a look-see.
14. I disremember what I said.
15. I don't understand it nohow.
16. They stole it on me.
17. He tickled the ivories.
18. He gave us a lot of bull.
19. It was a regular gyp-joint.
20. You said a mouthful.

—Answers—

There are several ways of correcting a slang expression. Any good English equivalent will do for each of the sentences in the above test. Here are some of the possible correct substitutions:

1. They are in collusion.
2. Stop making fun of me.
3. You entertain me tremendously (spoken sarcastically).
4. They showed her their disapproval.
5. Let him alone.
6. He told him the truth of the matter.
7. I'm falling in love with you, young lady.
8. He was a young gangster with an ugly face.
9. He's my best friend.
10. Stop the excessive flattery.
11. That talk is very insincere.
12. He's infatuated with her.
13. I'll have a look.
14. I don't remember what I said.
15. I don't understand it at all.
16. They stole it from me.

17. He played the piano.
18. His talk was full of bluff.
19. It was a place where the customers were generally cheated.
20. This inelegant remark is said to have been made by the wife of a former mayor of New York City. It was during the visit of Queen Marie of Roumania to the United States. When Marie told her hostess that New York had the finest buildings she had ever seen, the hostess beamed upon her and exclaimed: "You said a mouthful, Queen!"

What she meant to say was: "You are quite right, Your Majesty."

Time out for the Twenty-Second Word Game
WORDS THAT WILL ADD POWER
TO YOUR CONVERSATION

"There is a weird power," as Joseph Conrad reminds us, "in the spoken word . . . A word carries far—very far—deals destruction through time as the bullets go flying through space."

But the power of words can be constructive as well as destructive. Listen to Byron on this point:

". . . words are things; and a small drop of ink,
    Falling like dew upon a thought, produces
That which makes thousands, perhaps millions, think."

Here are 25 additional words that will add to your mental power—your ability to express your own thoughts and to make others think.

A

Check the correct synonym, or equivalent word or phrase, for each of the following words:

1. abstemious
    (a) temperate (b) vaporous (c) concealed
2. adulation
    (a) grown-up conduct (b) extravagant praise
    (c) excessive joy

3. ambiguous
   (a) adjacent (b) aspiring (c) having a double meaning

4. chauvinism
   (a) exaggerated patriotism (b) love for the theater (c) a determination to win

5. chimerical
   (a) ringing like a bell (b) cheerful (c) fanciful

6. condone
   (a) to forgive (b) to contribute (c) to conspire

7. desultory
   (a) deserted (b) insulting (c) fitful, random

8. equivocal
   (a) fair or just (b) impartial (c) doubtful, questionable

9. flagellate
   (a) to make flags (b) to whip (c) to harden into a jelly

10. germane
    (a) belonging to Germany (b) appropriate, closely related to (c) containing germs

11. garrulous
    (a) talkative (b) gallant (c) fond

12. iconoclast
    (a) an aristocrat (b) a classical work of art (c) an attacker of venerated beliefs

13. impecunious
    (a) habitually poor (b) queer (c) very rich, having much money

14. indubitable
    (a) in duty bound (b) unquestionable, certain (c) having debts to pay

15. intermittent
    (a) periodic (b) enclosed (c) forwarded

16. maritime
    (a) having a good time (b) a wedding anniversary (c) pertaining to the sea

17. obsequious
    (a) subservient (b) independent (c) pertaining to a funeral service

18. oligarchy
    (a) a spy ring (b) an oil mixture (c) a government restricted to a few powerful persons

19. peccable

(a) very old (b) capable of sinning (c) having a large capacity

20. peremptory

(a) authoritative, arbitrary (b) pertaining to a buyer (c) thoughtful

21. querulous

(a) cheerful (b) crazy (c) fault-finding, fretful

22. terrestrial

(a) frightening (b) pertaining to the earth (c) a summons to a trial

23. ubiquitous

(a) being everywhere at once (b) wicked (c) ready to quit

24. unctuous

(a) greasy (b) prompt (c) related by marriage

25. vociferous

(a) made of iron (b) noisy (c) speechless

—Answers—

1-a, 2-b, 3-c, 4-a, 5-c, 6-a, 7-c, 8-c, 9-b, 10-b, 11-a, 12-c, 13-a, 14-b, 15-a, 16-c, 17-a, 18-c, 19-b, 20-a, 21-c, 22-b, 23-a, 24-a, 25-b

B

Now try something harder. Check the correct antonym, or opposite word or phrase, for each of the following words:

1. abstemious

(a) forgiving (b) intemperate (c) cheerful

2. adulation

(a) abuse (b) sorrow (c) brightness

3. ambiguous

(a) certain (b) lazy (c) tiny

4. chauvinism

(a) friendliness (d) disinterest in one's country (c) dullness

5. chimerical

(a) real (b) flying by night (c) gloomy

6. condone

(a) to sympathize (b) to condemn (c) to conspire

7. desultory

(a) consistent (b) happy (c) quick

8. equivocal

(a) clear (b) unequal (c) silent

9. flagellate
(a) to lower the flag (b) to dissolve (c) to caress
10. germane
(a) unrelated (b) French (c) bald
11. garrulous
(a) ascetic (b) reticent (c) cruel
12. iconoclast
(a) a preserver of religious beliefs (b) a ne'er-do-well
(c) a hermit
13. impecunious
(a) extraordinary (b) spoiled (c) prosperous
14. indubitable
(a) doubtful (b) free from debt (c) avoidable
15. intermittent
(a) delayed (b) dug up (c) continuous
16. maritime
(a) pertaining to the land (b) dealing with sadness
(c) eternal
17. obsequious
(a) obliging (b) healthy (c) independent
18. oligarchy
(a) discipline (b) democracy (c) persuasion
19. peccable
(a) narrow (b) invisible (c) faultless, not liable to sin
20. peremptory
(a) lenient (b) disagreeable (c) exacting
21. querulous
(a) dull (b) inquisitive (c) uncomplaining
22. terrestrial
(a) unafraid (b) restless (c) celestial
23. ubiquitous
(a) merciful (b) just (c) not existing everywhere
24. unctuous
(a) not punctual (b) free from grease (c) unmanageable
25. vociferous
(a) timid (b) quiet (c) blind

—*Answers*—

1-b, 2-a, 3-a, 4-b, 5-a, 6-b, 7-a, 8-a, 9-c, 10-a, 11-b, 12-a, 13-c, 14-a, 15-c, 16-a, 17-c, 18-b, 19-c, 20-a, 21-c, 22-c, 23-c, 24-b, 25-b

C

Now that you are pretty familiar with these words, put the correct word into each of the following spaces:

1. He fl_____ himself for what he considered a terrible sin.

2. What you are now saying is not all ge_____ to the subject.

3. Patriotism with a chip on the shoulder has been defined as ch_____.

4. An interrupted electric current flowing in one direction is called in_____.

5. We live but a short time in our te_____ home before we are told to move on, as we hope, to our celestial home.

6. He was im_____ because he never could hold a job.

7. A good writer will abstain from am_____ expressions—that is, expressions which leave you in doubt as to their meaning.

8. His unrealistic plan to end the war was a ch_____ dream.

9. Good health frequently depends upon ab_____ habits in eating and drinking.

10. God's ub_____ presence, said Spinoza, fills every particle of the universe.

11. The judge sent a pe_____ summons for the appearance of the witness.

12. His voice had a qu_____ sound, as if he bore a a grudge against the world.

13. Franklin D. Roosevelt was opposed to what he called the financial ol_____ of our country—that is, the rule of the rich minority.

14. His plans were illogical, changeable, and de_____.

15. He spoke in a buttery, insincere, and un_____ voice.

16. England's ma_____ trade brings her products from all over the world.

17. To paraphrase Shakespeare, it is more noble to con_____ than to condemn.

18. To err is human; in other words, we are all pe_____ at times.

19. The ga_____ old fellow kept talking incessantly about his war exploits.

20. His testimony was shifty, evasive, and eq_____.

21. He flattered his superior with an ad_____ that was definitely insincere.

22. Ibsen, because of his attacks on widely held beliefs, was generally regarded as an ic_____.

23. He was boisterous, aggressive, and vo_____ in his demands.

24. The masses of the people were cowed and ob_____ to the dictator.

25. The prisoner was convicted because of the detailed and in_____ evidence of the witness.

—Answers—

1-flagellated, 2-germane, 3-chauvinism, 4-intermittent, 5-terrestrial, 6-impecunious, 7-ambiguous, 8-chimerical, 9-abstemious, 10-ubiquitous, 11-peremptory, 12-querulous, 13-oligarchy, 14-desultory, 15-unctuous, 16-maritime, 17-condone, 18-peccable, 19-garrulous, 20-equivocal, 21-adulation, 22-iconoclast, 23-vociferous, 24-obsequious, 25-indubitable

D

The more difficult words in this game are pronounced as follows:

1. abstemious: ab-STEE-mee-us
2. chauvinism: SHOW-vin-izm
3. chimerical, adjective: ki or kigh-MER-ik-l
   chimera, noun: ki or kigh-MEE-ra
4. desultory: DESS-ul-to-ree
5. equivocal: e-QUIV-o-kul
6. flagellate: FLAJ-el-late
7. garrulous: GAR-oo-lus
8. iconoclast: eye-KON-o-klast
9. impecunious: im-pe-KEW-ni-us
10. obsequious: ob-SEEK-wi-us
11. oligarchy: OL-ig-ar-kee
12. peccable: PEK-a-bl
13. peremptory: per-EMP-to-ree, or PER-emp-to-ree
14. querulous: KWER-you-lus
15. terrestrial: ter-RES-tree-ul
16. ubiquitous: you-BIK-wit-us
17. vociferous: vo-SIF-er-us

25

HOW TO WRITE BETTER LETTERS

Many of us look upon letter writing as a chore. Life is too rapid nowadays, we complain, for this leisurely method of friendly communication. How often do we neglect our correspondence with the excuse that we just "haven't the time to attend to that pile of unanswered letters."

The remedy for this sort of neglect is simple. *Organize* your time to include letter writing among your regular activities. Set aside a definite period every week—say an evening or a Sunday afternoon—for your correspondence and for nothing else. Before long, you will have turned this activity into a habit. You will look forward to your letter writing not as a distasteful chore but as a genuine pleasure—the pleasure of exchanging ideas and sympathies and hopes with your absent relatives and friends.

HOW TO DRESS UP A LETTER

A letter is a mental visit to a friend. Make your visits personable as well as pleasant. Use paper and envelopes of good quality if you want to make a good impression.

In general, you should write your informal social letters by hand, but your formal business letters on the typewriter. A typewritten social letter may seem too cold, a hand-written business letter too amateurish. With old friends, however, typewritten correspondence is usually considered acceptable, and it may even be desirable if your script is not easy to read. The business man will only be irritated if he can't decipher your message at once.

If you write your social letters by hand, try for courtesy's sake to be as legible as possible. Don't irritate your friend by carrying the obscurity of a poor handwriting too far.

Avoid too many abbreviations. Don't give your reader the impression that you have been anxious to get through with the letter as quickly as possible.

Don't crowd your letter. Have plenty of margin at the top, at the bottom, and on both sides. And don't cross out too many words, or drop ink blots on the page. If the letter is untidy, rewrite it.

Don't be too long-winded. A protracted visit, whether social or commercial, becomes a bore.

Above all, be tactful. In letter writing, as well as in conversation, always remember the other fellow's convenience and feelings if you want him to remember yours.

Letters are as a rule divided into five parts:

The Writer's Address and Date
The Salutation
The Body
The Conclusion
The Signature

SOCIAL LETTERS

An Informal Invitation:

Suppose you want to invite a friend for a week-end. Try to make the letter short and chatty and warm, like the following sample:

Scarsdale,
June 25, 19——

My dear Sally,

If you have no other plans for the week-end of July 2–4, we would love to have you spend it with us at Brewster. I'm having a few intimate friends—yours and mine—at our summer cottage; and, needless to say, the party will be incomplete without you.

So please don't say *no*. We are all looking forward to seeing you and hope you will be able to come.

Expectantly yours,
Joanne

In the above informal letter, please note the following points:

In the date, there are commas after the name of the city and the day of the month.

In the salutation, the word *dear* begins with a *small* instead of a *capital* letter, because it is preceded by *My*. At the end of the salutation, there is a comma.

In the body of this informal letter, the style is chatty and intimate and warm.

In the conclusion, the word *yours* begins with a small letter. There is a comma at the end.

In the signature, the last name is omitted.

An Informal Answer to an Informal Invitation:

Yonkers, June 27, 19—

Dear Joanne,

I shall be delighted to come for the week-end. With our mutual friends as your guests and you as the charming hostess, I look forward to having the time of my life. Thanks a million for the invitation.

Ever devotedly yours,
Sally

In the conclusion of this letter, please note that every word with the exception of the first begins with a small letter.

In the heading of a letter, it is customary to use no abbreviations, but to write out in full the names of cities, states, and months.

Salem, Massachusetts,
October 13, 19—

Some people prefer to put the date at the bottom, instead of at the top, of a letter. This is permissible. But note the customary usage of these two forms. If the date is at the top, it is placed on the right, and the day of the month is indicated by figures, as above. But if the date is at the bottom, it is placed on the left, and the day of the month is written out in full, as below.

Sincerely yours,
Helen Jackson

October the seventh

THE GOLDEN RULE IN LETTER WRITING

In your general correspondence with your friends, remember the Golden Rule of reciprocal good will. Write to others the way you would like them to write to you. In every letter to your friend, consider his convenience and tastes. Say nothing that will hurt. Even when your letter must bear a painful message, try to soften it with a kindly word.

Suppose, for example, your friend writes to you for a loan. Remember that he probably feels sensitive about his request, and answer him with consideration and tact. If you can grant the request, don't answer in a patronizing tone. And if you must refuse the loan, be sure to explain as warmly as you can that the refusal is beyond your control.

Some letters, as you can readily see, require considerable thoughtfulness on your part. But you will always find a sure guide to your thought in a simple question: How would you want *your friend* to write to *you* in a similar situation?

In all your correspondence, try to adopt what the letter-specialists call the "you-attitude." Try to put yourself into the other fellow's place. Avoid the excessive use of *I*, and be liberal with the flattering pronoun *you*. Even when you have to argue with your friend, try to impress your view upon him only when you can show him tactfully that it is to *his* interest to consider *your* argument.

BUSINESS LETTERS

In your business letters, just as in your social letters, try to remember the other fellow's point of view. Whether you sell goods or services, impress upon your customer that it is *his* convenience as well as your own that you have in mind.

Your business letter should be more formal, less chatty, than your social letter. Remember that the recipient of your business letter has no time to waste on unnecessary details. Be brief, frank, courteous, cooperative, and neat.

And be sure to have the letter properly typed. Leave plenty of white space at the top, the bottom, and the two sides. If your letter is short, arrange it in a narrow column down the center of the page. A letter of eight narrow lines looks more attractive than a letter of four wide lines. Your letter should form a box whose sides are as nearly parallel as possible to the edges of the paper on which it is typed.

In the heading of the letter, type the name of the recipient, his firm (if any), his address in full, and the repetition of the name, as follows:

Mr. John Clemens
The Hilton-Fletcher Company
342 Springdale Avenue
Hartford, Connecticut

Dear Mr. Clemens:

It used to be customary to place commas at the end of the first three lines in the heading, and a period at the end of the fourth line. Nowadays this practice is regarded as rather old-fashioned, but it isn't incorrect.

You may or you may not indent the first line in the body of the letter, and the first line in each subsequent paragraph. Both forms are correct.

Example 1:

Mr. John Clemens
The Hilton-Fletcher Company
342 Springdale Avenue
Hartford, Connecticut

Dear Mr. Clemens:

Thank you for your letter of April 21. We shall be happy to fill your order as soon as our new shipment arrives.

As for the other matter you mention in your letter, etc.

Example 2:

Mr. John Clemens
The Hilton-Fletcher Company
342 Springdale Avenue
Hartford, Connecticut

Dear Mr. Clemens:

Thank you for your letter of April 21. We shall be happy to fill your order as soon as our new shipment arrives.

As for the other matter you mention in your letter, etc.

WHAT TO SAY AND HOW TO SAY IT

Even more important than the layout of a business letter is the substance. Almost every letter written by a businessman, you must remember, is a sales letter. Whether you offer an article or a service, or try to adjust a claim, acknowledge a communication or collect a bill, your primary purpose is to sell goods or good will.

In business letters you must generally assume that the customer is right. He has a right to be treated promptly, patiently, and courteously. Consider every problem from the customer's point of view. Try to write and to do what will be to his advantage. And always address him by name. Whether you write an individual or a form letter, make your message *personal*. Never, if you can help it, head your letter with the mere words *Dear Sir* or *Dear Madam*, or, what is even worse, *Dear Sir or Madam*. If the name of the recipient of your circular letter is unknown to you, head it at least with the salutation *Dear Friend*.

Don't make your sales letters too long. On the other hand, don't make them too skimpy. Tell your story simply and vividly. Paint an adequate picture of the goods or the good will you are trying to sell. Organize your letter in such a way that it will *introduce* your product, *induce* your customer to consider it, and *produce* the sale.

This is true of every sales letter. Of the two specimen letters that follow, the first was unsuccessful and the second successful. Study them carefully and see if you can tell the reasons for the result in each case.

1. This letter was sent to the employment manager of a New York department store:

> 14 Prospect Street
> Worcester, Massachusetts
> March 14, 19—

Dear Sir:

I am looking for a job in your store. I would like, as a preliminary, to enter your training course with a view to employment either permanently or for the summer.

I am a graduate of Dartmouth College, class of 1948, and of the Harvard Graduate School of Business Administration, class of 1952. I have specialized in problems of retail distribution, and I want to supplement my academic training with actual experience. That is why I am asking for your help, so that I can have the opportunity to familiarize myself with department store management at first hand.

I trust you will send me a prompt and satisfactory reply.

> Yours truly,
> Henry Gordon

The young man did not get the job.

2. This letter was sent to an investment broker:

> 71 Chadwick Street
> Albany, New York
> January 4, 19—

Dear Mr. Hastings:

At the suggestion of Professor B——— of the Harvard

292

Graduate School of Business Administration, I am writing to offer my services to your company. I am 24 years old and I have just finished my post-graduate studies at the Harvard Business School. I am a member of the First Methodist Church, of which my uncle, the Reverend Dr. Saunders, is the minister.

Frankly, I know nothing about the practical side of the stock market. I have, however, made a thorough academic study of it under Professor B————, and I think I can learn the practical side in a short time. At least, I am going to try, as I find this field fascinating and I am eager to make good.

I think it will interest you to know that my father is a prominent surgeon. Personally, I am acquainted with quite a number of well-to-do physicians. These gentlemen are good prospects for a trustworthy investment company such as yours. Should I get this position, I will begin with them. And—if you will pardon my presumption—I *know* I can bring you business from the very start.

The initial salary is not too important to me. What concerns me most is to prove my value to your firm.

I am enclosing several references as to my character, my scholastic ability, and my practical workability. Busy as I know you are, I trust you will find the time to look at these references.

May I hope for a favorable reply, at your convenience, to this application?

Respectfully yours,
Donald Earle

This young man promptly landed the job.

WHAT MAKES OR BREAKS A LETTER

Now before you read the analysis of the two letters, jot down your own reasons for the failure of the first and the success of the second.

Have you done so? Then compare your own reasons with the following:

The first letter is little more than a plea for a job. It is based largely upon the "I-attitude" rather than upon the "you-attitude." For example: "*I* am looking for a job"—"*I* would like"—"*I* am a graduate"—"*I* have specialized"—"*I* want to supplement"—"*I* am asking for your help"—"*I* can have the opportunity."

In this letter, the writer merely asks for favors. He offers no services. He wants to be helped, but not to help in return. He shows no regard for the company in which he begs to be employed. He depicts himself, subconsciously, as a narrow and unsocial sort of person who is concerned only with his own problems. His letter contains not the slightest hint that he can arouse a customer's interest or produce a sale. Consequently, it fails to arouse the interest of the employment manager.

The only place for such a letter is the waste basket.

The second letter, on the other hand, is an offer of service rather than a request for a job. It contains the three important elements of a good sales letter:

1. It introduces the writer, modestly but adequately. It refers to an important person, Professor B———, as the basis for the introduction. It tells about the writer's background, including not only his own education, but his uncle's ecclesiastical calling and his father's medical profession. And it ties up his father's profession with his own possible ability to secure customers for the company.

2. In this way, the letter induces a definite interest on the part of the prospective employer. Note the "you-attitude" throughout the letter. Thus—"it will interest *you* to know" —"good prospects for a trustworthy company such as *yours*" —"I can bring *you* business"—"to prove my value to *your* firm"—"Busy as I know *you* are"—"a favorable reply at *your* convenience"—and so on. The reader of such a letter gets the impression that here is a young fellow who will work for the company's interests as well as for his own.

3. And, finally, the writer of this letter produces the sale —that is, he lands the job—through the inclusion of the proper references which show him not only as a bright young man of good character, but as a prospective employe who will very likely make good at his job.

AVOID THESE COMMON FAULTS

Keep your business letters free from such trite tags as *yours of 1st inst, thanking you for your favor, in re,* and so forth. And avoid the "telegraphic" style—that is, the omission of pronouns or of other words necessary to make your sentences complete. Don't give the recipient of your letter the idea that you have no time to treat him courteously, or to express your problem adequately. A letter with abbreviations and omissions is like a salesman with his hair uncombed and his shoes unlaced. In your letters, as in all your other writing, use clear English and complete sentences.

CLOSING YOUR BUSINESS LETTERS

A good business letter should have an effective conclusion as well as an effective salutation. The most successful conclusions, it has been found, convey a note of respect, tactful familiarity, whole-hearted enthusiasm, or genuine good will. Here are some of them:

Yours truly,
Very truly yours,
Yours respectfully,
Yours most sincerely,
Very sincerely yours,
Cordially yours,
Heartily yours,

The last two closings are generally used when you have some acquaintance with the person to whom you are writing.

And a final word. *Write* your name, instead of *typing* it, at the end of your letter. Your written name carries the warmth of a personal contact between your correspondent and yourself. In all your letters, try to stick to the *personal* note.

Time out for the Twenty-Third Word Game
WORDS ABOUT RELIGION AND GOD

Religion has given a large number of words to our language. Some are simple terms known to everyone, like *priest* and *church*. Others, however, describing church ritual and theological ideas, are not so familiar. These harder words are widely used in books, magazines, and speech, so you will find it valuable to know them, whether you are a believer in religion, in good English, or both.

A

Check whether each of the following statements is true or false:

1. *Absolution* is the declaration of forgiveness for sin.   True   False

2. The *apocalypse* is Judas's betrayal of Jesus.   True   False

3. *Apostasy* is belief in the Apostles.   True   False

4. *Beatitude* deals with the beauty of a cathedral or a synagogue.   True   False

5. The Book of Genesis presents a vivid *cosmogony*.   True   False

6. The *deification* of a man means that he is made a god.   True   False

7. *Expiation* is the transition from life to death.   True   False

8. A *fetish* is an ointment used in sacraments.   True   False

9. A *hierarchy* is a body of ecclesiastical rulers.   True   False

10. An *ineffable* statement is free from error.   True   False

11. An *infallible* idea is too sacred for expression.   True   False

12. A *liturgy* is a ritual, like the Mass.   True   False

13. Christianity may be regarded as a *Messianic* religion.   True   False

14. *Metempsychosis* means the transmigration of souls.   True   False

15. God is said to be *omnipotent*.   True   False

16. Another meaning for *omnipotent* is *omniscient*.   True   False

17. *Pantheism* is the belief in many gods.   True   False

18. According to the doctrine of *predestination*, you are master of your own destiny.   True   False

19. A *sacrilegious* person is a person of great piety.   True   False

20. A *theocracy* is the rule of one man.   True   False

—*Answers*—

1-true, 2-false, 3-false, 4-false, 5-true, 6-true, 7-false, 8-false, 9-true, 10-false, 11-false, 12-true, 13-true, 14-true, 15-true, 16-false, 17-false, 18-false, 19-false, 20-false

B

Match the words on the left with the definitions on the right:

1. absolution	a. desertion of one's faith
2. apocalypse	b. a body of ecclesiastical rulers, or other persons, belonging to various ranks
3. apostasy	c. too sacred for expression, indescribable
4. beatitude	d. an object of devotion among primitive peoples
5. cosmogony	e. atonement
6. deification	f. exaltation to divine honors
7. expiation	g. a theory of the world's creation
8. fetish	h. great bliss or blessedness
9. hierarchy	i. revelation
10. ineffable	j. forgiveness
11. infallible	k. a state that claims to be governed by God
12. liturgy	l. impious, wicked
13. messianic	m. destiny, fate, as ordained in advance by God
14. metempsychosis	n. the doctrine that God is in everything—that the Universe is God
15. omnipotent	o. all-knowing
16. omniscient	p. all-powerful
17. pantheism	q. the transmigration of souls; doctrine of the rebirth of souls in different bodies
18. predestination	r. pertaining to a messiah or deliverer of a nation, a group, or all mankind; (with a capital letter) pertaining to Jesus, the Messiah or Anointed One
19. sacrilegious	s. a ritual
20. theocracy	t. exempt from error of judgment

—*Answers*—

1-j, 2-i, 3-a, 4-h, 5-g, 6-f, 7-e, 8-d, 9-b, 10-c, 11-t, 12-s, 13-r, 14-q, 15-p, 16-o, 17-n, 18-m, 19-l, 20-k

C

Now that you are a little more familiar with these words, check the correct answer—a, b, or c—in each of the following:

1. A person who gets *absolution* is
   - a. all-powerful
   - b. exempt from error in judgment
   - c. forgiven for his sins

2. The *Apocalypse* is the Biblical book of
   - a. Exodus
   - b. Revelation
   - c. Genesis

3. When a man is an *apostate,* he
   - a. becomes an evangelist
   - b. deserts his religion
   - c. accepts the Apostles' creed

4. The *Beatitudes* are the
   - a. Eight Blessings of the Sermon on the Mount
   - b. Ten Commandments
   - c. Psalms of David

5. The *cosmogony* of the Bible is
   - a. the story of Creation
   - b. the conversion of St. Paul
   - c. the betrayal of Jesus at the hands of Judas

6. When Buddha received *deification,* he was
   - a. put to death
   - b. forgiven for his sins
   - c. made into a god

7. The *expiation* of a sinner means
   - a. his expulsion from church
   - b. the removal of his guilt through suffering
   - c. the end of his life

8. If a man made a *fetish* of anything, you could safely refer to him as
   - a. blindly devoted to it
   - b. festive
   - c. irreligious

9. The term *hierarchy* refers to
   - a. a body of priestly rulers
   - b. a higher grade of religious worship

c. The belief in one God

10. When an idea is *ineffable*, it is
   a. not subject to error
   b. too sacred for speech
   c. ineffectual as a prayer

11. When an idea is *infallible*, it is
   a. not subject to error
   b. too sacred for speech
   c. ineffectual as a prayer

12. The *liturgy* of the Catholic Church refers to
   a. the Mass
   b. the books of Catholic writers
   c. the vestments of the priests

13. The word *Messiah* means
   a. the Anointed One
   b. the Suffering One
   c. The Messenger

14. *Metempsychosis* is the belief in
   a. preordained destiny
   b. exemption from sin
   c. transmigration of souls

15. The *omnipotence* of God refers to
   a. His wisdom
   b. His goodness
   c. His power

16. The *omniscience* of God refers to
   a. His wisdom
   b. His goodness
   c. His power

17. A *pantheist* is a man who believes in
   a. the identity of God and the Universe
   b. the supremacy of God
   c. the trinity of God

18. If you believe in *predestination*, you are a
   a. fatalist
   b. man of destiny
   c. exempt from error

19. A *sacrilegious* person is prone to
   a. self-sacrifice
   b. deep reverence

c. violate something that is sacred

20. A *theocracy* is a state governed by

    a. the people

    b. God

    c. the men of aristocratic birth

—*Answers*—

1-c, 2-b (with a small letter, *apocalypse* means a prophetic revelation), 3-b, 4-a, 5-a, 6-c, 7-b, 8-a, 9-a, 10-b, 11-a, 12-a, 13-a, 14-c, 15-c, 16-a, 17-a, 18-a, 19-c, 20-b

D

Now check the word that fits each of the following definitions:

1. Jesus, the Anointed One   M_____
2. the Book of Revelation   A_____
3. the theory of the word's creation   c_____
4. the belief that God is identical with the world   p_____
5. the elevation of a person to godhood   d_____
6. exempt from error   i_____
7. the transmigration of souls   m_____
8. the desertion of one's faith   a_____
9. supreme blessedness   b_____
10. God's advance design for your fate   p_____
11. a church ritual   l_____
12. an object of blind devotion   f_____
13. all-knowing   o_____
14. all-powerful   o_____
15. atonement for sin through suffering   e_____
16. a God-government   t_____
17. impious   s_____
18. a body of ecclesiastical rulers   h_____
19. forgiveness for sin   a_____
20. too lofty or too sacred for expression   i_____

—*Answers*—

1-Messiah, 2-Apocalypse, 3-cosmogony, 4-pantheism, 5-deification, 6-infallible, 7-metempsychosis, 8-apostasy, 9-beatitude, 10-predestination, 11-liturgy, 12-fetish, 13-omniscient, 14-omnipotent, 15-expiation, 16-theocracy, 17-sacrilegious, 18-hierarchy, 19-absolution, 20-ineffable

E

Here is the correct pronunciation of the words:

absolution: ab-so-LEW-shun
Apocalypse: a-POK-al-ips
apostasy: a-POS-ta-see
beatitude: be-AT-it-yood
cosmogony: koz-MOG-o-nee
deification, noun: dee-i-fi-KAY-shun
deify, verb: DEE-i-figh
expiation, noun: ex-pee-AY (as in *day*)-shun
expiate, verb: EX-pee-ate
expiable, adjective: EX-pee-a-bl
fetish: FEE-tish or FET-ish
hierarchy: HIGH-ur-ar-kee
ineffable: in-EFF-a-bl
infallible: in-FAL (to rhyme with *pal*)-i-bl
liturgy: LIT-ur-gee
messianic, adjective: mes-see-AN-ik
Messiah, noun: mes-SIGH-a
metempsychosis: me-temp-si-KOE-sis
omnipotent: om-NIP-o-tent
omniscient: om-NISH-ent
pantheism: PAN-thee (as in *think*)-izm
predestination: pre-des-ti-NAY-shun
sacrilegious, adjective: sak-ri-LEE-jus, or sak-ri-LIJ-us
sacrilege, noun: SAK-ri-lej
theocracy, noun: thee (as in *think*)-OK-ra-see
theocratic, adjective: thee-o-KRAT-ik

26

YOUR FINAL TEST

We've come a long way since the start of this book, and school is just about ready to close. I hope your lessons have been fun and that they have been profitable too. How much have you really learned? There's nothing like an examination if you want to find out, and so this final chapter is given over to one.

There are some tricky questions in the test that follows. Still, every one has been answered in the foregoing pages. If you have studied this book very carefully, your score should be close to 150 correct, which is 100 per cent.

A review would be a good idea before taking this test. Don't, however, make the mistake of "cramming," as so many students do at school. You may waste half of your effort if you review simply for the purpose of getting a high mark. Psychologists tell us that intention is very important in mastering a subject and fastening it in your memory. If you plan to learn for keeps, you will learn better. They say, also, that the more often you go over a subject, the more lasting will be the impression it leaves on your mind. So treat your review as an important part of your reading of this book. Review for permanent remembering.

Our test consists of four parts—vocabulary, spelling, pronunciation, and grammar. It's fairly long, so sharpen your pencil and sharpen your wits and—good luck!

I. Vocabulary

A

Check the correct word in each of the following pairs enclosed by parentheses:

1. His argument was so (spacious, specious) that it appeared plausible.

2. The (Chronicles, Chronicals) are two of the historical books in the Old Testament.

3. Peter the Hermit, the apostle of the First Crusade, was an austere, self-denying and (esthetic, ascetic) monk.

4. His argument was clever and tricky, but certainly not (ingenious, ingenuous).

5. The grand jury (indited, indicted) the man as a spy.

6. And the attorney general proceeded with the (prosecution, persecution).

7. The map indicated the exact (typography, topography) of the country.

8. The prisoner (affected, effected) an air of innocence.

9. Many people in Europe are still (alliterate, illiterate).

10. His story sounded frank, friendly, and (veracious, voracious).

11. He was a (skeptic, septic) who believed nothing until it was proved true.

12. The old man was full of amusing (antidotes, anecdotes) about famous people.

13. The candidate had a glib tongue and a great (facility, felicity) of expression.

14. To make a long story short, let me (eliminate, illuminate) all the unnecessary passages.

15. France and Germany are (contiguous, contagious) countries.

16. The labor leader (castigated, instigated) a strike for better wages.

17. The judge refused the divorce on the ground of (collusion, collision) between the husband and the wife.

18. He refused to go to church, and was (irrelevant, irreverent) in his attitude toward God.

19. The judge (condemned, condoned) the offense when the prisoner promised to behave.

20. The child was fascinated by the regular (osculation, oscillation) of the pendulum.

B

Indicate whether each of the following statements is *true* or *false:*

21. The scientific study of the stars is called *astrology*.   True   False

22. A *pediatrician* is a specialist in children's diseases.   True   False

23. The disease resulting from the bite of a rabid dog is called *claustrophobia*.   True   False

24. A *stationary* store is a place where you can buy writing materials.   True   False

25. A *podiatrist* is a specialist who takes care of the feet.   True   False

26. An *optometrist* is a person who measures the powers of vision.   True   False

27. An *optician* is an eye doctor.   True   False

28. An *oculist* is a maker of eyeglasses.   True   False

29. A person who loves the pleasures of life may be defined as *uxorious*.   True   False

30. No person is so *ineffable* that he never makes a mistake.   True   False

31. *Metrology* is the scientific study of the weather.   True   False

32. *Vulnerable* people are worthy of reverence.   True   False

33. A *cynosure* is a competent judge of art.   True   False

34. A *pyromaniac* is a person addicted to setting fires.   True   False

35. *Arrogation* is the artificial watering of the land.   True   False

C

Match the words of the first column with the definitions of the second column:

36. dispersion   a. having a doubtful meaning
37. aspersion   b. a deadhouse or morgue
38. illegible   c. slander
39. ineligible   d. an animal with an armorlike covering
40. mortuary   e. not easy to read
41. moratorium   f. a slight or trifling sin
42. ambiguous   g. living both on land and in water
43. amphibious   h. a legal suspension of payments
44. armadillo   i. not qualified
45. peccadillo   j. the act of scattering or the state of being scattered

D

After each of the following words, check the definition that fits it best:

46. omnipotent
    (a) lacking in power, (b) a printed anthology,
    (c) all-powerful, (d) oppressive
47. masochistic
    (a) pertaining to a massage, (b) deriving pleasure
    from receiving cruel treatment, (c) disguised by
    mask, (d) adapted for chewing
48. presbyopia
    (a) long-sightedness, especially due to old age, (b)
    one of the Christian sects, (c) a reporter's news
    item, (d) a certain kind of drug
49. sycophancy
    (a) an oriental tree, (b) a dog bite, (c) a fantastic
    idea, (d) base flattery
50. aridity
    (a) a condition of dryness through excessive heat,
    (b) an inheritance, (c) a jingling song, (d) good
    riddance
51. polyglot
    (a) a figure of many sides and angles, (b) a person
    with an excessive appetite, (c) a person with
    several wives, (d) a speaker of many languages
52. chicanery
    (a) a plant used in adulterating coffee, (b) legal
    trickery, (c) a variety of sugar cane, (d) a can-
    ning factory
53. acrimony
    (a) scientific agriculture, (b) bitterness of speech or
    temper, (c) tainted money, (d) the scientific
    study of crime
54. surreptitious
    (a) stealthy, or accomplished by secret means, (b)
    pertaining to an irrational belief in the super-
    natural, (c) pertaining to a reptile, (d) charac-
    terized by useless repetition
55. metempsychosis
    (a) a mental disease, (b) mental telepathy, (c) mental
    healing, (d) transmigration of souls

II. Spelling

A

In each of the following groups, check the one word that
is spelled *wrong:*

56. (a) supersede, (b) precede, (c) indispensable,
    (d) percieve
57. (a) weird, (b) penitentiery, (c) siege, (d) exceed
58. (a) schizophrenia, (b) efervescent, (c) abscess,
    (d) permissible
59. (a) tyrrany, (b) drunkenness, (c) noticeable,
    (d) separate
60. (a) resistant, (b) priviledge, (c) analyze, (d) abscess
61. (a) annoint, (b) announce, (c) malign,
    (d) accommodate
62. (a) assassinate, (b) penitentiary, (c) picknicking
    (d) dissipate
63. (a) effervescent, (b) privilege, (c) acknowlege,
    (d) chrysanthemum
64. (a) anihilate, (b) beneficent, (c) hypocrisy,
    (d) permissible
65. (a) abcess, (b) picnicking, (c) anoint, (d) resistant

B

In each of the following groups, check the one word that
is spelled *right:*

66. (a) questionaire, (b) alright, (c) battalion,
    (d) anihilate
67. (a) sacrilegious, (b) superintendant,
    (c) conscienscious, (d) descriminate
68. (a) exhilirate, (b) questionnaire, (c) innoculate,
    (d) paralell
69. (a) dissapear, (b) innocuous, (c) inuendo,
    (d) dilletante
70. (a) vacillate, (b) dissention, (c) ocurrence,
    (d) dessicate
71. (a) concensus, (b) abstension, (c) tranquillity,
    (d) erisypelas
72. (a) liquefy, (b) apellation, (c) suppoena, (d) phlem
73. (a) villany, (b) fusillage, (c) gasseous, (d) secretarial
74. (a) cattarh, (b) incidently, (c) all right,
    (d) alltogether
75. (a) colonade, (b) fuselade, (c) Britannic,
    (d) hidrangea

C

In each of the following pairs, check A or B, whichever
spelling you think is correct.

	A	B
76.	concensus	consensus
77.	inuendo	innuendo
78.	inoculate	innoculate
79.	inocuous	innocuous
80.	desiccate	dessicate
81.	irridescent	iridescent
82.	imbrolio	imbroglio
83.	nemonick	mnemonic
84.	herbaceous	herbatious
85.	hors d'ouvers	hors d'oeuvres

III. Pronunciation

Check the correct pronunciation of the following words:

		(a)		(b)	
86.	grimace	(a)	grim-ACE	(b)	GRIM-iss
87.	cerebral	(a)	se-REE-bral	(b)	SER-e-bral
88.	museum	(a)	myou-ZEE-um	(b)	MYOU-zee-um
89.	genuine	(a)	JEN-you-in	(b)	JEN-you-wine
90.	adversary	(a)	ad-VERSE-e-ri	(b)	AD-ver-ser-ee
91.	infamous	(a)	IN-fam-us	(b)	in-FAME-us
92.	irrevocable	(a)	ir-REV-o-ka-bl	(b)	ir-re-VOKE-able
93.	sedentary	(a)	SED-en-ter-ee	(b)	se-DEN-ter-ee
94.	relapse	(a)	REE-laps	(b)	re-LAPS
95.	thyme	(a)	TIME	(b)	THIME
96.	lingerie	(a)	lon-zhe-RAY	(b)	lan-zhe-REE
97.	acumen	(a)	a-KEW-men	(b)	AK-you-men
98.	verbatim	(a)	ver-BAY-tim	(b)	ver-BAT-im
99.	impious	(a)	IM-pee-us	(b)	im-PIE-us
100.	culinary	(a)	KULL-in-er-ree	(b)	KEW-lin-er-ee
101.	comparable	(a)	COM-par-a-bl	(b)	com-PAR-a-bl
102.	gondola	(a)	GON-do-la	(b)	gon-DOE-la
103.	flaccid	(a)	FLAS-sid	(b)	FLAK-sid
104.	respite	(a)	re-SPITE	(b)	RES-pit
105.	secretive	(a)	se-KREE-tiv	(b)	SEE-kre-tiv
106.	heinous	(a)	HE-in-us	(b)	HAY-nus
107.	credence	(a)	KREE-dens	(b)	KRED-ens
108.	lichen	(a)	LITCH-en	(b)	LIKE-en
109.	ignominy	(a)	IG-no-min-ee	(b)	ig-NOM-in-ee
110.	dotage	(a)	DOE-tij	(b)	DOT-ij
111.	inchoate	(a)	IN-ko-ate	(b)	in-CHOE-ate
112.	viscount	(a)	VIE-count	(b)	VIS-count
113.	succinct	(a)	sus-SINKT	(b)	suk-SINKT

114. satiety   (a) sa-TIE-e-tee   (b) SAY-shee-et-ee
115. lascivious   (a) la-SHIV-ee-us   (b) las-SIV-ee-us

IV. Grammar

A

In each of the following sentences, check the correct word in the parentheses:

116. Come what (might, may), he was determined to see it through.
117. Galileo declared that the earth (moves, moved) around the sun.
118. I think he (don't, doesn't) know the truth.
119. "I wish he (were, was) out of danger," said the sick boy's mother.
120. Perhaps he would tell the truth if you (asked, ask) him.
121. Neither Gail nor Mary (has, have) been invited to the party.
122. Mrs. Smith told Johnny that the scissors (was, were) too sharp for little children to play with.
123. He got sick because he (laid, lay) too long in the sun.
124. They were afraid they hadn't (laid, lain) up enough money for their old age.
125. (Lay, Lie) quietly till the doctor comes.
126. Mrs. Woodruff organized a club for (mothers-in-law, mother-in-laws).
127. She used two (spoonsful, spoonfuls) of sugar in her cake recipe.

B

Correct the following sentences:

128. All dressed for the occasion, the party was called off.
129. Walking into the airport, the plane had already left.
130. To be appreciated, you must see it for yourself.
131. Speeding at 60 miles, two pedestrians were hit by the car.
132. Picking up his paper, the headline announced the result of the election.

C

Indicate whether the italicized word in each of the following sentences is right or wrong:

133. Harry has seen *less* plays than his sister.   Right   Wrong

134. He dislikes *this* sort of amusements.   Right   Wrong

135. The lion was restlessly growling in *it's* cage.   Right   Wrong

136. *Who'se* book is this?   Right   Wrong

137. *Who* do you expect will be the next lightweight champion?   Right   Wrong

138. He was so busy, he *most* forgot the appointment.   Right   Wrong

139. He did his job very *good*.   Right   Wrong

140. Nobody knows better than *he* how to do it.   Right   Wrong

141. Everybody except *he* would fall down on the job.   Right   Wrong

142. Let it remain a secret between you and *I*.   Right   Wrong

143. Peace is preferable *than* war.   Right   Wrong

144. She is identical *with* her twin sister.   Right   Wrong

145. He should *of* known better.   Right   Wrong

146. I disagree *with* him about the merits of the play.   Right   Wrong

147. Frank's job is similar *with* Bill's.   Right   Wrong

148. The idea originated *with* him.   Right   Wrong

149. No sooner had he sat down *than* the telephone rang.   Right   Wrong

150. He trusts nobody but you and *I*.   Right   Wrong

—*Answers*—

I A: 1-specious, 2-Chronicles, 3-ascetic, 4-ingenuous, 5-indicted, 6-prosecution, 7-topography, 8-affected, 9-illiterate, 10-veracious, 11-skeptic, 12-anecdotes, 13-facility, 14-eliminate, 15-contiguous, 16-instigated, 17-collusion, 18-irreverent, 19-condoned, 20-oscillation

I B: 21-false, 22-true, 23-false, 24-false, 25-true, 26-true, 27-false, 28-false, 29-false, 30-false, 31-false, 32-false, 33-false, 34-true, 35-false

I C: 36-j, 37-c, 38-e, 39-i, 40-b, 41-h, 42-a, 43-g, 44-d, 45-f

I D: 46-c, 47-b, 48-a, 49-d, 50-a, 51-d, 52-b, 53-b, 54-a, 55-d

II A: 56-d, 57-b, 58-b, 59-a, 60-b, 61-a, 62-c, 63-c, 64-a, 65-a

II B: 66-c, 67-a, 68-b, 69-b, 70-a, 71-c, 72-a, 73-d, 74-c, 75-c

II C: 76-b, 77-b, 78-a, 79-b, 80-a, 81-b, 82-b, 83-b, 84-a, 85-b

III : 86-a, 87-b, 88-a, 89-a, 90-b, 91-a, 92-a, 93-a, 94-b, 95-a, 96-b, 97-a, 98-a, 99-a, 100-b, 101-a, 102-a, 103-b, 104-b, 105-a, 106-b, 107-a, 108-b, 109-a, 110-a, 111-a, 112-a, 113-b, 114-a, 115-b

IV A: 116-might, 117-moves, 118-doesn't, 119-were, 120-asked, 121-has, 122-were, 123-lay, 124-laid, 125-Lie, 126-mothers-in-law, 127-spoonfuls

IV B: (There are several ways of correcting the sentences; among the possibilities are the following:) 128-When he was all dressed for the occasion, the party was called off. 129-When he walked into the airport, the plane had already left. 130-To appreciate it, you must see it for yourself. 131-Speeding at 60 miles, the car hit two pedestrians. 132-Picking up his paper, he read the headline announcing the result of the election.

IV C: 133-wrong, 134-right, 135-wrong, 136-wrong, 137-right, 138-wrong, 139-wrong, 140-right, 141-wrong, 142-wrong, 143-wrong, 144-right, 145-wrong, 146-right, 147-wrong, 148-right, 149-right, 150-wrong

Are you satisfied with your score, or are you still weak on some points? In either case, a re-reading of this book will help to fix the principles of good English more firmly in your mind. Even after you have mastered them, this volume will come in handy when you want to check up on various points.

Don't let the end of this book mean the end of your interest in good English. The things you have learned here are only the first harvest of your reading; there will be many more in store for you.

By applying the principles set forth in these pages, you will be able to enlarge not only your vocabulary but your mental horizons and your opportunities as well. Words stand for ideas—the more you know, the better equipped will you be to understand new situations, to think incisively, and to solve the problems of everyday life. Use your words wisely and correctly, and you will be able to express your thoughts with greater confidence and make a more favorable impres-

on on others. You will get better results in your work, open-
g up the way to increased earnings.

Knowledge is power, and a knowledge of how to use
nglish effectively is one of your most valuable tools for
ing.

INDEX

315

316

317